FUNDAMENTALS OF

ENGLISH GRAMMAR

Third Edition

Volume A

Longman

Betty Schrampfer Azar

Fundamentals of English Grammar, Third Edition
Volume A

Copyright © 2003, 1992, 1985 by Betty Schrampfer Azar
All rights reserved.

Azar Associates
Shelley Hartle, Editor
Susan Van Etten, Manager

Pearson Education, 10 Bank Street, White Plains, NY 10606

Vice president, director of publishing: Allen Ascher
Editorial manager: Pam Fishman
Project manager: Margo Grant
Development editor: Janet Johnston
Vice president, director of design and production: Rhea Banker
Director of electronic production: Aliza Greenblatt
Executive managing editor: Linda Moser
Production manager: Ray Keating
Production editor: Robert Ruvo
Director of manufacturing: Patrice Fraccio
Senior manufacturing buyer: Edie Pullman
Cover design: Monika Popowitz
Illustrations: Don Martinetti
Text composition: Carlisle Communications, Ltd.
Text font: 10.5/12 Plantin

ISBN: 0-13-013646-8

Printed in the United States of America
6 7 8 9 10–CRK–06 05

CONTENTS

Chapter 7 MODAL AUXILIARIES

Preface to the Third Edition

Fundamentals of English Grammar is a developmental skills text for lower-intermediate and intermediate students of English as a second or foreign language. It combines clear and understandable grammar information with a variety of exercises and activities.

Fundamentals of English Grammar is the second in a series of three texts: *Basic English Grammar* (red cover), *Fundamentals of English Grammar* (black cover), and *Understanding and Using English Grammar* (blue cover).

The principal aims of all three texts in this series are to present clear, cogent information about English grammar and usage, to provide extensive and varied practice that encourages growth in all areas of language use, and to be interesting, useful, and fun for student and teacher alike. The approach is eclectic, with the texts seeking to balance form-focused language-learning activities with abundant opportunities for engaged and purposeful communicative interaction.

The new editions of the texts in the Azar Grammar Series include these changes:

- The communicative aspects are more fully developed and explicit in the third editions. This edition of *Fundamentals of English Grammar* includes a greatly increased number of "real communication" opportunites for the teacher to exploit. The text often uses the students' own life experiences as context and regularly introduces topics of interest to stimulate the free expression of ideas in structured as well as open discussions.

    The Azar Grammar Series texts support the view of many experienced teachers that grammar-based and communicative approaches are not mutually exclusive, but rather mutually supportive, and can advantageously co-exist in the same language program, even in the same class, even in the same lesson.

- Similarly, the interactive aspects of the texts receive greater emphasis in the third editions. Many of the exercises formerly designated ORAL or ORAL (BOOKS CLOSED) are now reformatted to be more clearly available for pair work or group work, in addition to still being viable as class work led by a teacher. This edition of *Fundamentals of English Grammar* encourages interactivity but leaves it open for the users to decide what degree of interactivity best suits their needs.

- There is now an even wider variety of exercise types. This edition has a much larger number of free-response exercises and open-ended communicative tasks, while still providing ample controlled-response exercises to aid initial understanding of the form, meaning, and usage of the target structures. It also includes more writing topics, more speaking activities, new error-analysis exercises in every chapter, and additional extended-context exercises. Classroom teaching materials formerly found in the *Workbook* are now included in this student text, with the *Workbook* devoted solely to self-study exercises. The *Workbook* has a variety of practice approaches for independent study.

- A specific change in this edition of *Fundamentals of English Grammar* is the two Appendices, one with phrasal verbs and one with preposition combinations. Rather than asking students to study a whole chapter of these phrases at one time, the text uses appendices to present them in smaller groupings for teachers to intersperse throughout the teaching term. Another specific change is the omission of conditional sentences, which are presented in *Understanding and Using English Grammar.*

- The accompanying *Teacher's Guide* is written for both experienced and inexperienced teachers. It contains amplified grammar notes the teacher might want to present to the class or will find useful as background information. It outlines various ways of approaching the materials in the classroom and frequently suggests fresh teaching ideas for individual exercises beyond the directions in the text. It seeks to share with the teacher an understanding of the rationale behind the text's content and approaches. Its principal purpose is to make the busy teacher's job easier.

Fundamentals of English Grammar consists of
- a *Student Book* without an answer key
- a *Student Book* with an answer key
- a *Workbook,* consisting of self-study exercises for independent work
- a *Chartbook,* a reference book consisting of only the grammar charts
- a *Teacher's Guide,* with teaching suggestions and additional notes on grammar, as well as the answers to the exercises
- a *Test Bank*

ACKNOWLEDGMENTS

The third edition of *FEG* was reviewed by nine ESL/EFL professionals. I wish to express my thanks to these colleagues for their exceedingly helpful insights and suggestions. They are Stephanie La Qua, International Center for American English; Diane Mahin, University of Miami; Amy Parker, Embassy CES Intensive English Program; Gary Pietsch, Green River Community College; Thomas Pinkerton, North Miami Senior High School; Haydée Alvarado Santos, University of Puerto Rico; Hye-Young Um, Myongji University, Seoul, Korea; Lyn Waldie, Helenic-American Union, Athens, Greece; Aida Zic, Montgomery College.

My wholehearted thanks go to Shelley Hartle, who makes my job easy, and Editor Janet Johnston, who guides and assists us in so very many ways. Editor Margo Grant is simply super to work with, as are the many other skilled professionals at Pearson Education who have contributed to the publication of this work; in particular, Joanne Dresner, Anne Boynton-Trigg, Allen Ascher, Pam Fishman, Rhea Banker, Linda Moser, Aliza Greenblatt, Ray Keating, Barry Katzen, Kate McLoughlin, Sylvia Herrera-Alaniz, Bruno Paul, Hugo Loyola, Mike Bennett, Stacy Whitis, Monika Popowicz, Julie Hammond, and Amy Durfy.

A special thank you is reserved for Production Editor Robert Ruvo, who stayed on top of everything and remained unflappable.

I'd like to thank Carlisle Communications, Ltd., whose staff so excellently turned our disks into print pages. Without a doubt, they are the most skilled and reliable compositors I've worked with in twenty years.

I also once again thank Don Martinetti, the illustrator, whose touches of whimsy are so delightful. My appreciation also goes to graphic designer Christine Shrader, creator of the swallow that heralds this third edition.

My great appreciation goes to Stacy Hagen, an experienced ESL author,* who created new materials for the revised *Fundamentals of English Grammar Workbook,* bringing fresh approaches and ideas. Working with her was a very good experience.

I wish to express special acknowledgment of the contributing writers for the previous edition of the *Workbook:* Rachel Spack Koch, Susan Jamieson, Barbara Andrews, and Jeanie Francis. Some of the exercise material originally created for that workbook has been woven into this third edition of the student book, and I thank them for the ways in which this material has enriched the text. I am additionally very grateful to Rachel Spack Koch for her devotion and expertise in answering grammar and usage questions from teachers on the current Azar Companion Web Site.

I am indebted especially and always to my many students through the years; I learned so much from them. I also am indebted to my fellow ESL/EFL materials writers, past and present; we learn much from each other. I would like to make special mention of Thomas Crowell and Irene Schoenberg.

In addition, my thanks go to Donna Cowan, University of Washington, Patti Gulledge-White, Sue Van Etten, Joy Edwards, my great girls Chelsea and Rachel, and my wonderfully supportive husband, Larry Harris.

Sound Advice: A Basis for Listening, 2000, Pearson Education; *Better Writing Through Editing,* 1999, McGraw-Hill (co-author Jan Peterson); and *Sound Advantage: A Pronunciation Book,* 1992, Pearson Education (co-author Pat Grogan).

CHAPTER *1*
Present Time

☐ EXERCISE 1. Introductions.

Directions: You and your classmates are going to interview each other and then introduce each other to the rest of the class.

PART I.　Read and discuss the dialogue.

A:　Hi. My name is Kunio.

B:　Hi. My name is Maria. I'm glad to meet you.

KUNIO:　I'm glad to meet you, too. Where are you from?

MARIA:　I'm from Mexico. Where are you from?

KUNIO:　I'm from Japan.

MARIE:　Where are you living now?

KUNIO:　On Fifth Avenue in an apartment. And you?

MARIA:　I'm living in a dorm.

KUNIO:　How long have you been in (this city)?

MARIA:　Three days.

KUNIO:　Why did you come here?

MARIA:　To study English at this school before I go to another school to study computer programming. How about you?

KUNIO:　I came here two months ago. Right now I'm studying English. Later, I'm going to study engineering at this school.

MARIA:　What do you do in your free time?

KUNIO:　I read a lot. How about you?

MARIA:　I like to get on the Internet.

KUNIO:　Really? What do you do when you're online?

MARIA:　I visit many different Web sites. It's a good way to practice my English.

KUNIO:　That's interesting. I like to get on the Internet, too.

MARIA: I have to write your full name on the board when I introduce you to the class. How do you spell your name?

KUNIO: My first name is Kunio. K-U-N-I-O. My family name is Akiwa.

MARIA: Kunio Akiwa. Is that right?

KUNIO: Yes, it is. And what is your name again?

MARIA: My first name is Maria. M-A-R-I-A. My last name is Lopez.

KUNIO: Thanks. It's been nice talking with you.

MARIA: I enjoyed it, too.

PART II. Use the information in the dialogue to complete Kunio's introduction of Maria to the class.

KUNIO: I would like to introduce Maria Lopez. Maria, would you please stand up?

Thank you. Maria is from _____Mexico_____ . Right now, she's living

_____ . She has been here _____ .

She came here to _____ before she _____

_____ . In her free time, she _____

_____ .

PART III. Now it is Maria's turn to introduce Kunio to the class. What is she going to say? Create an introduction. Begin with *"I would like to introduce Kunio . . . ."*

PART IV. Pair up with another student in the class. Interview each other. Then introduce each other to the rest of the class. In your conversation, find out your classmate's:

name   **length of time in this city**
native country or hometown   **reason for being here**
residence   **free-time activities or hobbies**

Take notes during the interview.

PART V. Write the names of your classmates on a sheet of paper as they are introduced in class.

☐ EXERCISE 2. Introducing yourself in writing.
    Directions: Write answers to the questions. Use your own paper. With your teacher, decide what to do with your writing.

    Suggestions:
        a. Give it to a classmate to read. Your classmate can then summarize the information in a spoken report to a small group.
        b. Pair up with a classmate and correct errors in each other's writing.
        c. Read your composition aloud in a small group and answer any questions about it.
        d. Hand it in to the teacher, who will correct the errors and return it to you.
        e. Hand it in to the teacher, who will keep it and return it at the end of the term, when your English has progressed, for you to correct your own errors.

QUESTIONS:
1. What is your name?
2. Where are you from?
3. Where are you living?
4. Why are you here (in this city)?
   a. Are you a student? If so, what are you studying?
   b. Do you work? If so, what is your job?
   c. Do you have another reason for being here?
5. What do you like to do in your free time?
6. What is your favorite season of the year? Why?
7. What are your three favorite books? Why do you like them?
8. Describe your first day in this class.

☐ EXERCISE 3. Pretest (error analysis): present verbs. (Charts 1-1 → 1-6)
Directions: All the sentences contain mistakes. Find and correct the mistakes.

Example: I no like cold weather.
→ *I don't like cold weather.*

1. Student at this school.

2. I no living at home right now.

3. I be living in this city.

4. I am study English.

5. I am not knowing my teacher's name.

6. *(supply name)* teach our English class.

7. She/He* expect us to be in class on time.

8. We always are coming to class on time.

9. Omar does he going to school?

10. Tom no go to school.

11. My sister don't have a job.

12. Does Anna has a job?

———————

*Choose the appropriate pronoun for your teacher, *he* or *she*.

1-1 THE SIMPLE PRESENT AND THE PRESENT PROGRESSIVE

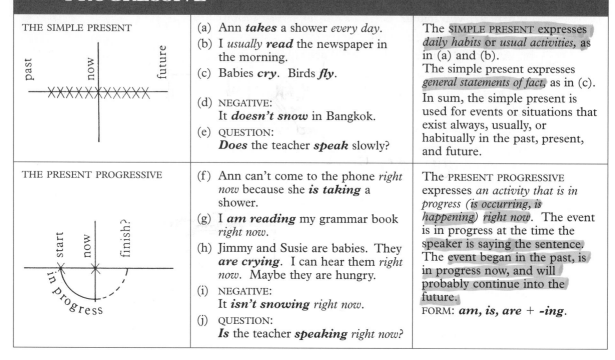

| THE SIMPLE PRESENT | (a) Ann **takes** a shower *every day*.
(b) I *usually* **read** the newspaper in the morning.
(c) Babies **cry**. Birds **fly**.

(d) NEGATIVE:
It **doesn't snow** in Bangkok.
(e) QUESTION:
Does the teacher **speak** slowly? | The SIMPLE PRESENT expresses *daily habits* or *usual activities*, as in (a) and (b).
The simple present expresses *general statements of fact*, as in (c).
In sum, the simple present is used for events or situations that exist always, usually, or habitually in the past, present, and future. |
| THE PRESENT PROGRESSIVE | (f) Ann can't come to the phone *right now* because she **is taking** a shower.
(g) I **am reading** my grammar book *right now*.
(h) Jimmy and Susie are babies. They **are crying**. I can hear them *right now*. Maybe they are hungry.
(i) NEGATIVE:
It **isn't snowing** *right now*.
(j) QUESTION:
Is the teacher **speaking** *right now*? | The PRESENT PROGRESSIVE expresses *an activity that is in progress (is occurring, is happening) right now*. The event is in progress at the time the speaker is saying the sentence. The event began in the past, is in progress now, and will probably continue into the future.
FORM: ***am, is, are*** + ***-ing***. |

1-2 FORMS OF THE SIMPLE PRESENT AND THE PRESENT PROGRESSIVE

	SIMPLE PRESENT	PRESENT PROGRESSIVE
STATEMENT	I-You-We-They **work**. He-She-It **works**.	I **am working**. You-We-They **are working**. He-She-It **is working**.
NEGATIVE	I-You-We-They **do not work**. He-She-It **does not work**.	I **am not working**. You-We-They **are not working**. He-She-It **is not working**.
QUESTION	**Do** I-you-we-they **work?** **Does** he-she-it **work?**	**Am** I **working?** **Are** you-we-they **working?** **Is** he-she-it **working?**
CONTRACTIONS pronoun + *be*	*I* + *am* = **I'm** working. *you, we, they* + *are* = **You're, We're, They're** working. *he, she, it* + *is* = **He's, She's, It's** working.	
do + *not*	*does* + *not* = **doesn't** *do* + *not* = **don't**	She **doesn't** work. I **don't** work.
be + *not*	*is* + *not* = **isn't** *are* + *not* = **aren't** (*am* + *not* = am not*	He **isn't** working. They **aren't** working. I am not working.)

*Note: *am* and *not* are not contracted.

□ EXERCISE 4. Simple present vs. present progressive. (Charts 1-1 and 1-2)
   Directions: Discuss the verbs in *italics*. Is the activity of the verb
   (a) a daily or usual habit? OR
   (b) happening right now (i.e., in progress in the picture)?

It's 7:30 A.M., and the Wilsons are in their kitchen. Mrs. Wilson *is sitting* at the
                                                                          b
                                                                          1
     b   *a*
breakfast table. She *is reading* a newspaper. She *reads* the newspaper every morning. Mr.
                2   3
       b   *b*
Wilson *is pouring* a cup of coffee. He *drinks* two cups of coffee every morning before he
     4   5
                                                            b
goes to work. There is a cartoon on TV, but the children *aren't watching* it. They
 6   *b*   7
                                               a
are playing with their toys instead. They usually *watch* cartoons in the morning, but this
   8   *b*   9   *b*
morning they *aren't paying* any attention to the TV. Mr. and Mrs. Wilson *aren't watching*
            10   *a*   *a*   11
the TV either. They often *watch* the news in the evening, but they *don't watch* cartoons.
                    12   13

□ EXERCISE 5. Simple present vs. present progressive. (Charts 1-1 and 1-2)
   Directions: Complete the sentences by using the words in parentheses. Use the simple
   present or the present progressive.

   1. Shhh. The baby *(sleep)* _____is sleeping_____ . The baby *(sleep)*

      _____sleeps_____ for ten hours every night.

2. Right now I'm in class. I *(sit)* _____I am sitting_____ at my desk. I usually

   (sit) _____sit_____ at the same desk in class every day.

3. Ali *(speak)* _____speaks_____ Arabic. Arabic is his native language, but

   right now he *(speak)* _____is speaking_____ English.

4. A: *(it, rain)* _____Does it rain_____ a lot in southern California?

   B: No. The weather *(be)* _____is_____ usually warm and sunny.

5. A: Look out the window. *(it, rain)* _____Is it raining_____ ? Should I take

      my umbrella?

   B: It *(start)* _____is starting_____ to sprinkle. _____hse_____

6. A: Look. It's ~~Youssef.~~ Yarself

   B: Where?

   A: Over there. He *(walk)* _____is walking_____ out of the bakery.

7. A: Oscar usually *(walk)* _____walks_____ to work. *(walk, you)*

      _____Do you walk_____ to work every day, too?

   B: Yes.

   A: *(Oscar, walk)* _____Does Oscar walk_____ with you?

   B: Sometimes.

8. A: Flowers! Flowers for sale!

      Yes sir! Can I help you?

   B: I'll take those—the yellow ones.

   A: Here you are, mister. Are they

      for a special occasion?

   B: I *(buy)* _____am buying_____

      them for my wife. I *(buy)*

      _____buy_____

   her flowers on the first day of every month.

☐ EXERCISE 6. Activity: using the present progressive. (Charts 1-1 and 1-2)
   Directions: Student A performs an action. Student B describes the action, using Student A's name and the present progressive.

   Example: stand next to your desk
      TEACHER: (Maria), would you please stand next to your desk? Thank you.
      STUDENT A: *(Student A stands up.)*
      TEACHER: Who is standing next to her desk? OR What is (Maria) doing?
      STUDENT B: (Maria) is standing next to her desk.

   1. stand up

   2. smile

   3. whistle

   4. open or close the door

   5. hum

   6. bite your fingernails

   7. read your grammar book

   8. erase the board

   9. look at the ceiling

   10. hold your pen in your left hand

   11. rub your palms together

   12. kick your desk (softly)

   13. knock on the door

   14. sit on the floor

   15. shake hands with someone

   16. look at your watch

   17. count aloud the number of people in the room

   18. shake your head "no"

   19. scratch your head

   20. Perform any action you choose. Use objects in the classroom if you wish.

☐ EXERCISE 7. Activity: using the present progressive. (Charts 1-1 and 1-2)
   Directions: Use the present progressive to discuss your classmates' immediate activities. Divide into two groups, I and II.

   GROUP I. Do anything you each feel like doing (stand up, talk, look out the window, etc.). You may wish to do some interesting or slightly unusual things. Perform these activities at the same time.

   GROUP II. Describe the immediate activities of the students in Group I (e.g., *Ali is talking to Ricardo. Yoko is scratching her chin. Spyros is leaning against the wall.*). Be sure to use your classmates' names.

   Later, Group I and Group II should reverse roles, with Group II acting and Group I describing.

Directions: Use the present progressive to describe activities in progress. Work in groups or as a class.

FIRST: One member of the group pretends to do something, and the rest of the group tries to guess what the action is and describe it, using the present progressive.

Example: painting a wall

STUDENT A: *(pretends to be painting a wall)*

OTHERS: You're conducting an orchestra. (No.)
Are you washing a window? (No.)
You're painting a wall. (Yes!)

SECOND: Student A repeats the performance and describes his/her actions aloud.

Example:

STUDENT A: I am standing in front of an unpainted wall. I'm opening a can of paint. Now I'm picking up a paintbrush. I'm dipping the brush in the can of paint. I'm lifting the brush. Now I'm painting the wall.

Suggestions for actions:

painting a wall	playing the piano
drinking a cup of tea / coffee	diving into a pool and swimming
petting a dog	driving a car
dialing a telephone	watching a tennis match
climbing a tree	pitching a baseball

1-3 FREQUENCY ADVERBS

| 100% | positive | always almost always usually† often† frequently† generally† sometimes† occasionally† | Frequency adverbs usually occur in the middle of a sentence and have special positions, as shown in examples (a) through (e) below. The adverbs with the symbol "†" may also occur at the beginning or end of a sentence. *I **sometimes** get up at 6:30.* ***Sometimes** I get up at 6:30.* *I get up at 6:30 **sometimes**.* |
| 0% | negative | seldom rarely hardly ever almost never not ever, never | The other adverbs in the list (the ones not marked by "†") rarely occur at the beginning or end of a sentence. Their usual position is in the middle of a sentence. |

(a) SUBJECT + FREQ ADV + VERB Karen **always** **tells** the truth.	Frequency adverbs usually come between the subject and the simple present verb (except main verb *be*).
(b) SUBJECT + BE + FREQ ADV Karen **is** **always** on time.	Frequency adverbs follow *be* in the simple present (*am, is, are*) and simple past (*was, were*).
(c) Do **you always** eat breakfast?	In a question, frequency adverbs come directly after the subject.
(d) Ann **usually doesn't eat** breakfast. (e) Sue **doesn't always** eat breakfast.	In a negative sentence, most frequency adverbs come in front of a negative verb (except *always* and *ever*). ***Always** follows a negative helping verb or negative be.*
(f) CORRECT: Anna **never eats** meat. (g) INCORRECT: Anna *doesn't never eat* meat.	Negative adverbs (*seldom, rarely, hardly ever, never*) are NOT used with a negative verb.
(h) — *Do* you **ever** *take* the bus to work? — Yes, I do. I often take the bus. (i) I **don't ever** walk to work. (j) INCORRECT: *I ever walk to work.*	***Ever** is used in questions about frequency, as in (h). It means "at any time."* ***Ever** is also used with **not**, as in (i).* ***Ever** is NOT used in statements.*

☐ **EXERCISE 9. The meaning of frequency adverbs. (Chart 1-3)**
Directions: Answer the questions. Discuss the meaning of the frequency adverbs.

What is something that . . .
1. you seldom do?
2. you often do before you go to bed?
3. a polite person often does?
4. a polite person never does?
5. I frequently do in class?
6. I usually don't do in class?
7. you rarely eat?
8. you occasionally do after class?
9. drivers generally do?
10. people in your country always or usually do to celebrate the New Year?

☐ **EXERCISE 10. Position of frequency adverbs. (Chart 1-3)**

Directions: Add the word in *italics* to the sentence. Put the word in its usual midsentence position.

1. *always*   Tom ⌃ studies at home in the evening.
                    always

2. *always*   Tom is at home in the evening.

3. *usually*   The mail comes at noon.

4. *usually*   The mail is here by noon.

5. *generally* I eat lunch around one o'clock.

6. *generally* Tom is in the lunch room around one o'clock.

7. *generally* What time do you eat lunch?

8. *usually*   Are you in bed by midnight?

☐ **EXERCISE 11. Frequency adverbs in negative sentences. (Chart 1-3)**

Directions: Add the given words to the sentence. Put the adverbs in their usual midsentence position. Make any necessary changes in the sentence.

1. *Sentence:* Jack doesn't shave in the morning.
   a. usually   → *Jack usually doesn't shave in the morning.*
   b. often   → *Jack often doesn't shave in the morning.*
   c. frequently   f. always   i. hardly ever
   d. occasionally   g. ever   j. rarely
   e. sometimes   h. never   k. seldom

2. I don't eat breakfast.
   a. usually   b. always   c. seldom   d. ever

3. My roommate isn't home in the evening.
   a. generally   b. sometimes   c. always   d. hardly ever

☐ **EXERCISE 12. Using the simple present with frequency adverbs. (Charts 1-1 → 1-3)**

Directions: Work in pairs. Use frequency adverbs to talk about yourself.
Speaker A: Your book is open. Tell your classmate about yourself, using the given ideas and frequency adverbs.
Speaker B: Your book is closed. Repeat the information Speaker A just gave you.
Speaker A: If Speaker B did not understand correctly, repeat the information.
           If Speaker B understood the information say, "Right. How about you?"
Speaker B: Answer the question, using a frequency adverb.

Example: walk to school
SPEAKER A *(book open):*   I usually walk to school.
SPEAKER B *(book closed):* You usually walk to school.
SPEAKER A *(book open):*   Right. How about you? Do you ever walk to school?
SPEAKER B *(book closed):* I seldom walk to school. I usually take the bus. OR I usually walk to school too.

1. wear a suit to class
2. go to sleep before eleven-thirty
3. get at least one e-mail a day
4. read in bed before I go to sleep
5. listen to the radio in the morning
6. speak to people who sit next to me on an airplane

Switch roles.
7. wear jeans to class
8. read poetry in my spare time
9. believe the things I read in newspapers
10. get up before nine o'clock in the morning
11. call my family or a friend if I feel homesick or lonely
12. have chocolate ice cream for dessert

☐ EXERCISE 13. Activity: topics for discussion or writing. (Charts 1-1 → 1-3)
Directions: Discuss the topics in pairs, in groups, or as a class. Topics can also be used for writing practice. Use several frequency adverbs with each topic. See Chart 1-3 for a list of frequency adverbs.

Example: What are some of the things you do when you get up in the morning?
→　*I generally turn on the news.*
I always brush my teeth.
I seldom make my bed.
I usually take a shower.
I never take a bath.

PART I. What are some things you do . . .
1. when you get ready to go to bed at night?
2. when you travel abroad?
3. in this classroom?
4. when you're on vacation?
5. when your airplane flight is delayed?
6. when you use a computer?

PART II. What are some things people in your country do . . .
7. at the dinner table?
8. to celebrate their birthdays?
9. when a child misbehaves?
10. when they meet someone for the first time?
11. when they want to have fun?
12. at a wedding?

1-4 FINAL -S

(a) SINGULAR: *one bird* (b) PLURAL: *two birds, three birds, many birds, all birds, etc.*	SINGULAR = one, not two or more PLURAL = two, three, or more
(c) **Birds** sing. (d) A bird **sings**.	**A plural noun** ends in **-s**, as in (c). **A singular verb** ends in **-s**, as in (d).

(e) **A bird** *sings* outside my window.
  It *sings* loudly.
  Ann *sings* beautifully.
  She *sings* songs to her children.
  Tom *sings* very well.
  He *sings* in a chorus.
	A singular verb follows a singular subject.
	Add **-s** to the simple present verb if the subject is
	  (1) a singular noun (e.g., *a bird, Ann, Tom*) or
	  (2) *he, she,* or *it.*★

★*He, she,* and *it* are third person singular personal pronouns. See Chart 6-10, p. 171, for more information about personal pronouns.

☐ EXERCISE 14. Using final -S. (Chart 1-4)
   Directions: Look at each word that ends in **-s**. Is it a noun or a verb? Is it singular or plural?

   1. Ali lives in an apartment. → *"lives" = a singular verb*
   2. Plants grow. → *"plants" = a plural noun*
   3. Ann listens to the radio in the morning.
   4. The students at this school work hard.
   5. A doctor helps sick people.
   6. Planets revolve around the sun.
   7. A dictionary lists words in alphabetical order.
   8. Mr. Lee likes to go to Forest Park in the spring. He takes the bus. He sits on a bench near a pond and feeds the birds. Ducks swim toward him for food, and pigeons land all around him.

☐ EXERCISE 15. Preview: spelling of final -S/-ES. (Chart 1-5)
   Directions: Add final **-s/-es**.

   1. talk **s**_____
   2. wish **es**_____
   3. hope _____
   4. reach _____
   5. move _____

   6. kiss _____
   7. push _____
   8. wait _____
   9. mix _____
   10. blow _____

   11. study _____
   12. buy _____
   13. enjoy _____
   14. fly _____
   15. carry _____

1-5 SPELLING OF FINAL -S/-ES

(a) visit → **visits**
   speak → **speaks**
(b) ride → **rides**
   write → **writes**
	Final **-s**, not **-es**, is added to most verbs.
	INCORRECT: *visites, speakes*
	Many verbs end in **-e**. Final **-s** is simply added.

(c) catch → **catches**
   wash → **washes**
   miss → **misses**
   fix → **fixes**
   buzz → **buzzes**
	Final **-es** is added to words that end in **-ch, -sh, -s, -x,** and **-z**.
	PRONUNCIATION NOTE: Final **-es** is pronounced /əz/ and adds a syllable.*

(d) fly → **flies** (e) pay → **pays**	If a word ends in a consonant + **-y**, change the **-y** to **-i** and add **-es**. (INCORRECT: *flys*) If a word ends in a vowel + **-y**, simply add **-s**.** (INCORRECT: *paies* or *payes*)

(f) go → **goes** /gowz/
   do → **does** /dəz/
   have → **has** /hæz/
	The singular forms of the verbs *go, do,* and *have* are irregular.

*See Chart 6-1 for more information about the pronunciation of final **-s/-es**.
**Vowels = a, e, i, o, u. Consonants = all other letters in the alphabet.

☐ EXERCISE 16. Simple present verbs: using final -S/-ES. (Charts 1-4 and 1-5)
   Directions: <u>Underline</u> the verb in each sentence. Add final **-s/-es** to the verb if **necessary**. Do not change any other words.

1. A dog <u>bark</u>. → barks

2. Dogs <u>bark</u>. → OK *(no change)*

3. Wood float on water.

4. Rivers flow toward the sea.

5. My mother worry about me.

6. A student buy a lot of books at the beginning of each term.

7. Airplanes fly all around the world.

8. Mr. Wong teach Chinese at the university.

9. The teacher ask us a lot of questions in class every day.

10. Mr. Cook watch game shows on TV every evening.

11. Music consist of pleasant sounds.

12. Cats usually sleep eighteen hours a day.

13. The front page of a newspaper contain the most important news of the day.

14. Water freeze at 32°F (0°C) and boil at 212°F (100°C).

15. Mrs. Taylor never cross the street in the middle of a block. She always walk to the

    corner and use the pedestrian walkway.

16. Many parts of the world enjoy four seasons: spring, summer, autumn, and winter.

    Each season last three months and bring changes in the weather.

☐ EXERCISE 17. Simple present verbs: using final -S/-ES. (Charts 1-4 and 1-5)
Directions: Count aloud around the class to the number 24. Find your number(s) in the exercise list, and write the words that appear beside it on a slip of paper. Then close your book.

    Walk around the classroom and read your words aloud to classmates. You are looking for the other half of your sentence.

    When you find the person with the other half, combine the information on your two slips of paper into a sentence. Write the sentence on the chalkboard or on a piece of paper. Make changes in the verb if necessary.

Example (using items 1 and 8): A star shines in the sky at night.

1. a star
2. causes air pollution
3. stretch when you pull on it
4. a hotel
5. newspaper ink
6. supports a huge variety of marine life
7. a bee
8. shine in the sky at night
9. cause great destruction when it reaches land
10. a river
11. improves your circulation and general health
12. an elephant
13. a hurricane
14. produce one-fourth of the world's coffee
15. oceans
16. use its long trunk like a hand to pick things up
17. Brazil
18. supply its guests with clean towels
19. a rubber band
20. gather nectar from flowers
21. flow downhill
22. stain my hands when I read the paper
23. automobiles
24. does physical exercise

□ EXERCISE 18. The simple present and the present progressive. (Charts 1-1 → 1-5)
Directions: Create three sentences about the activity shown in each picture. Work in pairs, in groups, or as a class.

Sentence 1: **Activity in progress:** Describe what the person in the picture is doing.
Sentence 2: **Usual frequency:** Describe how often this person probably does this activity.
Sentence 3: **Generalization:** Make a general statement or two about this activity.

Example:

Sentence 1: The man in the picture *is swimming*.
Sentence 2: It looks like he's near a tropical island. If he's on vacation there, he probably *swims* every day. If he lives there all the time, he probably *swims* once or twice a week.
Sentence 3: People *swim* for enjoyment and exercise. Swimming in the ocean *is* fun.

1-6 NON-ACTION VERBS

(a) I **know** Ms. Chen. INCORRECT: *I am knowing Ms. Chen.* (b) I'm hungry. I **want** a sandwich. INCORRECT: *I am wanting a sandwich.* (c) This book **belongs** to Mikhail. INCORRECT: *This book is belonging to Mikhail.*	Some verbs are not used in progressive tenses. These verbs are called "non-action verbs." They express a situation that exists, not an action in progress.

NON-ACTION VERBS★

hear	believe	be	own	need	like	forget
see	think†	exist	have†	want	love	remember
sound	understand		possess	prefer	hate	
	know		belong			

†COMPARE (d) I **think** that grammar is easy. (e) I **am thinking** about grammar right now. (f) Tom **has** a car. (g) I**'m having** a good time.	*Think* and *have* can be used in the progressive. In (d): When **think** means "believe," it is nonprogressive. In (e): When **think** expresses thoughts that are going through a person's mind, it can be progressive. In (f): When **have** means "own" or expresses possession, it is not used in the progressive. In (g): In expressions where **have** does not mean "own" (e.g., *have a good time, have a bad time, have trouble, have a problem, have company, have an operation*), **have** can be used in the progressive.

*Non-action verbs are also called "stative verbs" or "nonprogressive verbs."

☐ EXERCISE 19. Progressive verbs vs. non-action verbs. (Chart 1-6)
Directions: Complete the sentences with the words in parentheses. Use the simple present or the present progressive.

1. Right now I *(look)* _____am looking_____ at the board. I *(see)*
_____ some words on the board.

2. A: *(you, need)* _____ some help, Mrs. Brown?

   (you, want) _____ me to carry that box for you?

   B: Yes, thank you. That's very kind of you.

3. A: Who is that man? I *(think)* _____ that I *(know)*
   _____ him, but I *(forget)* _____ his name.

   B: That's Mr. Martinez.

   A: That's right! I *(remember)* _____ him now.

4. A: *(you, believe)* _____ in flying saucers?

   B: What *(you, talk)* _____ about?

   A: You know, spaceships from outer space with alien creatures aboard.

   B: In my opinion, flying saucers *(exist)* _____ only in people's
   imaginations.

5. Right now the children *(be)* _____ at the beach. They *(have)*

_____ a good time. They *(have)* _____ a beach

ball, and they *(play)* _____ catch with it. They *(like)*

_____ to play catch. Their parents *(sunbathe)* _____

_____ . They *(try)* _____ to get a tan.

They *(listen)* _____ to music on a radio. They also *(hear)*

_____ the sound of seagulls and the sound of the waves.

6. A: What *(you, think)* _____ about right now?

B: I *(think)* _____ about seagulls and waves.

A: *(you, like)* _____ seagulls?

B: Yes. I *(think)* _____ seagulls are interesting birds.

7. A: Which color *(you, prefer)* _____ , red or blue?

B: I *(like)* _____ blue better than red. Why?

A: I *(read)* _____ a magazine article right now. According

to the article, people who *(prefer)* _____ blue to red

(be) _____ calm and *(value)* _____ honesty and

loyalty in their friends. A preference for red *(mean)* _____ that a

person *(be)* _____ aggressive and *(love)* _____

excitement.

B: Oh? That *(sound)* _____ like a bunch of nonsense to me.

8. A: Does the earth turn around and around?

   B: Yes, Jimmy. The earth *(spin)* _____ around and around

   on its axis as it circles the sun. The earth *(spin)* _____

   rapidly at this very moment.

   B: Really? I can't feel it moving. *(you, try)* _____ to fool me?

   A: Of course not! *(you, think, really)* _____

   that the earth isn't moving?

   B: I guess so. Yes. I can't see it move. Yes. It isn't moving.

   A: *(you, believe)* _____ only those things that you can see?

   Look at the trees out the window. All of them *(grow)* _____

   at this very moment, but you can't see the growth. They *(get)* _____

   bigger and bigger with every second that passes. You can't see the trees grow, and

   you can't feel the earth spin, but both events *(take)* _____

   place at this moment while you and I *(speak)* _____ .

   B: Really? How do you know?

1-7 PRESENT VERBS: SHORT ANSWERS TO YES/NO QUESTIONS

	QUESTION	SHORT ANSWER	LONG ANSWER
QUESTIONS WITH *DO/DOES*	*Does* Bob *like* tea?	Yes, he **does**. No, he **doesn't**.	Yes, he likes tea. No, he doesn't like tea.
	Do you *like* tea?	Yes, I **do**. No, I **don't**.	Yes, I like tea. No, I don't like tea.
QUESTIONS WITH *BE*	*Are* you *studying?*	Yes, I **am**.★ No, I**'m not**.	Yes, I am (I'm) studying. No, I'm not studying.
	Is Yoko a student?	Yes, she **is**.★ No, she**'s not**. OR No, she **isn't**.	Yes, she is (she's) a student. No, she's not a student. OR No, she isn't a student.
	Are they *studying?*	Yes, they **are**.★ No, they**'re not**. OR No, they **aren't**.	Yes, they are (they're) studying. No, they're not studying. OR No, they aren't studying.

★*Am, is,* and *are* are not contracted with pronouns in short answers.
   INCORRECT SHORT ANSWERS: Yes, I'm. Yes, she's. Yes, they're.

□ EXERCISE 20. Short answers to yes/no questions. (Chart 1-7)
   Directions: Complete the following dialogues by using the words in parentheses. Also give short answers to the questions as necessary. Use the simple present or the present progressive.

1. A: *(Mary, have)* ___Does Mary have___ a bicycle?

   B: Yes, ___she does___ . She *(have)* ___has___ a ten-speed bike.

2. A: *(it, rain)* _____ right now?

   B: No, _____ . At least, I *(think, not)* _____ so.

3. A: *(your friends, write)* _____ a lot of e-mails?

   B: Yes, _____ . I *(get)* _____ lots of e-mails all the time.

4. A: *(the students, take)* _____ a test in class right now?

   B: No, _____ . They *(do)* _____ an exercise.

5. A: *(the weather, affect★)* _____ your mood?

   B: Yes, _____ . I *(get)* _____ grumpy when it's rainy.

6. A: *(Jean, study)* _____ at the library this evening?

   B: No, _____ . She *(be)* _____ at the recreation center.

   She *(play)* _____ pool with her friend.

   A: *(Jean, play)* _____ pool every evening?

   B: No, _____ . She usually *(study)*

   _____ at the library.

   A: *(she, be)* _____ a
   good player?

   B: Yes, _____ . She
   (play) _____ pool a lot.

   A: *(you, play)* _____ pool?

   B: Yes, _____ .
   But I *(be, not)* _____
   very good.

★The word *affect* is a verb: *The weather **affects** my mood.*

   The word *effect* is a noun: *Warm, sunny weather has a good **effect** on my mood.*

□ EXERCISE 21. Short answers to yes/no questions. (Chart 1-7)
Directions: Answer the questions with books closed. Give both a short and a long answer.
Work in pairs or as a class.

Example: Is Texas south of the equator?
→ No, it isn't. Texas isn't south of the equator. OR I don't know.

1. Do you wear a wristwatch every day?
2. Is (. . .) sitting next to (. . .) today?*
3. Does (. . .) usually sit in the same place every day?
4. Are (. . .) and (. . .) standing up?
5. Are you interested in politics?
6. Is Toronto in western Canada?

(Switch roles if working in pairs.)
7. Do whales lay eggs?
8. Does your country have bears in the wild?
9. Are dogs intelligent?
10. Is (. . .) from Cambodia?
11. Is the earth turning on its axis and rotating around the sun at the same time?
12. Do all mosquitoes carry malaria?

□ EXERCISE 22. Review: present verbs. (Chapter 1)
Directions: Complete the sentences by using the words in parentheses. Use the simple
present or the present progressive. Supply the short answer to a question if necessary.

1. A: My sister (have) _____has_____ a new car. She bought it last month.

   B: (you, have) ___Do you have___ a car?

   A: No, I ___don't___ . Do you?

   B: No, but I have a ten-speed bike.

2. A: Where are the children?

   B: In the living room.

   A: What are they doing? (they, watch) _____ TV?

   B: No, they _____ . They (play) _____ a game.

3. A: Shhh. I (hear) _____ a noise. (you, hear) _____ it, too?

   B: Yes, I _____ . I wonder what it is.

4. A: Johnny, (you, listen) _____ to me?

   B: Of course I am, Mom. You (want) _____ me to take out the

   garbage. Right?

   A: Right! And right now!

_____

*The symbol (. . .) means "supply the name of a person."

5. A: Knock, knock! Anybody home? Hey, Bill! Hi! It's me. I'm here with Tom. Where are you?

   B: I *(be)* _____ in the bedroom.

   A: What *(you, do)* _____ ?

   B: I *(try)* _____ to sleep!

   A: Oh. Sorry. I won't bother you. Tom, shhh. Bill *(rest)* _____ .

6. A: What *(you, think)* _____ about at night before you fall asleep?

   B: I *(think)* _____ about all of the pleasant things that happened during the day. I *(think, not)* _____ about my problems.

7. A: A penny for your thoughts.

   B: Huh?

   A: What *(you, think)* _____ about right now?

   B: I *(think)* _____ about English grammar. I *(think, not)* _____ about anything else right now.

   A: I *(believe, not)* _____ you!

8. A: *(you, see)* _____ that man over there?

   B: Which man? The man in the brown jacket?

   A: No, I *(talk)* _____ about the man who *(wear)* _____ the blue shirt.

   B: Oh, that man.

   A: *(you, know)* _____ him?

   B: No, I *(think, not)* _____ so.

9. A: *(you, know)* _____ any tongue-twisters?

   B: Yes, I _____ . Here's one: She sells seashells down by the seashore.

   A: That *(be)* _____ hard to say! Can you say this: Sharon wears Sue's shoes to zoos to look at cheap sheep?

   B: That *(make, not)* _____ any sense.

   A: I *(know)* _____ .

☐ **EXERCISE 23. Error analysis: present verbs. (Chapter 1)**

Directions: Correct the errors in verb tense usage.

(1) My friend Omar ~~is owning~~ *owns.* his own car now. It's brand new.* Today he driving to a small town north of the city to visit his aunt. He love to listen to music, so the CD player is play one of his favorite CDs—loudly. Omar is very happy: he is drive his own car and listen to loud music. He's look forward to his visit with his aunt.

(2) Omar is visiting his aunt once a week. She's elderly and live alone. She is thinking Omar a wonderful nephew. She love his visits. He try to be helpful and considerate in every way. His aunt don't hearing well, so Omar is speaks loudly and clearly when he's with her.

(3) When he's there, he fix things for her around her apartment and help her with her shopping. He isn't staying with her overnight. He usually is staying for a few hours and then is heading back to the city. He kiss his aunt good-bye and give her a hug before he is leaving. Omar is a very good nephew.

Brand new means "completely new."

CHAPTER 2
Past Time

CONTENTS

☐ **EXERCISE 1. Review of present verbs and preview of past verbs. (Chapters 1 and 2)**
Directions: Discuss the *italicized* verbs. Do they express present time or past time? Do the verbs describe an activity or situation that . . .
   a. is in progress right now?
   b. is usual or is a general statement of fact?
   c. began and ended in the past?
   d. was in progress at a time in the past?

B 1. Jennifer *works* for an insurance company.

B 2. When people *need* help with their automobile insurance, they *call* her.
   B

A 3. Right now it is 9:05 A.M., and Jennifer *is sitting* at her desk.

C 4. She *came* to work on time this morning.

C 5. Yesterday Jennifer *was* late to work because she *had* a minor auto accident.

D 6. While she *was driving* to work, her cell phone *rang*.
   C

C 7. She *answered* it. It *was* her friend Rob.
   C   C

   8. She *was* happy to hear from him because she *likes* Rob a lot and always *enjoys* her
   C   B   B
   conversations with him.

   9. While they *were talking*, Jennifer, who *is* allergic to bee stings, *noticed* two bees in her
   D   B   C
   car.

10. She quickly *opened* the car windows and *swatted* at the bees while she *was talking* to Rob on the phone.

11. Her hands *left* the steering wheel, and she *lost* control of the car. Her car *ran* into a row of mailboxes beside the road and *stopped.*

12. Fortunately, no one *was* hurt in the accident.

13. Jennifer *is* okay, but her car *isn't.* It *needs* repairs.

14. When Jennifer *got* to work this morning, she *talked* to her own automobile insurance agent.

15. That *was* easy to do because he *works* at the desk right next to hers.

2-1 EXPRESSING PAST TIME: THE SIMPLE PAST

(a) Mary **walked** downtown *yesterday*. (b) I **slept** for eight hours *last night*.	The simple past is used to talk about activities or situations that began and ended in the past (e.g., *yesterday, last night, two days ago, in 1999*).
(c) Bob **stayed** home yesterday morning. (d) Our plane **arrived** on time last night.	Most simple past verbs are formed by adding **-ed** to a verb, as in (a), (c), and (d).
(e) I **ate** breakfast this morning. (f) Sue **took** a taxi to the airport yesterday.	Some verbs have irregular past forms, as in (b), (e), and (f). See Chart 2-7, p. 33.
(g) I **was** busy yesterday. (h) They **were** at home last night.	The simple past forms of **be** are **was** and **were**.

2-2 FORMS OF THE SIMPLE PAST: REGULAR VERBS

STATEMENT	I-You-She-He-It-We-They **worked** yesterday.
NEGATIVE	I-You-She-He-It-We-They **did not (didn't) work** yesterday.
QUESTION	**Did** I-you-she-he-it-we-they **work** yesterday?
SHORT ANSWER	Yes, I-you-she-he-it-we-they **did**. No, I-you-she-he-it-we-they **didn't**.

2-3 FORMS OF THE SIMPLE PAST: *BE*

STATEMENT	I-She-He-It **was** in class yesterday. We-You-They **were** in class yesterday.
NEGATIVE	I-She-He-It **was not (wasn't)** in class yesterday. We-You-They **were not (weren't)** in class yesterday.
QUESTION	**Was** I-she-he-it in class yesterday? **Were** we-you-they in class yesterday?
SHORT ANSWER	Yes, I-she-he-it **was**. Yes, we-you-they **were**. No, I-she-he-it **wasn't**. No, we-you-they **weren't**.

☐ EXERCISE 2. Present and past time: statements and negatives.
(Chapter 1 and Charts 2-1 → 2-3)

Directions: All of the following sentences have inaccurate information. Correct them by
(a) making a negative statement, and
(b) making an affirmative statement with accurate information.

1. Thomas Edison invented the telephone.
   → (a) *Thomas Edison didn't invent the telephone.*
   (b) *Alexander Graham Bell invented the telephone.*

2. You live in a tree.

3. You took a taxi to school today.

4. You're sitting on a soft, comfortable sofa.

5. Our teacher wrote *Romeo and Juliet*.

6. Our teacher's name is William Shakespeare.

7. You were on a cruise ship in the Mediterranean Sea yesterday.

8. Rocks float and wood sinks.

9. The teacher flew into the classroom today.

10. Spiders have six legs.

□ EXERCISE 3. Present and past time: statements and negatives.
(Chapter 1 and Charts 2-1 → 2-3)

Directions: Correct the inaccurate statements by using negative then affirmative sentences. Some verbs are past, and some are present. Work as a class (with the teacher as Speaker A) or in pairs. Only Speaker A's book is open.

Example: (. . .)* left the classroom ten minutes ago.

SPEAKER A *(book open):*   Rosa left the classroom ten minutes ago.

SPEAKER B *(book closed):*   No, that's not true. Rosa didn't leave the classroom. Rosa is still here. She's sitting next to Kim.

1. You got up at 4:30 this morning.
2. (. . .) is standing in the corner of the classroom.
3. (. . .) stands in a corner of the classroom during class each day.
4. (. . .) stood in a corner during class yesterday.
5. This book has a green cover.
6. Shakespeare wrote novels.
7. A river flows from the bottom of a valley to the top of a mountain.
8. We cook food in a refrigerator.

(Switch roles if working in pairs.)
9. (. . .) taught this class yesterday.
10. Butterflies have ten legs.
11. This morning, you drove to school in a *(name of a kind of car).*
12. (. . .) takes a helicopter to get to school every day.
13. You speak (French and Arabic).
14. This room has *(supply an incorrect number)* windows.
15. (. . .) and you studied together at the library last night.
16. (. . .) went to *(an impossible place)* yesterday.

□ EXERCISE 4. Present and past time: statements and negatives.
(Chapter 1, Charts 2-1 → 2-3)

Directions: Work in pairs.

Speaker A: Your book is open. Complete each sentence to make an INACCURATE statement.

Speaker B: Your book is closed. Correct Speaker A's statement, first by using a negative sentence and then by giving correct information.

Example: . . . has/have tails.

SPEAKER A *(book open):*   People have tails.

SPEAKER B *(book closed):*   No, people don't have tails. Dogs have tails. Cats have tails. Birds have tails. But people don't have tails.

1. . . . is/are blue.
2. You ate . . . for breakfast this morning.

---

*The symbol (. . .) means "supply the name of a person."

3. Automobiles have . . . .

4. You . . . last night.

5. . . . sat next to you in class yesterday.

6. . . . is from Russia. He/She speaks Russian.

7. . . . is talking to . . . right now.

8. . . . was late for class today.

Switch roles.

9. . . . left class early yesterday.

10. . . . has/have six legs.

11. . . . was singing a song when the teacher walked into the room today.

12. . . . wore a black suit to class yesterday.

13. . . . is/are watching a video right now.

14. You . . . last weekend.

15. People . . . in ancient times.

16. . . . is/are delicious, inexpensive, and good for you.

2-4   REGULAR VERBS: PRONUNCIATION OF *-ED* ENDINGS

(a) talked = talk/t/ stopped = stop/t/ hissed = hiss/t/ watched = watch/t/ washed = wash/t/		Final *-ed* is pronounced /t/ after voiceless sounds. You make a voiceless sound by pushing air through your mouth. No sound comes from your throat. Examples of voiceless sounds: /k/, /p/, /s/, /ch/, /sh/.
(b) called = call/d/ rained = rain/d/ lived = live/d/ robbed = rob/d/ stayed = stay/d/		Final *-ed* is pronounced /d/ after voiced sounds. You make a voiced sound from your throat. Your voice box vibrates. Examples of voiced sounds: /l/, /n/, /v/, /b/, and all vowel sounds.
(c) waited = wait/əd/ needed = need/əd/		Final *-ed* is pronounced /əd/ after "t" and "d" sounds. /əd/ adds a syllable to a word.

☐ **EXERCISE 5. Pronunciation of -ED endings. (Chart 2-4)**

Directions: Write the correct pronunciations and practice saying the words aloud.

1. cooked = cook/ t /

2. served = serve/ d /

3. wanted = want/ əd /

4. asked = ask/ t /

5. started = start/ id /

6. dropped = drop/ t /

7. pulled = pull/ d /

8. pushed = push/ t /

9. added = add/ id /

10. passed = pass/ t /

11. returned = return/ d /

12. touched = touch/ t /

13. waved = wave/ d /

14. pointed = point/ id /

15. agreed = agree/ d /

☐ EXERCISE 6. Pronunciation of -ED endings. (Chart 2-4)

Directions: Practice saying these words. Use them in sentences.

1. answered	6. finished	11. worked
2. arrived	7. fixed	12. invited
3. continued	8. helped	13. suggested
4. ended	9. looked	14. smelled
5. explained	10. planned	15. crossed

2-5 SPELLING OF *-ING* AND *-ED* FORMS

END OF VERB	DOUBLE THE CONSONANT?	SIMPLE FORM	*-ING*	*-ED*	
-e	NO	(a) smil**e** hop**e**	smil**ing** hop**ing**	smil**ed** hop**ed**	*-ing* form: Drop the *-e*, add *-ing*. *-ed* form: Just add *-d*.
Two Consonants	NO	(b) hel**p** lea**rn**	help**ing** learn**ing**	help**ed** learn**ed**	If the verb ends in two consonants, just add *-ing* or *-ed*.
Two Vowels + One Consonant	NO	(c) **rain** **heat**	rain**ing** heat**ing**	rain**ed** heat**ed**	If the verb ends in two vowels + a consonant, just add *-ing* or *-ed*.
One Vowel + One Consonant	YES	ONE-SYLLABLE VERBS (d) sto**p** pla**n**	stop**ping** plan**ning**	stop**ped** plan**ned**	If the verb has one syllable and ends in one vowel + one consonant, double the consonant to make the *-ing* or *-ed* form.★
	NO	TWO-SYLLABLE VERBS (e) **vís**it **óf**fer	visit**ing** offer**ing**	visit**ed** offer**ed**	If the first syllable of a two-syllable verb is stressed, do not double the consonant.
	YES	(f) pre**fér** ad**mít**	prefer**ring** admit**ting**	prefer**red** admit**ted**	If the second syllable of a two-syllable verb is stressed, double the consonant.
-y	NO	(g) pla**y** enjo**y**	play**ing** enjoy**ing**	play**ed** enjoy**ed**	If the verb ends in a vowel + *-y*, keep the *-y*. Do not change the *-y* to *-i*.
		(h) wor**ry** stu**dy**	worr**ying** study**ing**	worr**ied** stud**ied**	If the verb ends in a consonant + *-y*, keep the *-y* for the *-ing* form, but change the *-y* to *-i* to make the *-ed* form.
-ie		(i) **die** **tie**	**dying** **tying**	**died** **tied**	*-ing* form: Change the *-ie* to *-y* and add *-ing*. *-ed* form: Just add *-d*.

★Exceptions: Do not double "w" or "x": *snow, snowing, snowed, fix, fixing, fixed.*

□ EXERCISE 7. -ING and -ED forms. (Chart 2-5)
   Directions: Write the **-ing** and **-ed** forms of the following verbs. (The simple past/past participle of irregular verbs is given in parentheses.)

		-ING	**-ED**
1.	start	*starting*	*started*
2.	wait		
3.	hit		*(hit)*
4.	write		*(wrote/written)*
5.	shout		
6.	cut		*(cut)*
7.	meet		*(met)*
8.	hope		
9.	hop		
10.	help		
11.	sleep		*(slept)*
12.	step		
13.	tape		
14.	tap		
15.	rain		
16.	run		*(ran/run)*
17.	whine		
18.	win		*(won)*
19.	explain		
20.	burn		

□ EXERCISE 8. -ING and -ED forms. (Chart 2-5)
   Directions: Write the **-ing** and **-ed** forms of the following verbs.

		-ING	**-ED**
1.	open		
2.	begin		*(began/begun)*
3.	occur		
4.	happen		

5. refer _____ _____

6. offer _____ _____

7. listen _____ _____

8. admit _____ _____

9. visit _____ _____

10. omit _____ _____

11. hurry _____ _____

12. study _____ _____

13. enjoy _____ _____

14. reply _____ _____

15. stay _____ _____

16. buy _____ _____ (bought) _____

17. try _____ _____

18. tie _____ _____

19. die _____ _____

20. lie* _____ _____

□ EXERCISE 9. -ING and -ED forms. (Chart 2-5)
   Directions: Write the **-ing** and **-ed** forms of the following verbs.

	-ING	**-ED**
1. lift	lifting	lifted
2. promise		
3. slap		
4. wipe		
5. carry		
6. cry		
7. pray		
8. smile		

---

*Lie** is a regular verb when it means "not tell the truth." **Lie** is an irregular verb when it means "put one's body flat on a bed or another surface": *lie, lay, lain.*

9. fail   _____   _____

10. file   _____   _____

11. drag   _____   _____

12. use   _____   _____

13. prefer   _____   _____

14. sign   _____   _____

15. point   _____   _____

16. appear   _____   _____

17. relax   _____   _____

18. borrow   _____   _____

19. aim   _____   _____

20. cram   _____   _____

2-6 THE PRINCIPAL PARTS OF A VERB

	SIMPLE FORM	SIMPLE PAST	PAST PARTICIPLE	PRESENT PARTICIPLE
REGULAR VERBS	finish	finished	finished	finishing
	stop	stopped	stopped	stopping
	hope	hoped	hoped	hoping
	wait	waited	waited	waiting
	play	played	played	playing
	try	tried	tried	trying
IRREGULAR VERBS	see	saw	seen	seeing
	make	made	made	making
	sing	sang	sung	singing
	eat	ate	eaten	eating
	put	put	put	putting
	go	went	gone	going
PRINCIPAL PARTS OF A VERB (1) the simple form	English verbs have four principal forms or "parts." **The simple form** is the form that is found in a dictionary. It is the base form with no endings on it (no final *-s*, *-ed*, or *-ing*).
(2) the simple past	**The simple past** form ends in *-ed* for regular verbs. Most verbs are regular, but many common verbs have irregular past forms. See the reference list of irregular verbs that follows in Chart 2-7.
(3) the past participle	**The past participle** also ends in *-ed* for regular verbs. Some verbs are irregular. It is used in perfect tenses (see Chapter 4) and the passive (Chapter 10).
(4) the present participle	**The present participle** ends in *-ing* (for both regular and irregular verbs). It is used in progressive tenses (e.g., the present progressive and the past progressive).

2-7 IRREGULAR VERBS: A REFERENCE LIST

SIMPLE FORM	SIMPLE PAST	PAST PARTICIPLE	SIMPLE FORM	SIMPLE PAST	PAST PARTICIPLE
awake	awoke	awoken	lie	lay	lain
be	was, were	been	light	lit/lighted	lit/lighted
beat	beat	beaten	lose	lost	lost
become	became	become	make	made	made
begin	began	begun	mean	meant	meant
bend	bent	bent	meet	met	met
bite	bit	bitten	pay	paid	paid
blow	blew	blown	prove	proved	proved/proven
break	broke	broken	put	put	put
bring	brought	brought	quit	quit	quit
broadcast	broadcast	broadcast	read	read	read
build	built	built	ride	rode	ridden
burn	burned/burnt	burned/burnt	ring	rang	rung
buy	bought	bought	rise	rose	risen
catch	caught	caught	run	ran	run
choose	chose	chosen	say	said	said
come	came	come	see	saw	seen
cost	cost	cost	seek	sought	sought
cut	cut	cut	sell	sold	sold
dig	dug	dug	send	sent	sent
dive	dived/dove	dived	set	set	set
do	did	done	shake	shook	shaken
draw	drew	drawn	shave	shaved	shaved/shaven
dream	dreamed/dreamt	dreamed/dreamt	shoot	shot	shot
drink	drank	drunk	shut	shut	shut
drive	drove	driven	sing	sang	sung
eat	ate	eaten	sink	sank	sunk
fall	fell	fallen	sit	sat	sat
feed	fed	fed	sleep	slept	slept
feel	felt	felt	slide	slid	slid
fight	fought	fought	speak	spoke	spoken
find	found	found	spend	spent	spent
fit	fit	fit	spread	spread	spread
fly	flew	flown	stand	stood	stood
forget	forgot	forgotten	steal	stole	stolen
forgive	forgave	forgiven	stick	stuck	stuck
freeze	froze	frozen	strike	struck	struck
get	got	got/gotten	swear	swore	sworn
give	gave	given	sweep	swept	swept
go	went	gone	swim	swam	swum
grow	grew	grown	take	took	taken
hang	hung	hung	teach	taught	taught
have	had	had	tear	tore	torn
hear	heard	heard	tell	told	told
hide	hid	hidden	think	thought	thought
hit	hit	hit	throw	threw	thrown
hold	held	held	understand	understood	understood
hurt	hurt	hurt	upset	upset	upset
keep	kept	kept	wake	woke/waked	woken/waked
know	knew	known	wear	wore	worn
lay	laid	laid	weave	wove	woven
lead	led	led	weep	wept	wept
leave	left	left	win	won	won
lend	lent	lent	withdraw	withdrew	withdrawn
let	let	let	write	wrote	written

□ EXERCISE 10. Simple past: irregular verbs. (Chart 2-7)
Directions: Complete each sentence with the simple past of any irregular verb that makes sense. There may be more than one possible completion.

1. Maria walked to school today. Rebecca _____drove_____ her car. Olga _____rode_____ her bicycle. Yoko _____took_____ the bus.

2. Last night I had a good night's sleep. I _____slept_____ nine hours.

3. Ann _____wore_____ a beautiful dress to the wedding reception.

area that smaller than lake

4. It got so cold last night that the water in the pond _____froze_____ .

5. Frank was really thirsty. He _____drank_____ four glasses of water.

6. Karen had to choose between a blue raincoat and a tan one. She finally _____chose_____ the blue one.

7. My husband gave me a painting for my birthday. I _____hung_____ it on a wall in my office.

8. Last night around midnight, when I was sound asleep, the telephone _____rang_____ . It _____woke_____ me up.

9. The sun _____rose_____ at 6:04 this morning and will set at 6:59.

10. I _____sent_____ an e-mail to my cousin after I finished studying yesterday evening.

11. Ms. Manning _____taught_____ chemistry at the local high school last year.

12. The police _____caught_____ the bank robbers. They are in jail now.

13. Oh my gosh! Call the police! Someone _____stole_____ my car!

14. Today Victor has on slacks and a sports jacket, but yesterday he _____wore_____ jeans and a sweatshirt to work.

15. My friend told me that he had a singing dog. When the dog _____sang_____ , I _____put_____ my hands over my ears.

16. When I introduced Pedro to Ming, they ___shook___ hands and greeted each other.

17. I ___swept___ the kitchen floor with a broom.

18. A bird ___came , flew___ into our apartment through an open window.

19. I caught the bird and ___held___ it gently in my hands until I could put it back outside.

20. The children had a good time at the park yesterday. They ___threw___ the ducks small pieces of bread.

21. My dog ___dug___ a hole in the yard and buried his bone.

22. Ahmed ___left___ his apartment in a hurry this morning because he was late for school. That's why he ___forgot___ to bring his books to class.

☐ EXERCISE 11. Simple past: irregular verbs. (Chart 2-7)
Directions: Complete each sentence with the simple past of any irregular verb that makes sense. There may be more than one possible completion.

1. Alex hurt his finger when he was fixing his dinner last night. He accidentally ___cut___ it with a sharp knife.

2. I don't have any money in my pocket. I ___spent___ it all yesterday. I'm flat broke.

3. Ann didn't throw her old shoes away. She ___wore , kept___ them because they were comfortable.

4. I ___read___ an interesting article in the newspaper yesterday.

5. Jack ___forgot___ his pocketknife at the park yesterday. This morning he ___came , went___ back to the park to look for it. Finally, he ___found___ it in the grass. He was glad to have it back.

6. Mr. Litovchenko was very happy but a little nervous when he ___held___ his baby in his arms for the first time.

7. I ___met___ Jennifer's parents when they visited her. She introduced me to them.

8. A: Is Natasha still angry with you?

   B: No, she ___forgave___ me for what I did, and she's speaking to me again.

9. I dropped my favorite vase. It fell on the floor and _____broke_____ into a hundred pieces.

10. When I went shopping yesterday, I _____bought_____ some light bulbs and a cooking pot.

11. The soldiers _____fought_____ the battle through the night and into the morning.

12. I used to have a camera, but I _____sold_____ it because I needed the money.

13. Jane didn't want anyone to find her diary, so she _____hid_____ it in a shoe box in her closet.

14. I didn't want anyone else to see the note, so I _____tore_____ it into tiny pieces and _____threw_____ them in the wastebasket.

15. The children _____drew_____ pictures of themselves in art class yesterday.

16. I have a cold. Yesterday I _____felt_____ terrible, but I'm feeling better today.

17. Last night I _____heard_____ a strange noise in the house around 2:00 A.M., so I _____got_____ up to investigate.

18. Sam ran the fastest, so he _____won_____ the race.

19. My dog isn't very friendly. Yesterday she _____bit_____ my neighbor's leg. Luckily, my dog is very old and doesn't have sharp teeth, so she didn't hurt my neighbor.

20. Steve _____blew_____ on the campfire to make it burn.

21. When I went fishing yesterday, I _____caught_____ a fish right away. But the fish was too small to keep. I carefully returned it to the water. It quickly _____swam_____ away.

22. Amanda _____told_____ a lie. I didn't believe her because I _____knew_____ the truth.

☐ EXERCISE 12. Simple past. (Charts 2-1 → 2-7)
Directions: Perform the action and then describe the action, using the simple past. Most of the verbs are irregular; some are regular.
Work in groups or as a class. Only Speaker A's book is open.

Example: Give (. . .) your pen.
SPEAKER A (book open): Give Pablo your pen.
SPEAKER B (book closed): (Speaker B performs the action.)
SPEAKER A (book open): What did you do?
SPEAKER B (book closed): I gave Pablo my pen.

1. Give (. . .) your dictionary.
2. Open your book.
3. Shut your book.
4. Stand up.
5. Hold your book above your head.
6. Put your book in your lap.
7. Bend your elbow.
8. Touch the tip of your nose.
9. Spell the word "happened."
10. Shake hands with (. . .).
11. Bite your finger.
12. Hide your pen.
13. Leave the room.
14. Speak to (. . .).
15. Tear a piece of paper.
16. Tell (. . .) to stand up.
17. Throw your pen to (. . .).
18. Draw a triangle on the board.
19. Turn to page ten in your book.
20. Choose a pen, this one or that one.
21. Invite (. . .) to have lunch with you.
22. Thank (. . .) for the invitation.
23. Steal (. . .)'s pen.
24. Sell your pen to (. . .) for a (penny).
25. Hit your desk with your hand.
26. Stick your pen in your pocket/purse.
27. Read a sentence from your book.
28. Repeat my sentence: This book is black.
29. Hang your (jacket) on your chair.
30. Take (. . .)'s grammar book.
31. Write your name on the board.

☐ EXERCISE 13. Simple past: questions and short answers. (Charts 2-1 → 2-7)
Directions: Use the words in parentheses. Give short answers to questions where necessary.

1. A: (you, sleep) _____Did you sleep_____ well last night?

   B: Yes, _____I did_____. I (sleep) _____slept_____ very well.

2. A: (Tom's plane, arrive) _____ on time yesterday?

   B: Yes, _____. It (get) _____ in at 6:05 on the dot.

3. A: (you, go) _____ to class yesterday?

   B: No, _____. I (stay) _____ home because I

   (feel, not) _____ good.

4. A: (Mark Twain, write) _____

   Tom Sawyer?

   B: Yes, _____. He also (write)

   _____ Huckleberry Finn.

5. A: *(you, eat)* _____ breakfast this morning?

   B: No, _____ . I *(have, not)* _____ enough

      time. I was late for class because my alarm clock *(ring, not)* _____ .

☐ EXERCISE 14. Simple past: questions, short answers, and irregular verbs.
              (Charts 2-1 → 2-7)

Directions: Pair up with a classmate.

Speaker A: Ask questions beginning with *"Did you . . . ?"* Listen carefully to Speaker B's
           answers to make sure he or she is using the irregular verbs correctly. Look at
           Chart 2-7 if necessary to check the correct form of an irregular verb. Your
           book is open.

Speaker B: In order to practice using irregular verbs, answer "yes" to all of Speaker A's
           questions. Give both a short answer and a long answer. Your book is closed.

Example: eat breakfast this morning

SPEAKER A *(book open):* Did you eat breakfast this morning?

SPEAKER B *(book closed):* Yes, I did. I ate breakfast this morning.

1. sleep well last night	6. lose your grammar book yesterday
2. wake up early this morning	7. find your grammar book
3. come to class early today	8. take a bus somewhere yesterday
4. bring your books to class	9. ride in a car yesterday
5. put your books on your desk	10. drive a car

Switch roles.

11. hear about the earthquake	17. have a good time
12. read the newspaper this morning	18. think about me
13. catch a cold last week	19. meet (. . .) the first day of class
14. feel terrible	20. shake hands with (. . .) when you first met him/her
15. see a doctor	
16. go to a party last night	

Switch roles.

21. buy some books yesterday	26. send your parents a letter
22. begin to read a new novel	27. lend (. . .) some money
23. fly to this city	28. wear a coat yesterday
24. run to class today	29. go to the zoo last week
25. write your parents a letter	30. feed the birds at the park

Switch roles.

31. make your own dinner last night	36. break your arm
32. leave home at eight this morning	37. understand the question
33. drink a cup of tea before class	38. speak to (. . .) yesterday
34. fall down yesterday	39. tell him/her your opinion of this class
35. hurt yourself when you fell down	40. mean what you said

□ EXERCISE 15. Past time. (Charts 2-1 → 2-7)

Directions: Pair up with a classmate.

Speaker A: Tell Speaker B about your activities yesterday. Think of at least five things you did yesterday to tell Speaker B about. Also think of two or three things you didn't do yesterday.

Speaker B: Listen carefully to Speaker A. Make sure that Speaker A is using past tenses correctly. Ask Speaker A questions about his/her activities if you wish. Take notes while Student A is talking.

When Speaker A finishes talking, switch roles: Speaker B tells Speaker A about his/her activities yesterday.

Use the notes from the conversation to write a composition about the other student's activities yesterday.

2-8 THE SIMPLE PAST AND THE PAST PROGRESSIVE

THE SIMPLE PAST	(a) Mary **walked** downtown yesterday. (b) I **slept** for eight hours last night.	The SIMPLE PAST is used to talk about *an activity or situation that began and ended at a particular time in the past* (e.g., *yesterday, last night, two days ago, in 1999*), as in (a) and (b).
THE PAST PROGRESSIVE	(c) I sat down at the dinner table at 6:00 P.M. yesterday. Tom came to my house at 6:10 P.M. I **was eating** dinner *when Tom came.* (d) I went to bed at 10:00. The phone rang at 11:00. I **was sleeping** *when the phone rang.*	The PAST PROGRESSIVE expresses *an activity that was in progress (was occurring, was happening)* at a point of time in the past (e.g., *at 6:10*) or at the time of another action (e.g., *when Tom came*). In (c): eating was in progress at 6:10; eating was in progress *when Tom came.* FORM: ***was/were*** + ***-ing***.

(e) **When** *the phone rang,* I was sleeping. (f) The phone rang **while** *I was sleeping.*	**when** = at that time **while** = during that time (e) and (f) have the same meaning.

2-9 FORMS OF THE PAST PROGRESSIVE

STATEMENT	I-She-He-It **was working**. You-We-They **were working**.	
NEGATIVE	I-She-He-It **was not (wasn't) working**. You-We-They **were not (weren't) working**.	
QUESTION	**Was** I-she-he-it **working?** **Were** you-we-they **working?**	
SHORT ANSWER	Yes, I-she-he-it **was**. No, I-she-he-it **wasn't**.	Yes, you-we-they **were**. No, you-we-they **weren't**.

☐ EXERCISE 16. Simple past and past progressive. (Charts 2-8 and 2-9)
Directions: Complete the sentences with the words in parentheses. Use the simple past or the past progressive.

1. At 6:00 P.M., Bob sat down at the table and began to eat. At 6:05, Bob *(eat)* __**was eating**__ dinner.

2. While Bob *(eat)* __was eating__ dinner, Ann *(come)* __came__ through the door.

3. In other words, when Ann *(come)* __came__ through the door, Bob *(eat)* __was eating__ dinner.

4. Bob went to bed at 10:30. At 11:00 Bob *(sleep)* __was sleeping__.

5. While Bob *(sleep)* __was sleeping__, the phone *(ring)* __rang__.

6. In other words, when the phone *(ring)* __rang__, Bob *(sleep)* __was sleeping__.

7. Bob left his house at 8:00 A.M. and *(begin)* __began__ to walk to class.

8. While he *(walk)* __was walking__ to class, he *(see)* __saw__ Mrs. Smith.

9. When Bob *(see)* __saw__ Mrs. Smith, she *(stand)* __was standing__ on her front porch. She *(hold)* __was holding__ a broom.

10. Mrs. Smith *(wave)* __waved__ at Bob when she *(see)* __saw__ him.

□ **EXERCISE 17. Using the past progressive.** (Charts 2-8 and 2-9)
Directions: Perform the actions and answer the questions. Only the teacher's book is open.

    Example: A: write on the board   B: open the door
To STUDENT A: Please write on the board. Write anything you wish. *(Student A writes on the board.)* What are you doing?
    Response: I'm writing on the board.
To STUDENT A: Good. Please continue.
To STUDENT B: Open the door. *(Student B opens the door.)* What did you just do?
    Response: I opened that door.
To STUDENT A: *(Student A),* thank you. You may stop now.
To STUDENT C: Describe the two actions that just occurred, using *when.*
    Response: When *(Student B)* opened the door, *(Student A)* was writing on the board.
To STUDENT D: Again, using *while.*
    Response: While *(Student A)* was writing on the board, *(Student B)* opened the door.

1. A: write a note to (. . .)   B: knock on the door

2. A: walk around the room   B: clap your hands once

3. A: talk to (. . .)   B: come into the room

4. A: read your book   B: tap (Student A)'s shoulder

5. A: look out the window   B: ask (Student A) a question

6. A: whistle   B: leave the room

7. A: look at your watch   B: ask (Student A) a question

8. A: pantomime eating (pretend to eat)   B: sit down next to (Student A)

9. A: pantomime sleeping   B: take (Student A)'s grammar book

10. A: pantomime drinking a glass of water   B: come into the room

□ **EXERCISE 18. Present progressive and past progressive.** (Charts 1-1, 2-8, and 2-9)
Directions: <u>Underline</u> the present progressive and past progressive verbs in the following pairs of sentences. Discuss their use. What are the similarities between the two tenses?

1. A: Where are Ann and Rob? I haven't seen them for a couple of weeks.
  B: They're out of town. They<u>'re traveling.</u>

2. A: I invited Ann and Rob to my birthday party, but they didn't come.
  B: Why not?
  A: They were out of town. They <u>were traveling</u>.

3. A: What was I talking about when the phone interrupted me? I lost my train of thought.
  B: You <u>were describing</u> the website you found on the Internet yesterday.

4. A: I missed the beginning of the news report. What's the announcer talking about?
  B: She's describing conditions in Bangladesh after the flood.

5. A: Good morning, Kim.

    B: Hello, Tom. Good to see you.

    A: Good to see you, too. On your way to work?

    B: Yup. I'm walking to work today to take advantage of the beautiful spring morning.

    A: It certainly is a beautiful spring morning.

6. A: Guess who I saw this morning.

    B: Who?

    A: Jim.

    B: Oh? How is he?

    A: He looks fine.

    B: Where did you see him?

    A: On the sidewalk near the corner of 5th and Pine. He was walking to work.

☐ EXERCISE 19. Present and past verbs. (Chapters 1 and 2)
   Directions: Complete the sentences with the simple present, present progressive, simple past, or past progressive.

   PART I. PRESENT TIME

   SITUATION:

   Right now Toshi *(sit)* _____is sitting_____ at his desk. He

   (study) _____ his grammar book. His roommate, Oscar, *(sit)*

   _____ at his desk, but he *(study, not)* _____.

   He *(stare)* _____ out the window. Toshi *(want)*

   _____ to know what Oscar *(look)* _____ at.

   TOSHI: Oscar, what *(you, look)* _____ at?

OSCAR: I *(watch)* _____(9)_____ the bicyclists. They are very skillful. I

(know, not) _____(10)_____ how to ride a bike, so I *(admire)*

_____(11)_____ anyone who can. Come over to the window. Look at

that guy in the blue shirt. He *(steer)* _____(12)_____ his bike with one

hand while he *(drink)* _____(13)_____ a soda with the other. At the

same time, he *(weave)* _____(14)_____ in and out of the heavy street

traffic. He *(seem)* _____(15)_____ fearless.

TOSHI: Riding a bike *(be, not)* _____(16)_____ as hard as it *(look)* _____(17)_____.
I'll teach you to ride a bicycle if you'd like.

OSCAR: Really? Great!

TOSHI: How come you don't know how to ride a bike?*

OSCAR: I *(have, never)* _____(18)_____ a bike when I *(be)* _____(19)_____

a kid. My family *(be)* _____(20)_____ too poor. Once I *(try)*

_____(21)_____ to learn on the bike of one of my friends, but the other kids

all *(laugh)* _____(22)_____ at me. I never *(try)* _____(23)_____ again

because I *(be)* _____(24)_____ too embarrassed. But I'd really like to learn

now! When can we start?

PART II. PAST TIME

Yesterday, Toshi *(sit)* _____**was sitting**_____(25) at his desk and *(study)*

_____(26)_____ his grammar book. His roommate, Oscar, *(sit)*

_____(27)_____ at his desk, but he *(study, not)* _____(28)_____.

He *(stare)* _____(29)_____ out the window. He *(watch)* _____(30)_____

bicyclists on the street below.

_____

*"How come?" means "Why?" For example, "How come you don't know how to ride a bike?" means "Why don't you know how to ride a bike?"

Toshi *(walk)* _____ over to the window. Oscar *(point)* _____
<u>31</u>   <u>32</u>

out one bicyclist in particular. This bicyclist *(steer)* _____ with one
<u>33</u>

hand while he *(drink)* _____ a soda with the other. At the same
<u>34</u>

time, he *(weave)* _____ in and out of the heavy traffic. To Oscar,
<u>35</u>

the bicyclist *(seem)* _____ fearless.
<u>36</u>

    Oscar *(learn, never)* _____ how to ride a bike when he *(be)*
<u>37</u>

_____ a child, so Toshi *(offer)* _____ to teach him. Oscar
<u>38</u>   <u>39</u>

(accept) _____ gladly.
<u>40</u>

☐ **EXERCISE 20. Verb tense and irregular verb review. (Chapters 1 and 2)**
    Directions: Complete the sentences with the verbs in parentheses. Use the simple past, simple present, or past progressive.

(1) Once upon a time, a king and his three daughters *(live)* _____<u>lived</u>_____ in a castle in a faraway land. One day while the king *(think)* __<u>was thinking</u>__ about his daughters, he *(have)* _____<u>had</u>_____ an idea. He *(form)* _____<u>formed</u>_____ a plan for finding husbands for them.

(2) When it *(come)* _____<u>came</u>_____ time for the three daughters to marry, the king *(announce)* __<u>announced</u>__ his plan. He said, "I'm going to take three jewels to the fountain in the center of the village. The young men *(meet)* _____<u>meet*</u>_____ together there every day. The three young men who find the jewels will become my daughters' husbands."

(3) The next day, the king *(choose)* _____ three jewels—an emerald, a ruby, and a diamond—and *(take)* _____ them into the village. He *(hold)* _____ them in his hand and *(walk)* _____ among the young men. First he *(drop)* _____ the emerald, then the ruby, and then the diamond. A handsome man *(pick)* _____ up the emerald. Then a wealthy prince *(spot)* _____ the ruby and *(bend)* _____ down to pick it up. The king *(be)* _____ very pleased.

_____

*The simple present is used here because the story is giving the king's exact words in a quotation. Notice that quotation marks ("...") are used. See Chart 14-8, p. 420, for more information about quotations.

(4) But then a frog *(hop)* _____ toward the diamond and *(pick)* _____ it up. The frog *(bring)* _____ the diamond to the king and said, "I *(be)* _____ the Frog Prince. I *(claim)* _____ your third daughter as my wife."

(5) When the king *(tell)* _____ Tina, his third daughter, about the Frog Prince, she *(refuse)* _____ to marry him. When the people of the land *(hear)* _____ the news about the frog and the princess, they *(laugh)* _____ and *(laugh)* _____ . "Have you heard the news?" the people *(say)* _____ to each other. "Princess Tina is going to marry a frog!"

(6) Tina *(feel)* _____ terrible. She said, "I *(be)* _____ the unluckiest person in the world." She *(fall)* _____ to the floor and *(sob)* _____ . No one *(love)* _____ her, she *(believe)* _____ . Her father *(understand, not)* _____ her. She *(hide)* _____ from her friends and *(keep)* _____ her pain in her heart. Every day, she *(grow)* _____ sadder and sadder. Her two sisters *(have)* _____ grand weddings. Their wedding bells *(ring)* _____ with joy across the land.

(7) Eventually, Tina (leave) _____ the castle. She (run)

_____ away from her family and (go) _____ to live in the

woods by herself. She (eat) _____ simple food, (drink) _____

water from the lake, (cut) _____ her own firewood, (wash)

_____ her own clothes, (sweep) _____ the floor herself,

(make) _____ her own bed, and (take) _____ care of all her

own needs. But she (be) _____ very lonely and unhappy.

(8) One day Tina (go) _____ swimming. The water (be) _____

deep and cold. Tina (swim) _____ for a long time and (become)

_____ very tired. While she (swim) _____ back

toward the shore, she (lose) _____ the desire to live. She (quit)

_____ trying to swim to safety. She (drown) _____

when the frog suddenly (appear) _____ and with all his strength

(push) _____ Tina to the shore. He (save) _____ her life.

(9) "Why (save, you) _____ my life, Frog?"

"Because you (be) _____ very young and you (have) _____

a lot to live for."

"No, I (do, not) _____," said the princess. "I (be) _____

the most miserable person in the whole universe."

(10) "Let's talk about it," (say) _____ the frog. And they (begin)

_____ to talk. Tina and the Frog Prince (sit) _____

together for hours and hours. Frog (listen) _____ and (understand)

_____ . He (tell) _____ her about himself and his own

unhappiness and loneliness. They *(share)* _____ their minds and hearts.
Day after day, they *(spend)* _____ hours with each other. They
(talk) _____ , *(laugh)* _____ , *(play)* _____ ,
and *(work)* _____ together.

(11) One day while they *(sit)* _____ near the lake, Tina *(bend)*
_____ down and, with great affection, *(kiss)* _____ the frog
on his forehead. Poof! Suddenly the frog *(turn)* _____ into a man!
He *(take)* _____ Tina in his arms, and said, "You *(save)* _____

me with your kiss. Outside, I *(look)* _____ like a frog, but you *(see)*
_____ inside and *(find)* _____ the real me. Now I *(be)*
_____ free. An evil wizard had turned me into a frog until I found the love
of a woman with a truly good heart." When Tina *(see)* _____ through
outside appearances, she *(find)* _____ true love.

(12) Tina and the prince *(return)* _____ to the castle and *(get)*
_____ married. Her two sisters, she discovered, *(be)* _____
very unhappy. The handsome husband *(ignore)* _____ his wife and
(talk, not) _____ to her. The wealthy husband *(make)* _____
fun of his wife and *(give)* _____ her orders all the time. But Tina and her
Frog Prince *(live)* _____ happily ever after.

□ **EXERCISE 21. Past time. (Chapter 2)**

   Directions: Write a story that begins "Once upon a time, ..."

   Choose one:

   1. Invent your own story. For example, write about a lonely bee who finds happiness, a poor orphan who succeeds in life with the help of a fairy godmother, a hermit who rediscovers the joys of human companionship, etc. Discuss possible story ideas in class.

   2. Write a fable that you are familiar with, perhaps one that is well known in your culture.

   3. Write a story with your classmates. Each student writes one or two sentences at a time. One student begins the story. Then he or she passes the paper on to another student, who then writes a sentence or two and passes the paper on—until everyone in the class has had a chance to write part of the story, or until the story has an ending. This story can then be reproduced for the class to revise and correct together. The class may want to "publish" the final product on the Internet or in a small booklet.

2-10 EXPRESSING PAST TIME: USING TIME CLAUSES

(a) time clause: *After I finished my work,* main clause: *I went to bed.*	*After I finished my work* = a time clause★
	I went to bed = a main clause★
	(a) and (b) have the same meaning.
	A time clause can
	  (1) come in front of a main clause, as in (a).
	  (2) follow a main clause, as in (b).

(b) main clause: *I went to bed* time clause: *after I finished my work.*	

(c) I went to bed *after I finished my work.*
 	
(d) *Before I went to bed,* I finished my work.
 	
(e) I stayed up *until I finished my work.*
 	
(f) *As soon as I finished my work,* I went to bed.
 	
(g) The phone rang *while I was watching* TV.
 	
(h) *When the phone rang,* I was watching TV.
	These words introduce time clauses:
	  after
	  before
	  until } + *subject and verb* = a time clause
	  as soon as
	  while
	  when<hr>In (e): *until* = "to that time and then no longer"★★
	In (f): *as soon as* = "immediately after"<hr>PUNCTUATION: Put a comma at the end of a time clause when the time clause comes first in a sentence (comes in front of the main clause):
	  time clause + **comma** + **main clause**
	  main clause + NO **comma** + **time clause**

(i) When the phone *rang,* I *answered* it.	In a sentence with a time clause introduced by *when*, both the time clause verb and the main verb can be simple past. In this case, the action in the *when*-clause happened first. In (i): *First: The phone rang. Then: I answered it.*
(j) While I *was doing* my homework, my roommate *was watching* TV.	In (j): When two actions are in progress at the same time, the past progressive can be used in both parts of the sentence.

   ★A *clause* is a structure that has a subject and a verb.
   ★★*Until* can also be used to say that something does NOT happen before a particular time: *I didn't go to bed until I finished my work.*

☐ EXERCISE 22. Past time clauses. (Chart 2-10)

Directions: Combine the two sentences into one sentence by using time clauses. Discuss correct punctuation.

1. *First:* I got home.
    Then: I ate dinner.

    → After ....   OR   ... after ....
       After I got home, I ate dinner.   OR   *I ate dinner after I got home.*

2. *First:* I unplugged the coffee pot.
    Then: I left my apartment this morning.
    → Before ....   OR   ... before ....

3. *First:* I lived on a farm.
    Then: I was seven years old.
    → Until ....   OR   ... until ....

4. *First:* I heard the doorbell.
    Then: I opened the door.
    → As soon as ....   OR   ... as soon as ....

5. *First:* The rabbit was sleeping.
    Then: The fox climbed through the window.
    → While ....   OR   ... while ....
    → When ....   OR   ... when ....

6. *First:* It began to rain.
    Then: I stood under a tree.
    → When ....   OR   ... when ....

7. *At the same time:* I was lying in bed with the flu.
                        My friends were swimming at the beach.
    → While ....   OR   ... while ....

□ **EXERCISE 23. Past time clauses. (Charts 2-1 → 2-10)**

  Directions: Complete the sentences using the words in parentheses. Use the simple past or the past progressive. Identify the time clauses.

1. My mother called me around 5:00. My husband came home a little after that.

   [When he *(come)* _____ came _____ home,] I *(talk)* _____ **was talking** _____ to my mother on the phone.

2. I *(buy)* _____ bought _____ a small gift before I *(go)* _____ went _____ to the hospital yesterday to visit my friend.

3. Yesterday afternoon I *(go)* _____ went _____ to visit the Smith family. When I *(get)* _____ got _____ there around two o'clock, Mrs. Smith *(be)* _____ was _____ in the yard. She *(plant)* _____ was planting _____ flowers in her garden. Mr. Smith *(be)* _____ was _____ in the garage. He *(work)* _____ was working _____ on their car. He *(change)* _____ was changing _____ the oil. The children *(play)* _____ were playing _____ in the front yard. In other words, while Mr. Smith *(change)* _____ was changing _____ the oil in the car, the children *(play)* _____ were playing _____ with a ball in the yard.

4. I (hit) _____hit_____ my thumb while I (use) _____was using_____ the hammer. Ouch! That (hurt) _____hurt_____.

5. As soon as we (hear) _____heard_____ the news of the approaching hurricane, we (begin) _____began_____ our preparations for the storm.

6. It was a long walk home. Mr. Chu (walk) _____walked_____ until he (get) _____got_____ tired. Then he (stop) _____stoped_____ and (rest) _____rested_____ until he (be) _____was_____ strong enough to continue.

7. While I (lie) _____was lying_____ in bed last night, I (hear) _____was hearing_____ a strange noise. When I (hear) _____heard_____ this strange noise, I (turn) _____turned_____ on the light. I (hold) _____held_____ my breath and (listen) _____listened_____ carefully. A mouse (chew) _____was chewing_____ on something under the floor.

8. I work at a computer all day long. Yesterday while I (look) _____was looking_____ at my computer screen, I (start) _____started_____ to feel a little dizzy, so I (take) _____took_____ a break. While I (take) _____was taking_____ a short break outdoors and (enjoy) _____enjoying_____ the warmth of the sun on my face, an elderly gentleman (come) _____came_____ up to me and (ask) _____asked_____ me for directions to the public library. After I (tell) _____told_____ him how to get there, he (thank) _____thanked_____ me and (go) _____went_____ on his way. I (stay) _____stayed_____ outside until a big cloud (come) _____came_____ and (cover) _____covered_____ the sun, and then I reluctantly (go) _____went_____ back inside to work. As soon as I (return) _____returned_____ to my desk, I (notice) _____notice_____ that my computer (make) _____was making_____ a funny noise. It (hum) _____was humming_____ loudly, and my screen was frozen. I (think) _____thought_____ for a moment, then I (shut) _____shut_____ my computer off, (get) _____got_____ up from my desk, and (leave) _____left_____. I (spend) _____spent_____ the rest of the day in the sunshine.

2-11 EXPRESSING PAST HABIT: *USED TO*

(a) I *used to live* with my parents. Now I live in my own apartment. (b) Ann *used to be* afraid of dogs, but now she likes dogs. (c) Al *used to smoke,* but he doesn't anymore.	*Used to* expresses a past situation or habit that no longer exists at present. FORM: *used to* + *the simple form of a verb*
(d) *Did* you *used to* live in Paris? (OR *Did* you *use to* live in Paris?)	QUESTION FORM: *did* + *subject* + *used to* (OR *did* + *subject* + *use to*)*
(e) I *didn't used to* drink coffee at breakfast, but now I always have coffee in the morning. (OR I *didn't use to* drink coffee.) (f) I *never used to* drink coffee at breakfast, but now I always have coffee in the morning.	NEGATIVE FORM: *didn't used to* (OR *didn't use to*)* *Didn't use(d) to* occurs infrequently. More commonly, people use *never* to express a negative idea with *used to,* as in (f).

*Both forms (spelled *used to* or *use to* in questions and negatives) are possible. There is no consensus among English language authorities on which is preferable.

☐ EXERCISE 24. Past habit with USED TO. (Chart 2-11)
Directions: Correct the errors.

1. Alex used to ~~living~~ live in Cairo.

2. Jane used to worked at an insurance company.

3. Margo was used to teach English, but now she works at a publishing company.

4. Where you used to live?

5. I didn't was used to get up early, but now I do.

6. Were you used to live in Singapore?

7. My family used to going to the beach every weekend, but now I don't.

☐ EXERCISE 25. Past habit with USED TO. (Chart 2-11)
Directions: Make sentences with a similar meaning by using *used to.* Some of the sentences are negatives, and some of them are questions.

1. When I was a child, I was shy. Now I'm not shy.

→ I ___used to be___ shy, but now I'm not.

2. When I was young, I thought that people over forty were old.

→ I _____ that people over forty were old.

3. Now you live in this city. Where did you live before you came here?

→ Where _____?

4. Did you at some time in the past work for the telephone company?

→ _____ for the telephone company?

5. When I was younger I slept through the night. I never woke up in the middle of the night.

→ I _____ in the middle of the night, but now I do.

→ I _____ through the night, but now I don't.

6. When I was a child, I watched cartoons on TV. I don't watch cartoons anymore. Now I watch news programs. How about you?

→ I _____ cartoons on TV, but I don't anymore.

→ I _____ news programs, but now I do.

→ What _____ on TV when you were a little kid?

☐ **EXERCISE 26. Past habit with USED TO. (Chart 2-11)**
Directions: Complete the sentences with a form of **used to** and your own words.

1. I _____used to ride_____ my bicycle to work, but now I take the bus.

2. What time _____did you use(d) to go_____ to bed when you were a child?

3. I _____didn't use(d) to stay up_____ past midnight, but now I often go to bed very late because I have to study.

4. Tom _____ tennis after work every day, but now he doesn't.

5. I _____ breakfast, but now I always have something to eat in the morning because I read that students who eat breakfast do better in school.

6. I _____ interested in _____ , but now I am.

7. A: When you were a little kid, what _____ after school?

B: I _____ . How about you?

A: I _____ .

☐ **EXERCISE 27. Past habit with USED TO.** (Chart 2-11)

Directions: Work in pairs. Use **used to**.
Speaker A: Ask the given question.
Speaker B: Answer the question, using **used to**. Then ask Speaker A the same question.

Example: Where did you used to live?
SPEAKER A: Where did you used to live?
SPEAKER B: I used to live in Tel Aviv. How about you? Where did you used to live?
SPEAKER A: I used to live in Manila.

1. What did you used to watch on TV when you were a child, and what do you watch now?

2. You are living in a foreign country (OR a different city). What did you used to do in your own country (OR your hometown) that you don't do now?

3. You are an adult now. What did you used to do when you were a child that you don't do now?

4. Think of a particular time in your past (for example, when you were in elementary school, when you lived in Paris, when you worked at your uncle's store). Describe a typical day in your life at that time. What did you used to do?

☐ **EXERCISE 28. Past habit with USED TO.** (Chart 2-11)

Directions: Write about the following topics. Use **used to**. Try to think of at least two or three differences for each topic.

Topics:

1. Compare past and present clothing. How are they different?
   (e.g., *Shoes used to have buttons, but now they don't.*)

2. Compare past and present means of transportation.
   (e.g., *It used to take months to cross the Atlantic Ocean by ship, but now people fly from one continent to another in a few hours.*)

3. Compare the daily lives of people fifty years ago to the daily lives of people today.
   (e.g., *Fifty years ago people didn't use to watch rented movies on TV, but today people often watch movies at home for entertainment.*)

4. Compare past and present beliefs.
   (e.g., *Some people used to believe the sun revolved around the earth, but now we know that the earth revolves around the sun.*)

CHAPTER 3
Future Time

☐ EXERCISE 1. Preview: future time. (Charts 3-1 → 3-6)
   Directions: Use the given words to make sentences about the future. Work in pairs, in groups, or as a class.

   Examples: I . . . around four this afternoon.
                  → *I'm going to go home around four this afternoon.*

                you . . . tomorrow?
                  → *Will you be in class tomorrow?*

   1. I . . . this evening.
   2. the teacher . . . next week?
   3. I . . . probably . . . later today.
   4. what time . . . you . . . tomorrow morning?
   5. you . . . later this (morning/afternoon/evening)?
   6. computers . . . in the future.★
   7. what . . . you . . . this weekend?
   8. I may . . . in a few days.
   9. we . . . after we finish this exercise.
   10. I . . . before I . . . tomorrow.

   ───────────

   ★*In the future* = American English; *in future* = British English.

3-1 EXPRESSING FUTURE TIME: *BE GOING TO* AND *WILL*

FUTURE 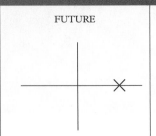	(a) I **am going to leave** at nine tomorrow morning. (b) I **will leave** at nine tomorrow morning. (c) Marie **is going to be** at the meeting today.★ (d) Marie **will be** at the meeting today.	**Be going to** and **will** are used to express future time. (a) and (b) have the same meaning. (c) and (d) have the same meaning. **Will** and **be going to** often give the same meaning, but sometimes they express different meanings. The differences are discussed in Chart 3-5, p. 63.
(e) **I shall** leave at nine tomorrow morning. (f) **We shall** leave at nine tomorrow morning.		The use of *shall* (with *I* or *we*) to express future time is possible but infrequent.

★**Today**, **tonight**, and **this** + **morning**, **afternoon**, **evening**, **week**, etc., can express present, past, or future time.
PRESENT: *Sam is in his office this morning.*
PAST: *Ann was in her office this morning at eight, but now she's at a meeting.*
FUTURE: *Bob is going to be in his office this morning after his dentist appointment.*

3-2 FORMS WITH *BE GOING TO*

(a) We *are going to* **be** late. (b) She's *going to* **come** tomorrow. INCORRECT: *She's going to comes tomorrow.*	**Be going to** is followed by the simple form of the verb, as in (a) and (b).
(c) **Am** I **Is** he, she, it } **going to be** late? **Are** they, we, you	QUESTION: **be** + *subject* + **going to**
(d) I **am not** He, she, it **is not** } **going to be** late. They, we, you **are not**	NEGATIVE: **be** + **not** + **going to**
(e) "Hurry up! We're **gonna** be late!"	**Be going to** is more common in speaking and in informal writing than in formal writing. In informal speaking, it is sometimes pronounced "gonna" /gənə/. "Gonna" is not usually a written form.

☐ **EXERCISE 2. BE GOING TO. (Charts 3-1 and 3-2)**
  Directions: Complete the sentences with **be going to** and the words in parentheses.

  1. A: What (*you, do*) _____are you going to do_____ this afternoon?

     B: I (*work*) _____am going to work_____ on my report.

  2. A: Where (*Alex, be*) _____ later tonight?

     B: He (*be*) _____ at Kim's house.

3. A: *(you, finish)* _____ this exercise soon?

   B: Yes, I *(finish)* _____ it in less than a minute.

4. A: When *(you, call)* _____ your sister?

   B: I *(call, not)* _____ her. I *(send)*

   _____ her an e-mail.

5. A: What *(Dr. Price, talk)* _____ about in her

   speech tonight?

   B: She *(discuss)* _____ the economy of Southeast

   Asia.

☐ **EXERCISE 3. BE GOING TO. (Charts 3-1 and 3-2)**
Directions: Pair up with a classmate. Use ***be going to*** to talk about plans and intentions.
(NOTE: You may wish to practice saying "gonna," but also practice enunciating the full
form.)
Speaker A: Ask a question using ***be going to*** and the given words. Your book is open.
Speaker B: Answer the question in a complete sentence, using ***be going to***. Your book is
closed.

Example: What . . . do next Monday?
SPEAKER A *(book open):* What are you going to do next Monday?
SPEAKER B *(book closed):* I'm going to go to my classes as usual.

Example: watch TV tonight?
SPEAKER A *(book open):* Are you going to watch TV tonight?
SPEAKER B *(book closed):* Yes, I'm going to watch TV tonight. OR No, I'm not going to
watch TV tonight.

1. where . . . go after your last class today?
2. have pizza for dinner tonight?
3. what . . . do this evening?
4. when . . . visit my hometown?
5. visit . . . sometime in the future?
6. what . . . do this coming Saturday?

Switch roles.
7. what time . . . go to bed tonight?
8. what . . . wear tomorrow?
9. wear your . . . tomorrow too?
10. how long . . . stay in this city?
11. take a trip sometime this year or next?
12. where . . . go and what . . . do?

□ EXERCISE 4. Review of verb forms: past, present, and future.
        (Chapters 1 and 2; Charts 3-1 and 3-2)
    Directions: Complete the dialogue with your own words. The dialogue reviews the forms
    (statement, negative, question, short answer) of the simple present, simple past, and ***be***
    going to.

Example:
A: I *hitchhiked to school* yesterday.
B: Oh? That's interesting. *Do* you *hitchhike to school* every day?
A: Yes, I *do*. I *hitchhike to school* every day.
B: *Do* you also *hitchhike home* every day?
A: No, I *don't*. Etc.

1. A: I _____ yesterday.

2. B: Oh? That's interesting. _____ you _____ every day?

3. A: Yes, I _____ . I _____ every day.

4. B: _____ you also _____ every day?

5. A: No, I _____ . I _____ every day.

6. B: _____ you _____ yesterday?

7. A: Yes, I _____ . I _____ yesterday.

8. B: _____ you also _____ yesterday?

9. A: No, I _____ . I _____ yesterday.

10. B: _____Are_____ you _____ tomorrow?

11. A: Yes, I _____ . I _____ tomorrow.

12. B: _____ you also _____ tomorrow?

13. A: No, I _____ . I _____ tomorrow.

□ EXERCISE 5. Present, past, and future time. (Chapters 1 and 2; Charts 3-1 and 3-2)
    Directions: Pair up with a classmate.
    Speaker A: Ask Speaker B a question about his or her activities. Use ***what*** and the given
             time expressions. Your book is open.
    Speaker B: Answer the question in a complete sentence. Your book is closed.

Example: this evening
SPEAKER A *(book open):* What are you going to do this evening?
SPEAKER B *(book closed):* I'm going to get on the Internet for a while and then read.

Switch roles.

1. yesterday
2. tomorrow
3. right now
4. every day
5. later today
6. the day before yesterday

7. tonight
8. the day after tomorrow
9. last week
10. next week
11. every week
12. this weekend

3-3 FORMS WITH *WILL*

STATEMENT	I-You-She-He-It-We-They ***will come*** tomorrow.
NEGATIVE	I-You-She-He-It-We-They ***will not (won't) come*** tomorrow.
QUESTION	***Will*** I-you-she-he-it-we-they ***come*** tomorrow?
SHORT ANSWER	Yes,} I-you-she-he-it-we-they {***will.***★ No,} {***won't.***

CONTRACTIONS	*I'll* *she'll* *we'll* *you'll* *he'll* *they'll* *it'll*	***Will*** is usually contracted with pronouns in both speech and informal writing.
	Bob + ***will*** = "Bob***'ll***" the teacher + ***will*** = "the teacher***'ll***"	***Will*** is often contracted with nouns in speech, but usually not in writing.

★Pronouns are NOT contracted with helping verbs in short answers.
> CORRECT: *Yes, I will.*
> INCORRECT: *Yes, I'll.*

☐ EXERCISE 6. Forms with WILL. (Chart 3-3)
> *Directions:* Practice using contractions with ***will***. Write the correct contraction for the words in parentheses. Practice pronunciation.

1. *(I will)* _____I'll_____ be home at eight tonight.
2. *(We will)* _____ do well in the game tomorrow.
3. *(You will)* _____ probably get a letter today.
4. Karen is collecting shells at the beach. *(She will)* _____ be home around sundown.
5. Henry hurt his heel climbing a hill. *(He will)* _____ probably stay home today.
6. *(It will)* _____ probably be too cold to go swimming tomorrow.
7. I invited some guests for dinner. *(They will)* _____ probably get here around seven.

☐ EXERCISE 7. Forms with WILL. (Chart 3-3)
> *Directions:* Read the following sentences aloud. Practice contracting ***will*** with nouns in speech.

1. Rob will probably call tonight. *("Rob'll probably call tonight.")*
2. Dinner will be at seven.
3. Mary will be here at six tomorrow.
4. The weather will probably be a little colder tomorrow.
5. The party will start at eight.
6. Sam will help us move into our new apartment.
7. My friends will be here soon.
8. The sun will rise at 6:08 tomorrow morning.

3-4 SURENESS ABOUT THE FUTURE

100% sure	(a) I **will be** in class tomorrow. OR I **am going to be** in class tomorrow.	In (a): The speaker uses **will** or **be going to** because he feels sure about his future activity. He is stating a fact about the future.

90% sure	(b) Po **will probably be** in class tomorrow.
	OR
	Po **is probably going to be** in class tomorrow.
	(c) Anna **probably won't be** in class tomorrow. OR
	Anna **probably isn't going to be** in class tomorrow.
		In (b): The speaker uses **probably** to say that he expects Po to be in class tomorrow, but he is not 100% sure. He's almost sure, but not completely sure.
		Word order with **probably:***
		  (1) in a statement, as in (b):
		    helping verb + **probably**
		  (2) with a negative verb, as in (c):
		    probably + *helping verb*

50% sure	(d) Ali **may come** to class tomorrow, or Ali **may not come** to class tomorrow. I don't know what he's going to do.	**May** expresses a future possibility: maybe something will happen, and maybe it won't happen.** In (d): The speaker is saying that maybe Ali will come to class, or maybe he won't come to class. The speaker is guessing.
	(e) **Maybe** Ali **will come** to class, and **maybe** he **won't**. OR **Maybe** Ali **is going to come** to class, and **maybe** he **isn't**.	**Maybe** + **will/be going to** gives the same meaning as **may**. (d) and (e) have the same meaning. **Maybe** comes at the beginning of a sentence.

*See Chart 1-3, p. 9, for more information about placement of midsentence adverbs such as **probably**.
See Chart 7-3, p. 193, for more information about **may.

☐ **EXERCISE 8. Sureness about the future. (Chart 3-4)**
    Directions: Discuss how sure the speaker is in each sentence.

1. The bank will be open tomorrow.
    → *The speaker is very sure.*

2. I'm going to go to the bank tomorrow.

3. I'll probably go to the post office too.

4. I may stop at the market on my way home.

5. Ms. White will probably be in the office around nine tomorrow morning.

6. Mr. Wu will be in the office at seven tomorrow morning.

7. Mr. Alvarez may be in the office early tomorrow morning.

8. The sun will rise tomorrow.

9. I'm going to go to the art museum this Saturday, and I may go to the natural history museum too.

10. Abdul is probably going to come with me.

□ **EXERCISE 9. Sureness about the future: using PROBABLY. (Chart 3-4)**

> *Directions:* For each situation, predict what will probably happen and what probably won't happen. Include *probably* in your prediction. Use either *will* or *be going to*.

1. Antonio is late to class almost every day.
   (be on time tomorrow? be late again?)
   → *Antonio probably won't be on time tomorrow. He'll probably be late again.*

2. Rosa has a terrible cold. She feels miserable.
   (go to work tomorrow? stay home and rest?)

3. Sam didn't sleep at all last night.
   (go to bed early tonight? stay up all night again tonight?)

4. Ms. Bok needs to travel to a nearby city. She hates to fly.
   (take a plane? travel by bus or train?)

5. Mr. Chu is out of town on business. He needs to contact his assistant right away.
   (call her on the phone or e-mail her? wait until she calls him?)

6. Gina loves to run, but right now she has sore knees and a sore ankle.
   (run in the marathon race this week? skip the race?)

□ **EXERCISE 10. Sureness about the future. (Chart 3-4)**

> *Directions:* First the teacher will find out some information from Speaker A, and then ask Speaker B a question. Speaker B will answer using *may* or *maybe* if s/he's simply guessing or *probably* if s/he's fairly sure. Only the teacher's book is open.

Example:

TEACHER *(book open):* Who's going to visit an interesting place in this city soon?

SPEAKER A *(book closed):* *(Speaker A raises his/her hand.)* I am.

TEACHER *(book open):* Where are you going to go?

SPEAKER A *(book closed):* To the zoo.

TEACHER *(book open):* *(Speaker B),* how is *(Speaker A)* going to get to the zoo?

SPEAKER B *(book closed):* I have no idea. He may walk, or he may take a bus. Maybe he'll ride his bike. OR Well, it's pretty far from here, so he'll probably take a bus.

1. Who's going to visit an interesting place soon?
   Where are you going to go?
   Question to Speaker B: How is *(Speaker A)* going to get to *(name of place)*?

2. Who is going to stay home tonight?
   Question to Speaker B: What is *(Speaker A)* going to do at home tonight?

3. Who's going to go out this evening?
   Question to Speaker B: What is *(Speaker A)* going to do this evening?

4. Who's going to take a trip soon?
   Where are you going?
   Question to Speaker B: How is *(Speaker A)* going to get to *(name of place)*?

5. *(Speaker A),* please tell us three things you would like to do this weekend.
   Question to Speaker B: What is *(Speaker A)* going to do this weekend?

☐ EXERCISE 11. Sureness about the future. (Chart 3-4)
Directions: Answer the questions using ***will, be going to,*** or ***may.*** Include ***probably*** or ***maybe*** as appropriate. Work in pairs or as a class.

Example: What will you do after class tomorrow?
> → *I'll probably go back to my apartment.* OR
> *I'm not sure. I may go to the bookstore.*

1. Will you be in class tomorrow?

2. Will (. . .) be in class tomorrow?

3. Is (. . .) going to be in class a month from now?

4. What will the weather be like tomorrow?

5. Will the sun rise tomorrow morning?

6. Is (. . .) going to sit in the same seat in class again tomorrow?

(Switch roles if working in pairs.)
7. What are you going to do after class tomorrow?

8. What is (. . .) going to do after class tomorrow?

9. Will we *(do a particular activity)* in class tomorrow?

10. Who will be the next *(head of state in this country)*?

11. How will the Internet change students' lives?

12. How will the Internet change everyone's life?

☐ EXERCISE 12. Activity: using WILL, BE GOING TO, and MAY. (Charts 3-1 → 3-4)
Directions: In groups or as a class, use the given topics to discuss the future. The topics can also be used for writing practice.

1. *Clothes:* Will clothing styles change much in the next 10 years? The next 100 years? What kind of clothing will people wear in the year 3000?

2. *Education:* Will computers replace teachers?

3. *Communications:* Will computers take the place of telephones? Will we be able to see the people we're talking to?

4. *Space:* Will we discover other forms of life in the universe? Will humans colonize other planets someday?

5. *Environment:* What will the earth's environment—its water, air, and land—be like in 100 years? Will we still have rainforests? Will animals live in the wild? Will the sea still be a plentiful source of food for humans?

6. *Music:* Will any of today's popular music still be popular 50 years from now? Which songs or singers will last?

7. *Transportation:* Will we still use fossil fuels to power automobiles by the end of this century? Will most automobiles use electric motors in the future? Will cars use other sources of power?

8. *Science:* How will genetic engineering affect our food supply in the future?

3-5 BE GOING TO vs. WILL

(a) She *is going to succeed* because she works hard. (b) She *will succeed* because she works hard.	*Be going to* and *will* mean the same when they are used to make predictions about the future. (a) and (b) have the same meaning.
(c) I bought some wood because I *am going to build* a bookcase for my apartment.	*Be going to* (but not *will*) is used to express a prior plan (i.e., a plan made before the moment of speaking). In (c): The speaker plans to build a bookcase.
(d) This chair is too heavy for you to carry alone. I'*ll help* you.	*Will* (but not *be going to*) is used to express a decision the speaker makes at the moment of speaking. In (d): The speaker decides to help at the immediate present moment; he did not have a prior plan or intention to help.

□ **EXERCISE 13. BE GOING TO vs. WILL.** (Charts 3-1 → 3-5)

Directions: Discuss the *italicized* verbs in the following dialogues. Are the speakers expressing

    (1) plans they made **before** the moment of speaking, or

    (2) decisions they are making **at** the moment of speaking?

  1. A: Did you return Pam's phone call?

      B: No, I forgot. Thanks for reminding me. I'*ll call* her right away.

      → *Speaker B makes the decision at the moment of speaking.*

  2. A: I'*m going to call* Martha later this evening. Do you want to talk to her too?

      B: No, I don't think so.

  3. A: Jack is in town for a few days.

      B: Really? Great! I'*ll give* him a call. Is he staying at his Aunt Rosa's?

  4. A: Alex is in town for a few days.

      B: I know. He called me yesterday. We'*re going to get* together for a drink after I get off work tonight.

  5. A: Are you leaving?

      B: Yes. I'*m going to go* for a short walk. I need some fresh air.

      A: I'*ll join* you.

      B: Great! Where should we go?

  6. A: I'*m going to take* Mohammed to the airport tomorrow morning. Do you want to come along?

      B: Sure.

  7. A: We'*re going to go* to Uncle Jacob's over the holiday. Do you want to come with us?

      B: Gee, I don't know. I'*ll think* about it. When do you need to know?

  8. A: Children, I have a very special job to do, and I need some help. I'*m going to feed* Mr. Whiskers, the rabbit. Who would like to help me?

      B: Me!

      C: I *will!*

      D: Me! Me! I *will!*

      E: I *will!* I *will!*

☐ **EXERCISE 14. BE GOING TO vs. WILL. (Charts 3-1 → 3-5)**
   Directions: Complete the sentences with *be going to* or *will*.

1. A: Why did you buy this flour?

   B: I __'m going to__ make some bread.

2. A: Could someone get me a glass of water?

   B: Certainly. I __'ll__ get you one. Would you like some ice in it?

3. A: Are you going to go to the post office soon?

   B: Yes. Why?

   A: I need to send this letter today.

   B: I _____ mail it for you.

   A: Thanks.

4. A: Why are you carrying that box?

   B: I _____ mail it to my sister. I'm on my way to the post office.

5. A: Could someone please open the window?

   B: I _____ do it.

   A: Thanks.

6: A: What are your vacation plans?

   B: We _____ spend two weeks on a Greek island.

7. A: I have a note for Joe from Rachel. I don't know what to do with it.

   B: Let me have it. I _____ give it to him. He's in my algebra class.

   A: Thanks. But you have to promise not to read it.

8. A: Did you know that Sara and I are moving? We found a great apartment on
      45th Street.

   B: That's terrific. I _____ help you on moving day if you like.

   A: Hey, great! We'd really appreciate that.

9. A: Do you have a car?

   B: Yes, but I _____ sell it. I don't need it now that I live in the city.

10. A: Do you want to walk to the meeting together?

    B: Okay. I _____ meet you by the elevator. Okay?

    A: Okay. I _____ wait for you there.

3-6 EXPRESSING THE FUTURE IN TIME CLAUSES AND *IF*-CLAUSES

time clause (a) ⌐**Before I go** to class tomorrow⌐ , I'm going to eat breakfast. (b) I'm going to eat breakfast ⌐**before I go** to class tomorrow.⌐	In (a) and (b): *before I go to class tomorrow* is a future time clause. $\left.\begin{array}{l}\textbf{\textit{before}}\\\textbf{\textit{after}}\\\textbf{\textit{when}}\\\textbf{\textit{as soon as}}\\\textbf{\textit{until}}\\\textbf{\textit{while}}\end{array}\right\}$ + *subject and verb* = a time clause
(c) *Before I* **go** *home tonight,* I'm going to stop at the market. (d) I'm going to eat dinner at 6:00 tonight. *After I* **eat** *dinner,* I'm going to study in my room. (e) I'll give Rita your message *when I* **see** *her.* (f) It's raining right now. *As soon as the rain* **stops**, I'm going to walk downtown. (g) I'll stay home *until the rain* **stops**. (h) *While you're at school tomorrow,* I'll be at work.	The simple present is used in a future time clause. **Will** and **be going to** are NOT used in a future time clause. INCORRECT: Before I will go to class, I'm going to eat breakfast. INCORRECT: Before I am going to go to class tomorrow, I'm going to eat breakfast. All of the example sentences, (c) through (h), contain future time clauses.
(i) Maybe it will rain tomorrow. *If it* **rains** *tomorrow,* I'm going to stay home.	In (i): *If it rains tomorrow* is an ***if***-clause. ***if*** + *subject and verb* = an ***if***-clause When the meaning is future, the simple present (not **will** or **be going to**) is used in an ***if***-clause.

☐ **EXERCISE 15. Future time clauses and IF-clauses. (Chart 3-6)**
Directions: Underline the time clauses and correct any errors in verb use.

1. <u>Before I ~~'m going to~~ return to my country next year,</u> I'm going to finish my graduate

   degree in computer science.

2. The boss will review your work after she will return from vacation next week.

3. I'll give you a call on my cell phone as soon as my plane will land.

4. I don't especially like my current job, but I'm going to stay with this company until I

   will find something better.

5. I need to know what time the meeting starts. Please be sure to call me as soon as you

   will find out anything about it.

6. When you will be in Australia next month, are you going to go snorkeling at the Great

   Barrier Reef?

7. If it won't be cold tomorrow, we'll go to the beach. If it will be cold tomorrow, we'll

   go to a movie.

☐ **EXERCISE 16. Future time clauses and IF-clauses. (Chart 3-6)**
   Directions: Use the given verbs to complete the sentences. Give a future meaning to the
   sentences.

   1. *take/read*

      I __'ll read__ the textbook **before** I ___take___ the final exam next month.

   2. *return/call*

      Mr. Lee _____ his wife **as soon as** he _____ to the

      hotel tonight.

   3. *come/be, not*

      I _____ home tomorrow **when** the painters _____ to

      paint my apartment. Someone else will have to let them in.

   4. *prepare/go*

      Before I _____ to my job interview tomorrow, I _____

      a list of questions I want to ask about the company.

5. *visit/take*

    When Sandra _____ us this coming weekend, we _____
    her to our favorite seafood restaurant.

6. *stay/call*

    I _____ by the phone **until** Rosa _____.★

7. *miss/come, not*

    If Adam _____ to work tomorrow morning, he _____ a
    very important meeting.

8. *get/be/eat*

    If Barbara _____ home on time tonight, we _____
    dinner at 6:30. **If** she _____ late, dinner _____ late.

□ EXERCISE 17. Future IF-clauses. (Chart 3-6)
Directions: Make sentences about the following possible conditions. Use *if* and add your
own ideas. Pay special attention to the verb in the *if*-clause. Work in pairs.
Speaker A: Give the cue as written in the text. Your book is open.
Speaker B: Use the cue to create a sentence with an *if*-clause. Your book is closed.

Example:
SPEAKER A: Maybe you'll go downtown tomorrow.
SPEAKER B: If I **go** downtown tomorrow, I'm going to buy some new clothes/go to the post
office/etc.

1. Maybe you'll have some free time tomorrow.

2. Maybe it'll rain tomorrow.

3. Maybe it won't rain tomorrow.

4. Maybe the teacher will be absent tomorrow.

Switch roles.

5. Maybe you'll be tired tonight.

6. Maybe you won't be tired tonight.

7. Maybe it'll be nice tomorrow.

8. Maybe we won't have class tomorrow.

★Time clauses beginning with **until** usually **follow** the main clause.
　　Usual: I'm going to stay by the phone **until** *Rosa calls.*
　　Possible but less usual: **Until** *Rosa calls,* I'm going to stay by the phone.

☐ **EXERCISE 18. Future time clauses with BEFORE and AFTER.** (Chart 3-6)

Directions: Each item consists of two actions. Decide which action you want to do first. Use **before** or **after** to say what you intend to do. Then perform the actions. Work in pairs, groups, or as a class. Pay special attention to the verb in the time clause.

1. touch your ear / close your grammar book
    → *I'm going to close my grammar book before/after I touch my ear.* OR
      Before/After I close my grammar book, I'm going to touch my ear.

2. raise your hand, touch your foot

3. sit down, stand up

4. clap your hands, slap your knee

5. shake hands with (. . .), shake hands with (. . .)

6. scratch your chin, pick up your pen

7. *Think of other actions to perform.*

☐ **EXERCISE 19. Future time clauses with UNTIL and AS SOON AS.** (Chart 3-6)

Directions: Listen to the directions; state what you're going to do; then perform the actions. Work as a class with the teacher as the leader or in groups with one student designated as leader. Only the leader's book is open; everyone else has a closed book.

Example: *(Student A)*, stand up **until** *(Student B)* stands up. Then sit down.
    (Student A), please tell us what you're going to do.
    (Student B), please tell us what *(Student A)* is going to do.
    (Student C), please tell us what *(Student A)* is going to do **until** *(Student B)*
      stands up.
LEADER: Ali, I'd like you to stand up **until** Kim stands up, and then sit down.
    Ali, please tell us what you're going to do.
    ALI: I'm going to stand up **until** Kim stands up. Then I'm going to sit down.
LEADER: Kim, please tell us what Ali is going to do.
    KIM: He's going to stand up **until** I stand up. Then he's going to sit down.
LEADER: Maria, tell us what Ali is going to do **as soon as** Kim stands up.
    MARIA: **As soon as** Kim stands up, Ali is going to sit down.

Students A and B then perform the actions.

1. *(Student A)*, sit at your desk **until** *(Student B)* knocks on the door. Then get up and
      walk to the door.
    (Student A), please tell us what you're going to do.
    (Student B), please tell us what *(Student A)* is going to do.
    (Student C), please tell us what *(Student A)* is going to do **as soon as** *(Student B)*
      knocks on the door.

2. *(Student A)*, hold your breath **until** *(Student B)* snaps his/her fingers. Then breathe
      again.
    (Student A), please tell us what you're going to do.
    (Student B), please tell us what *(Student A)* is going to do.
    (Student C), please tell us what *(Student A)* is going to do **as soon as** *(Student B)*
      snaps his/her fingers.

3. *(Student A)*, clap your hands **until** *(Student B)* bows. Then stop clapping your hands.
   (Student A), please tell us what you're going to do.
   (Student B), please tell us what *(Student A)* is going to do.
   (Student C), please tell us what *(Student A)* is going to do **as soon as** *(Student B)*
      bows.

□ EXERCISE 20. Review of time clauses and IF-clauses. (Chapters 1 → 3)
   Directions: Complete the sentences by using a form of the words in parentheses. Read
   carefully for time expressions.

1. a. Before Tom *(go)* _____goes_____ to bed, he always *(brush)* _____
      his teeth.

   b. Before Tom *(go)* _____ to bed later tonight, he *(e-mail)* _____
      his girlfriend.

   c. Before Tom *(go)* _____ to bed last night, he *(take)* _____
      a shower.

   d. While Tom *(take)* _____ a shower last night, the phone *(ring)*
      _____ .

   e. As soon as the phone *(ring)* _____ last night, Tom *(jump)*
      _____ out of the shower to answer it.

   f. As soon as Tom *(get)* _____ up tomorrow morning, he *(brush)*
      _____ his teeth.

   g. Tom always *(brush)* _____ his teeth as soon as he *(get)*
      _____ up.

2. a. After I *(get)* _____ home from work every afternoon, I usually
      (drink) _____ a cup of tea.

   b. After I *(get)* _____ home from work tomorrow afternoon, I *(drink)*
      _____ a cup of tea.

   c. I *(have, not)* _____ any tea until I *(get)* _____
      home from work tomorrow.

   d. After I *(get)* _____ home from work yesterday, I *(drink)*
      _____ a cup of tea.

   e. While I *(drink)* _____ a cup of tea yesterday afternoon,
      my neighbor *(come)* _____ over, so I *(offer)* _____
      her a cup of tea too.

   f. My neighbor *(drop, probably)* _____ over again
      tomorrow. If she *(come)* _____ , I *(make)* _____
      a cup of tea for her.

☐ EXERCISE 21. Writing about the past and the future. (Chapters 2 and 3)
   Directions: Write two paragraphs. Show the time relationships by using words such as
   before, after, when, while, as soon as, next, then, later, after that.

   Paragraph 1: a detailed description of your day yesterday.
   Paragraph 2: a detailed description of your day tomorrow.

3-7 USING THE PRESENT PROGRESSIVE TO EXPRESS FUTURE TIME

(a) Tom *is going to come* to the party tomorrow. (b) Tom *is coming* to the party tomorrow. (c) We*'re going to go* to a movie tonight. (d) We*'re going* to a movie tonight. (e) I*'m going to stay* home this evening. (f) I*'m staying* home this evening.	The present progressive can be used to express future time. Each pair of example sentences has the same meaning. The present progressive describes *definite plans for the future, plans that were made before the moment of speaking.*
(g) Ann *is going to fly* to Chicago next week. (h) Ann *is flying* to Chicago next week.	A future meaning for the present progressive is indicated either by future time words (e.g., *tomorrow*) or by the situation.*
(i) You*'re going to laugh* when you hear this joke. (j) INCORRECT: *You're laughing when you hear this joke.*	The present progressive is NOT used for predictions about the future. In (i): The speaker is predicting a future event. In (j): The present progressive is not possible; laughing is a prediction, not a planned future event.

*COMPARE: Present situation: *Look! Mary's coming. Do you see her?*
          Future situation: *Are you planning to come to the party? Mary's coming. So is Alex.*

☐ EXERCISE 22. Using the present progressive to express future time. (Chart 3-7)
   Directions: Complete the dialogues with any of the following verbs that make sense. Use
   the present progressive if possible. Discuss whether the present progressive expresses
   present or future time.

cut	*go*	*spend*
do	*leave*	*stay*
drive	*meet*	*take*
fly		

1. A: What _____ are _____ you _____ doing _____ tomorrow afternoon?

   B: I _____ am going _____ to the mall.

   A: Why?

   B: I _____ am going _____ shopping for some new clothes. How about you?
       What ___ are ___ you _ going to do _ tomorrow afternoon?

   A: I _^{'m} going_ to a movie with Tom. After the movie, we
       _ are   going _ out to dinner. Would you like to meet us for dinner?

B: No, thanks. I can't. I _____'m going to_____ Heidi at 6:30 at the new seafood restaurant on Fifth Street.

2. A: What courses _____are_____ you _____taking_____ this year?

   B: I _____'m taking_____ English, biology, math, and psychology.

   A: What courses _____are_____ you _____going to take_____ next year?

   B: I _____'m going to take_____ English literature, chemistry, calculus, and history.

   A: That should keep you busy!

3. A: I _____'m taking_____ on vacation tomorrow.

   B: Where _____are_____ you _____going_____ ?

   A: To San Francisco.

   B: How are getting there? _____Are_____ you _____flying_____ or _____driving_____ your car?

   A: I _____'m leaving_____ . I have to be at the airport by seven tomorrow morning.

   B: Do you need a ride to the airport?

   A: No, thanks. I _____'m taking_____ a taxi. Are you planning to go somewhere over vacation?

   B: No. I _____'m going to stay_____ here.

4. A: Stop! Annie! What _____are_____ you _____doing_____ ?

   B: I _____am cutting_____ my hair, Mom.

   A: Oh dear!

5. A: You haven't seen my passport, have you?

B: No. Why?

A: I need it because I _'m going to stay_ for Taipei next Monday.

B: Oh? How long will you be there?

A: A week. I _'m going to spend_ the first few days with my brother, who _is going to go_ to school there. After that I _'m going to meet_ some old friends I went to school with in Australia several years ago. They've invited me to be their house guest.

B: Sounds like a great trip. Hope you find your passport.

☐ EXERCISE 23. Using the present progressive to express future time. (Chart 3-7)
Directions: Pair up with a classmate. Tell each other your plans. Use the present progressive.

Example: What are your plans for this evening?
SPEAKER A: I'm staying home. How about you?
SPEAKER B: I'm going to a cybercafe to send some e-mails. Then I'm going to the English Conversation Club. I'm meeting Anna there.

What are your plans . . .
1. for the rest of today?
2. for tomorrow or the next day?
3. for this coming weekend?
4. for the rest of this month?

☐ EXERCISE 24. Writing: using the present progressive to express future time. (Chart 3-7)
Directions: Think of a place you would like to visit. Pretend you are going to take a trip there this weekend. You have already made all of your plans. Write a paragraph in which you describe your trip. Use the present progressive where appropriate.

Example: This coming weekend, my friend Gisella and I are taking a trip. We're going to Nashville, Tennessee. Gisella likes country music and wants to go to some shows. I don't know anything about country music, but I'm looking forward to going to Nashville. We're leaving Friday afternoon as soon as Gisella gets off work. (Etc.)

Possible questions to answer in your paragraph:
1. Where are you going?
2. When are you leaving?
3. Are you traveling alone?
4. How are you getting there?
5. Where are you staying?
6. Are you visiting anyone? Who?
7. How long are you staying there?
8. When are you getting back?

3-8 USING THE SIMPLE PRESENT TO EXPRESS FUTURE TIME

(a) My plane *arrives* at 7:35 *tomorrow evening*. (b) Tom's new job *starts* *next week*. (c) The semester *ends* *in two more weeks*. (d) There *is* a meeting at ten *tomorrow morning*.	The simple present can express future time when events are on a definite schedule or timetable. Only a few verbs are used in the simple present to express future time. The most common are *arrive, leave, start, begin, end, finish, open, close, be*.
(e) INCORRECT: *I wear my new suit to the wedding next week*. CORRECT: *I am wearing/am going to wear my new suit to the wedding next week*.	Most verbs **cannot** be used in the simple present to express future time. For example, in (e): The verb *wear* does not express an event on a schedule or timetable. It cannot be used in the simple present to express future time.

□ EXERCISE 25. Using present verb forms to express future time. (Charts 3-7 and 3-8)

Directions: Circle the correct possible completions and cross out those that are incorrect.

1. The concert _____ at eight tonight.

   (a.) begins   (b.) is beginning/is going to begin

2. I _____ seafood pasta for dinner tonight.

   a. make   (b.) am making/am going to make

3. I _____ to school tomorrow morning. I need the exercise.

   a. walk   (b.) am walking/am going to walk

4. The bus _____ at 8:15 tomorrow morning.

   (a.) leaves   b. is leaving/is going to leave

5. I _____ the championship game on TV at Jim's house tomorrow.

   a. watch   (b.) am watching/am going to watch

6. The game _____ at one tomorrow afternoon.

   (a.) starts   b. is starting/is going to start

7. Alex's plane _____ at 10:14 tomorrow morning.

   (a.) arrives   b. is arriving/is going to arrive

8. I can't pick him up tomorrow, so he _____ the airport bus into the city.

   a. takes   (b.) is taking/is going to take

3-9 IMMEDIATE FUTURE: USING *BE ABOUT TO*

(a) Ann's bags are packed, and she is wearing her coat. She *is about to leave* for the airport. (b) Shhh. The movie *is about to begin*.	The idiom "be about to do something" expresses an activity that will happen *in the immediate future*, usually within minutes or seconds. In (a): Ann is going to leave sometime in the next few minutes.

☐ **EXERCISE 26. Using BE ABOUT TO.** (Chart 3-9)

Directions: Describe the actions that are about to happen in the pictures. Use *be about to*.

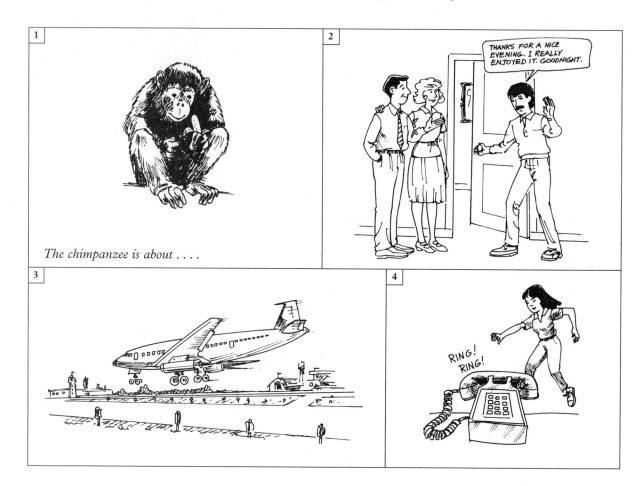

The chimpanzee is about . . . .

☐ **EXERCISE 27. Using BE ABOUT TO.** (Chart 3-9)

Directions: What are the following people probably about to do? Create pictures of them in your imagination.

1. Jack is holding his camera to his eye. He has his finger on the button.
   → *He's about to take a picture.*

2. The door is closed. Sally has her hand on the doorknob.

3. Eric is on the last question of the examination.

4. Nancy has dirty hands from working in the garden. She is holding a bar of soap. She is standing at the bathroom sink.

5. Ben is putting on his coat and heading for the door.

6. Rita is holding a fly swatter and staring at a fly on the kitchen table.

7. Mr. Tomko has just checked to make sure the doors are locked and turned off the lights in the living room. He's heading toward the bedroom.

☐ **EXERCISE 28. Using BE ABOUT TO. (Chart 3-9)**
Directions: Think of an action to perform. Don't reveal what it is. Get ready to do it, but just before you perform the action, ask the class to describe what you are about to do. Perform with a partner if you wish.

Examples: (. . .) walks to the chalkboard and picks up the eraser. The class guesses correctly that he is about to erase the board.

(. . .) and (. . .) hold out their hands to each other. They are about to shake hands.

Suggestions for actions to prepare to perform:
1. stand up
2. open the door
3. close the window
4. pick up your pen
5. close your book
6. etc.

☐ **EXERCISE 29. Preview: parallel verbs. (Chart 3-10)**
Directions: Correct the errors.

1. Fifteen years from now, my wife and I will retire and travel ~~ing~~ all over the world.

2. I opened the door and invite my friend to come in.

3. If I feel tense, I close my eyes and thinking about nothing at all.

4. Pete is in the other room. He's listening to music and study for his chemistry exam.

5. It's hot in here. I'm going to open the window and turning on the fan.

3-10 PARALLEL VERBS

v   ***and***   **v**
(a) Jim ⌐*makes*⌐ his bed ⌐*and*⌐ ⌐*cleans*⌐ up his room every morning.
	Often a subject has two verbs that are connected by ***and***. We say that the two verbs are parallel:
	      v + *and* + v
	     makes and cleans = parallel verbs

(b) Ann ***is cooking*** dinner *and (is)* ***talking*** on the phone at the same time. (c) I ***will stay*** home and *(will)* ***study*** tonight. (d) I ***am going to stay*** home and *(am going to)* ***study*** tonight.	It is not necessary to repeat a helping verb (an auxiliary verb) when two verbs are connected by ***and***.

☐ EXERCISE 30. Parallel verbs. (Chart 3-10)

Directions: Complete the sentences with the correct forms of the words in parentheses.

1. When I *(walk)* _____walked_____ into the living room yesterday, Grandpa *(read)* _____ a newspaper and *(smoke)* _____ his pipe.

2. Helen will graduate soon. She *(move)* _____ to New York and *(look)* _____ for a job after she *(graduate)* _____ .

3. Every day my neighbor *(call)* _____ me on the phone and *(complain)* _____ about the weather.

4. Look at Erin! She *(cry)* _____ and *(laugh)* _____ at the same time. I wonder if she is happy or sad?

5. I'm beat! I can't wait to get home. After I *(get)* _____ home, I *(take)* _____ a hot shower and *(go)* _____ to bed.

6. Yesterday my dog *(dig)* _____ a hole in the back yard and *(bury)* _____ a bone.

7. I'm tired of this cold weather. As soon as spring *(come)* _____ , I *(play)* _____ tennis and *(jog)* _____ in the park as often as possible.

8. While Paul *(carry)* _____ brushes and paint and *(climb)* _____ a ladder, a bird *(fly)* _____ down and *(sit)* _____ on his head. Paul *(drop)* _____ the paint and *(spill)* _____ it all over the ground.

9. When I first (arrive) _____ in this city and (start) _____

going to school here, I knew no one. I was lonely and felt that I didn't have a friend in

the world.

     One day while I (watch) _____ TV alone in my room

and (feel) _____ sorry for myself, a woman I had met in one of

my classes (knock) _____ on my door and (ask) _____

me if I wanted to accompany her to the student center. That was the beginning of my

friendship with Lisa King.

     Now we (see) _____ each other every day and usually (spend)

_____ time talking on the phone, too. Later this week we (borrow)

_____ her brother's car and (go) _____ to visit her

aunt in the country. Next week we (take) _____ a bus to

Fall City and (go) _____ to a football game. I'm really enjoying our

friendship.

□ **EXERCISE 31. Review: verb forms. (Chapters 1 → 3)**
    Directions: Complete the sentences with the correct forms of the words in parentheses.

1. I usually (ride) __*ride*__ my bicycle to work in the morning, but it (rain)

_____ when I left my house early this morning, so I (take)

_____ the bus. After I (arrive) _____ at work, I

(discover) _____ that I had left my briefcase at home.

2. A: Are you going to take the kids to the amusement park tomorrow morning?

   B: Yes. It (open) _____ at 10:00. If we (leave) _____

     here at 9:30, we'll get there at 9:55. The kids can be the first ones in the park.

3. A: Ouch!

   B: What happened?

   A: I (cut) _____ my finger.

   B: It (bleed) _____!

   A: I know!

   B: Put pressure on it. I (get) _____ some antibiotic and a

     bandage.

   A: Thanks.

4. A: I *(go)* _____ to a lecture on Shakespeare tomorrow evening. Want to join me?

   B: Nah. Brian and I *(go)* _____ to a movie—*Godzilla Eats the Earth.*

5. A: Your phone *(ring)* _____ .

   B: I *(know)* _____ .

   A: *(you, answer)* _____ it?

   B: No.

   A: *(you, want)* _____ me to get it?

   B: No thanks.

   A: Why *(you, want, not)* _____ to answer your phone?

   B: I *(expect)* _____ another call from the bill collector. I have a bunch of bills I haven't paid. I *(want, not)* _____ to talk to her.

   A: Oh.

6. A: What *(you, wear)* _____ to Eric's wedding tomorrow?

   B: My blue dress, I guess. How about you?

   A: I *(plan)* _____ to wear my new outfit. I *(buy)* _____ it just a few days ago. It *(be)* _____ a yellow suit with a white blouse. Just a minute. I *(show)* _____ it to you. Wait right here. I *(get)* _____ it from my closet and *(bring)* _____ it out.

7. A: Look! There *(be)* _____ a police car behind us. Its lights *(flash)* _____ .

   B: I *(know)* _____! I *(know)* _____! I *(see)* _____ it.

   A: What *(go)* _____ on? *(you, speed)* _____ ?

   B: No, I'm not. I *(drive)* _____ the speed limit.

   A: Ah, look. The police car *(pass)* _____ us.

   B: Whew!

8. A: *(the sun, keep)* _____ burning forever, or *(it, burn, eventually)* _____ itself out?

   B: It *(burn, eventually)* _____ itself out, but that *(happen, not)* _____ for billions of years.

9. Sometime in the next twenty-five years, a spaceship with a human crew *(land)* _____ on Mars. I *(think)* _____ they *(find)* _____ evidence of some kind of life forms there, but I *(expect, not)* _____ _____ them to encounter sentient beings. Someday, however, I *(believe)* _____ that humans *(make)* _____ contact with other intelligent beings in the universe.

☐ EXERCISE 32. Review: verb forms. (Chapters 1 → 3)
Directions: Complete the sentences with a form of the verb in parentheses.

(1) Three hundred and fifty years ago, people *(make)* _____**made**_____ their own clothes. They *(have, not)* _____ machines for making clothes. There *(be, not)* _____ any clothing factories. People *(wear)* _____ homemade clothes that were sewn by hand.

(2) Today, very few people *(make)* _____ their own clothes. Clothing *(come)* _____ ready-made from factories. People *(buy)* _____ almost all their clothes from stores.

(3) The modern clothing industry *(be)* _____ international. As a result, people from different countries often *(wear)* _____ similar clothes. For example, people in many different countries throughout the world *(wear)* _____ jeans and T-shirts.

(4) However, some regional differences in clothing still *(exist)* _____ . For instance, people of the Arabian deserts *(wear)* _____ loose, flowing robes to protect themselves from the heat of the sun. In parts of northern Europe, fur hats *(be)* _____ common in the winter.

(5) In the future, there *(be, probably)* _____ fewer and fewer differences in clothing. People throughout the world *(wear)* _____ clothes from the same factories. *(we all, dress)* _____ alike in the future? TV shows and movies about the future often *(show)* _____ everybody in a uniform of some kind. What *(you, think)* _____ ?

☐ **EXERCISE 33. Error analysis: summary review of present, past, and future time.**
(Chapters 1 → 3)

Directions: Correct the errors.

1. I used to kick ~~ed~~ my sister's legs.

2. We had a test last week, and I past it.

3. I not like the food in the United State.

4. I use to get up at noon, but now I have to be at work by eight.

5. I study hardly every day, but my english is not be improve.

6. Everyone enjoy these English classes.

7. At the picnic, we sang songs and talk to each other.

8. I learn the english in my school in hong Kong before I come here.

9. I like to travel. I gonna go to new and interesting places all my life.

10. Now I study at this school and I living with my cousin. I am always meet my friends

    in the cafeteria and we talking about our classes.

11. When I wake up in the morning. I am turning on the radio. Before get up.

12. I am live with an American family. They are having four childrens.

13. When I was at the outdoor market, I pointed at the chicken I wanted to buy. The man

    was taking it from a wooden cage and kill it without mercy.

14. Every day I wake up when the birds begin to sing. If the weather not to be cloudy, I

    am seeing a beautiful sunrise from my bed.

15. My husband and children they are going to join me after I will finish my English

    course.

Directions: Rewrite the paragraphs. Correct any errors in grammar, spelling, or punctuation. If you wish, change the wording to improve the expression of the ideas.

1. I want to tell you about Oscar. He my cousin. He comes here four years ago. Before he came here, he study statistics in Chile. When he leaves Chile to come here. He came with four friends. They were studying English in Ohio. Then he went to New york stayed there for three years. He graduated from New York University. Now he study at this school. After he finish his Master's degree, he return to Chile.

2. Long ago in a faraway place, a lonely man move into a new neighborhood. His first project is his new garden. He begun to work on it right away. He wanting to make a perfect garden. One day some friendly neighbors and their children visitted the man in his garden and helpped him with the work. They planting flowers and build a small bridge across a little stream. All of them were very happy during they were building the bridge and work on the garden. The man was especially happy because he's no longer lonely. While the adults working, some of their children plaied with a ball in the garden while they were play, one of them step on a flower. Suddenly the man was getting very angry and tell everyone to leave. All the neighbors leaved and go back to their own homes. After that, the man builded a wall around his garden and lock the gate. For the rest of his life, the man sat alone in his garden every evening and crying.

☐ EXERCISE 35. Review: verb forms. (Chapters 1 → 3)

Directions: Complete the sentences with the correct forms of the words in parentheses.

A: Okay, let's all open our fortune cookies.

B: What *(yours, say)* _____ ?
 1

A: Mine says, "An unexpected gift *(add)* _____ to your pleasure."
 2

 Great! *(you, plan)* _____ to give me a gift soon?
 3

B: Not that I know of. Mine says, "Your trust in a friend *(prove)* _____
4

well-founded." Good. I *(like)* _____ having trustworthy friends.
5

C: This one says, "A smile *(overcome)* _____ a language
6

barrier." Well, that's good! After this, when I *(understand, not)* _____
7

people who *(speak)* _____ English to me, I *(smile, just)*
8

_____ at them!
9

D: My fortune is this: "Your determination *(make)* _____ you
10

succeed in everything."

A: Well, it *(look)* _____ like all of us *(have)* _____
11   12

good luck in the future!

☐ EXERCISE 36. Future time. (Chapter 3)
Directions: Do you believe that some people are able to predict the future? Pretend that
you have the ability to see into the future. Choose several people you know (classmates,
teachers, family members, friends) and tell them in writing about their future lives.
Discuss such topics as jobs, contributions to humankind, marriage, children, fame, and
exciting adventures. With your words, paint interesting and fun pictures of their future
lives.

CHAPTER 4
The Present Perfect and the Past Perfect

CONTENTS			
4-1	Past participle	4-6	Present perfect progressive
4-2	Forms of the present perfect	4-7	Present perfect progressive vs. present
4-3	Meanings of the present perfect		perfect
4-4	Simple past vs. present perfect	4-8	Using *already*, *yet*, *still*, and *anymore*
4-5	Using *since* and *for*	4-9	Past perfect

☐ EXERCISE 1. Review and preview: present and past verbs. (Chapters 1, 2, and 4)
Directions: Complete the sentences with the words in parentheses. Some of the completions review verb tenses studied in Chapters 1 and 2. Some of them preview verb tenses that will be studied in this chapter: the present perfect and the past perfect. Discuss the form and meaning of the new tenses.

There may be more than one possible correct completion.

My name *(be)* __is__ Surasuk Jutukanyaprateep. I *(be)* __am__ from

Thailand. Right now I *(study)* __'m studying__ English at this school. I *(be)*

__have been__ at this school since the beginning of January. I *(arrive)*

__arrived__ here January 2, and my classes *(begin)* __began__

January 6.

Since I *(come)* __came__ here, I *(do)* __did__

many things, and I *(meet)* __met__ many people. Last week, I *(go)*

__went__ to a party at my friend's house. I *(meet)* __met__

some of the other students from Thailand at the party. Of course, we *(speak)*

__spoke__ Thai, so I *(practice, not)* __didn't practice__ my English

that night. There *(be)* __were__ only people from Thailand at the party.

However, since I *(come)* _____came_____ here, I *(meet)* __have met__

15   16

a lot of other people, too. I *(meet)* _____ people from Latin America,

17

Africa, the Middle East, and Asia. I enjoy meeting people from other countries. Before I

came here, I *(meet, never)* _____ anyone from the Ukraine

18

or Bolivia. Now I *(know)* _____ people from both these places, and they

19

(become) _____ my friends.

20

4-1 PAST PARTICIPLE

	SIMPLE FORM	SIMPLE PAST	PAST PARTICIPLE
REGULAR VERBS	finish stop wait	finished stopped waited	**finished** **stopped** **waited**
IRREGULAR VERBS	see make put	saw made put	**seen** **made** **put**

The **past participle** is one of the principal parts of a verb. (See Chart 2-6, p. 32.)

The past participle is used in the PRESENT PERFECT tense and the PAST PERFECT tense.*

The past participle of regular verbs is the same as the simple past form: both end in *-ed*.

See Chart 2-7, p. 33, for a list of irregular verbs.

*The past participle is also used in the passive. See Chapter 10.

☐ EXERCISE 2. Past participle. (Chart 4-1)

Directions: Write the past participle.

	SIMPLE FORM	SIMPLE PAST	PAST PARTICIPLE		SIMPLE FORM	SIMPLE PAST	PAST PARTICIPLE
1.	finish	finished	__finished__	11.	come	came	come
2.	see	saw	__seen__	12.	study	studied	studied
3.	go	went	gone	13.	stay	stayed	stayed
4.	have	had	had	14.	begin	began	begun
5.	meet	met	met	15.	start	started	started
6.	call	called	called	16.	write	wrote	written
7.	fall	fell	fallen	17.	eat	ate	eaten
8.	do	did	done	18.	cut	cut	cut
9.	know	knew	known	19.	read	read	read
10.	fly	flew	flown	20.	be	was/were	been

4-2 FORMS OF THE PRESENT PERFECT

(a) I *have finished* my work. (b) The students *have finished* Chapter 3. (c) Jim *has eaten* lunch.	STATEMENT: *have/has* + *past participle*
(d) *I've/You've/We've/They've* eaten lunch. (e) *She's/He's* eaten lunch. (f) *It's* been cold for the last three days.	CONTRACTION *pronoun* + *have* = *'ve* *pronoun* + *has* = *'s*★
(g) I *have not (haven't) finished* my work. (h) Ann *has not (hasn't) eaten* lunch.	NEGATIVE: *have/has* + *not* + *past participle* NEGATIVE CONTRACTION *have* + *not* = *haven't* *has* + *not* = *hasn't*
(i) *Have you finished* your work? (j) *Has Jim eaten* lunch? (k) How long *have you lived* here?	QUESTION: *have/has* + *subject* + *past participle*
(l) A: Have you seen that movie? B: *Yes, I have.* OR *No, I haven't.* (m) A: Has Jim eaten lunch? B: *Yes, he has.* OR *No, he hasn't.*	SHORT ANSWER: *have/haven't* or *has/hasn't* Note: The helping verb in the short answer is not contracted with the pronoun. *INCORRECT: Yes, I've.* OR *Yes, he's.*

★COMPARE: *It's* cold today. [*It's = It is: It is* cold today.]
     It's been cold since December. [*It's = It has: It has* been cold since December.]

☐ EXERCISE 3. Forms of the present perfect. (Chart 4-2)

Directions: Complete the dialogues with the words in parentheses. Use the present perfect.

1. A: *(you, eat, ever)* ___Have you ever eaten___ seaweed?

   B: No, I ___haven't___ . I *(eat, never)* ___'ve never eaten___ seaweed.

2. A: *(you, stay, ever)* _____ at a big hotel?

   B: Yes, I _____ . I *(stay)* _____ at a big hotel
   lots of times.

3. A: *(you, meet, ever)* _____ a movie star?

   B: No, I _____ . I *(meet, never)* _____
   a movie star.

4. A: *(Tom, visit, ever)* _____ you at your house?

   B: Yes, he _____ . He *(visit)* _____ me lots
   of times.

5. A: *(Ann, be, ever)* _____ in Mexico?

   B: No, she _____ . She *(be, never)* _____ in
   Mexico. She *(be, not)* _____ in any Spanish-speaking
   countries.

4-3 MEANINGS OF THE PRESENT PERFECT

Jim has eaten lunch.

Ann hasn't eaten lunch.

PRESENT PERFECT, MEANING #1: SOMETHING HAPPENED BEFORE NOW AT AN UNSPECIFIED TIME.

(diagram: before now — time? — now)	(a) Jim **has** already **eaten** lunch. (b) Ann **hasn't eaten** lunch yet. (c) **Have** you ever **eaten** at that restaurant?	The PRESENT PERFECT expresses an activity or situation that occurred (or did not occur) *before now, at some unspecified time in the past.* In (a): Jim's lunch occurred before the present time. The exact time is not mentioned; it is unimportant or unknown. For the speaker, the only important information is that Jim's lunch occurred in the past, sometime before now.
(diagram: before now — now)	(d) Pete **has eaten** at that restaurant *many times.* (e) I **have eaten** there *twice.*	An activity may be repeated two, several, or more times *before now,* at *unspecified times in the past,* as in (d) and (e).

PRESENT PERFECT, MEANING #2: A SITUATION BEGAN IN THE PAST AND CONTINUES TO THE PRESENT.

(diagram: 10:00 A.M. — now)	(f) We**'ve been** in class **since** *ten o'clock this morning.* (g) I **have known** Ben **for** *ten years.* I met him ten years ago. I still know him today. We are friends.	When the present perfect is used with **since** or **for**, it expresses situations that began in the past and continue to the present. In (f): Class started at ten. We are still in class now, at the moment of speaking. *INCORRECT: We are in class since ten o'clock this morning.*

Directions: When speakers use the present perfect, they often contract **have** and **has** with nouns in everyday speech. Listen to your teacher say these sentences in normal contracted speech and practice saying them yourself. Discuss the meaning of the present perfect.

1. Bob has been in Montreal since last Tuesday. *("Bob's been in . . . .")*
2. Jane has been out of town for two days.
3. The weather has been warm since the beginning of April.
4. My parents have been active in politics for forty years.
5. Mike has already eaten breakfast.
6. My friends have moved into a new apartment.
7. My roommate has traveled a lot. She's visited many different countries.
8. My aunt and uncle have lived in the same house for twenty-five years.

4-4 SIMPLE PAST vs. PRESENT PERFECT

SIMPLE PAST (a) I **finished** my work *two hours ago*. PRESENT PERFECT (b) I **have** already* **finished** my work.	In (a): I finished my work at a specific time in the past *(two hours ago)*. In (b): I finished my work at an unspecified time in the past *(sometime before now)*.
SIMPLE PAST (c) I **was** in Europe *last year/three years ago/in 1999/in 1995 and 1999/when I was ten years old*. PRESENT PERFECT (d) I **have been** in Europe *many times/several times/a couple of times/once/(no mention of time)*.	The SIMPLE PAST expresses an activity that occurred at a specific time (or times) in the past, as in (a) and (c). The PRESENT PERFECT expresses an activity that occurred at an unspecified time (or times) in the past, as in (b) and (d).
SIMPLE PAST (e) Ann **was** in Miami *for two weeks*. PRESENT PERFECT (f) Bob **has been** in Miami *for two weeks/since May first*.	In (e): In sentences where *for* is used in a time expression, the simple past expresses an activity that began and ended in the past. In (f): In sentences with *for* or *since,* the present perfect expresses an activity that began in the past and continues to the present.

*For more information about **already**, see Chart 4-8, p. 102.

□ EXERCISE 5. Simple past vs. present perfect. (Chart 4-4)
Directions: Discuss the meanings of the verb tenses.

1. All of the verbs in the following talk about past time, but the verb in (a) is different from the other three verbs. What is the difference?

(a) I *have had* several bicycles in my lifetime.

(b) I *had* a red bicycle when I was in elementary school.

(c) I *had* a blue bicycle when I was a teenager.

(d) I *had* a green bicycle when I lived and worked in Hong Kong.

2. What are the differences in the ideas the verb tenses express?

   (e) I *had* a wonderful bicycle last year.

   (f) I've *had* many wonderful bicycles.

3. What are the differences in the ideas the verb tenses express?

   (g) Ann *had* a red bike for two years.

   (h) Sue *has had* a red bike for two years.

4. Who is still alive, and who is dead?

   (i) In his lifetime, Uncle Alex *had* several red bicycles.

   (j) In his lifetime, Grandpa *has had* several red bicycles.

☐ **EXERCISE 6. Simple past vs. present perfect. (Chart 4-4)**

Directions: Look at the verb in *italics*. Is it simple past, or is it present perfect? Check the box that describes whether the verb expresses something that happened at a specified time in the past or at an unspecified time in the past.

SPECIFIED TIME IN THE PAST	UNSPECIFIED TIME IN THE PAST	
☐	☒	1. Ms. Parker *has been* in Tokyo many times. (→ *present perfect*)
☒	☐	2. Ms. Parker *was* in Tokyo last week. (→ *simple past*)
☐	☒	3. I've *met* Ann's husband. He's a nice guy.
☒	☐	4. I *met* Ann's husband at a party last week.
☒	☐	5. Mr. White *was* in Rome three times last month.
☐	☒	6. Mr. White *has been* in Rome many times.
☐	☒	7. I like to travel. I've *been* in more than thirty foreign countries.
☒	☐	8. I *was* in Morocco in 2001.
☐	☒	9. Mary *has never been* in Morocco.
☒	☐	10. Mary *wasn't* in Morocco when I was there in 2001.

☐ **EXERCISE 7. Simple past vs. present perfect. (Chart 4-4)**

Directions: Complete the sentences with the words in parentheses. Use the present perfect or the simple past.

1. A: Have you ever been in Europe?

   B: Yes, I _____have_____ . I *(be)* _____have been_____ in Europe several times.

   In fact, I *(be)* _____was_____ in Europe last year.

2. A: Are you going to finish your work before you go to bed?

   B: I *(finish, already*)* ___have already finished___ it. I *(finish)* ___finished___

   my work two hours ago.

---

*In informal spoken English, the simple past is sometimes used with ***already***. Practice using the present perfect with ***already*** in this exercise.

3. A: Have you ever eaten at Al's Steak House?

   B: Yes, I __have__. I *(eat)* __have eaten__ there many times. In fact, my wife and I *(eat)* __ate__ there last night.

4. A: Do you and Erica want to go to the movie at the Palace Theater with us tonight?

   B: No thanks. We *(see, already)* __have already seen__ it. We *(see)* __saw__ it last week.

5. A: When are you going to write your report for Mr. Goldberg?

   B: I *(write, already)* __have already written__ it. I *(write)* __wrote__ it two days ago and gave it to him.

6. A: *(Antonio, have, ever)* __Has Antonio ever had__ a job?

   B: Yes, he __has__. He *(have)* __has had__ lots of part-time jobs. Last summer he *(have)* __had__ a job at his uncle's waterbed store.

7. A: This is a good book. Would you like to read it when I'm finished?

   B: Thanks, but I *(read, already)* __have already read__ it. I *(read)* __read__ it a couple of months ago.

8. A: What European countries *(you, visit)* __have you visited__?

   B: I *(visit)* __have visited__ Hungary, Germany, and Switzerland. I *(visit)* __visited__ Hungary in 1998. I *(be)* __was__ in Germany and Switzerland in 2001.

☐ EXERCISE 8. Simple past vs. present perfect. (Chart 4-4)

Directions: Ask and answer questions, using the present perfect and the simple past.

Speaker A: You are the questioner. Ask a question using the present perfect, and then immediately follow up with a related question that prompts the use of the simple past. Ask two or three people the same question.

Work as a class with the teacher as Speaker A or in groups with one person selected to be the leader.

Example:

SPEAKER A: (. . .), what countries have you been in?

SPEAKER B: Well, I've been in Norway, and I've been in Peru.

SPEAKER A: Oh? When were you in Norway?

SPEAKER B: I was in Norway three years ago.

SPEAKER A: How about you, (. . .)? What countries have you been in?

SPEAKER C: I've never been in Norway or Peru, but I've been in . . . .

ETC.

1. What countries have you been in?
   When were you in . . . ?

2. What cities *(in Canada, in the United States, etc.)* have you been in?
   When were you in . . . ?

3. What are some of the things you have done since you came to *(this city)*?
   When did you . . . ?

4. What are some of the things we've done in class since the beginning of the term?
   When did we . . . ?

5. What are some of the most interesting or unusual things you have done in your lifetime?
   When did you . . . ?

□ EXERCISE 9. Present perfect. (Charts 4-2 → 4-4)
Directions: Ask and answer questions using the present perfect. Work in pairs.
SPEAKER A: Use *ever* in the question. *Ever* comes between the subject *(you)* and the main verb.*
SPEAKER B: Give a short answer first and then a complete sentence answer.

Use
$\begin{cases} \textbf{\textit{many times}} \\ \textbf{\textit{lots of times}} \\ \textbf{\textit{several times}} \\ \textbf{\textit{a couple of times}} \\ \textbf{\textit{once in my lifetime}} \\ \textbf{\textit{never}} \end{cases}$
in the complete sentence.

Example: be in Florida**
SPEAKER A: Have you ever been in Florida?
SPEAKER B: Yes, I have. I've been in Florida many times. OR
            No, I haven't. I've never been in Florida.

No, I haven't ever

	Switch roles.
1. be in Europe	10. be in *(name of a city)*
2. be in Africa	11. be in *(name of a state/province)*
3. be in Asia	12. be in love
4. eat Chinese food	13. play soccer
5. eat Italian food	14. play chess
6. eat *(a certain kind of)* food	15. play a video game
7. ride a horse	16. walk to *(a place in this city)*
8. ride a motorcycle	17. stay up all night
9. ride an elephant	18. buy something on the Internet

---

*In these questions, **ever** means *in your lifetime, at any time(s) in your life before now.*

When using the present perfect, a speaker might also use the idiom **be to *(a place): Have you ever been **to** Florida?*

□ EXERCISE 10. Irregular verbs. (Chart 2-5)

Directions: Write the simple past and the past participles. You will use these irregular verbs in the next exercise (Exercise 11).

1. see   <u>saw</u>   <u>seen</u>
2. eat   <u>ate</u>   <u>eaten</u>
3. give   <u>gave</u>   <u>given</u>
4. fall   <u>fell</u>   <u>fallen</u>
5. take   <u>took</u>   <u>taken</u>
6. shake   <u>shook</u>   <u>shaken</u>
7. drive   <u>drove</u>   <u>driven</u>
8. ride   <u>rode</u>   <u>ridden</u>
9. write   <u>wrote</u>   <u>written</u>
10. bite   <u>bit</u>   <u>bitten</u>
11. hide   <u>hid</u>   <u>hidden</u>

□ EXERCISE 11. Practicing irregular verbs. (Charts 2-5 and 4-2 → 4-4)

Directions: In order to practice using the past participles of irregular verbs, ask and answer questions that use the present perfect. Work in pairs, in groups, or as a class.
Speaker A: Ask a question beginning with "Have you ever . . . ?"
Speaker B: Answer the question, using the present perfect. Add another sentence about the topic if you wish.

Example: eat at the student cafeteria

SPEAKER A: Have you ever eaten at the student cafeteria?

SPEAKER B: Yes, I have. I've eaten there many times. In fact, I ate breakfast there this morning. OR No, I haven't. I usually eat all my meals at home.

1. take a course in chemistry
2. ride in a hot-air balloon
3. write a poem
4. give the teacher an apple
5. shake hands with (. . .)
6. bite into an apple that had a worm inside

(Switch roles if working in pairs.)
7. drive a semi (a very large truck)
8. eat raw fish
9. hide money under your mattress
10. fall down stairs
11. see the skeleton of a dinosaur

☐ **EXERCISE 12. Irregular verbs. (Chart 2-5)**
Directions: Write the simple past and the past participles.

1. break _broke_ _broken_
2. speak _spoke_ _spoken_
3. steal _stole_ _stolen_
4. get _got_ _got_
5. wear _wore_ _worn_
6. draw _drew_ _drawn_
7. grow _grew_ _grown_

8. throw _threw_ _thrown_
9. blow _blew_ _blown_
10. fly _flew_ _flown_
11. drink _drank_ _drunk_
12. sing _sang_ _sung_
13. swim _swam_ _swum_
14. go _went_ _gone_

☐ **EXERCISE 13. Practicing irregular verbs. (Charts 2-5 and 4-2 → 4-4)**
Directions: Ask questions beginning with "Have you ever . . . ?" and give answers.

1. fly a private plane
2. break your arm
3. draw a picture of a mountain
4. swim in the ocean
5. speak to (. . .) on the phone
6. wear a costume to a party
7. go to a costume party

(Switch roles if working in pairs.)
8. get a package in the mail
9. steal anything
10. grow tomatoes
11. sing *(name of a song)*
12. drink carrot juice
13. throw a football
14. blow a whistle

☐ **EXERCISE 14. Irregular verbs. (Chart 2-5)**
Directions: Write the simple past and the past participles.

1. have _had_ _had_
2. make _made_ _made_
3. build _built_ _built_
4. lend _lent_ _lent_
5. send _sent_ _sent_
6. spend _spent_ _spent_
7. leave _left_ _left_

8. lose _lost_ _lost_
9. sleep _slept_ _slept_
10. feel _felt_ _felt_
11. meet _met_ _met_
12. sit _sat_ _sat_
13. win _won_ _won_
14. hang* _hung_ _hung_

---

*Hang is a regular verb *(hang, hanged, hanged)* when it means to kill a person by putting a rope around his/her neck.
   Hang is an irregular verb when it refers to suspending a thing on a wall, in a closet, on a hook, etc.

☐ **EXERCISE 15. Practicing irregular verbs. (Charts 2-5 and 4-2 → 4-5)**

Directions: Ask questions beginning with "Have you ever . . . ?" and give answers.

1. lose the key to your house
2. meet (. . .)
3. have the flu
4. feel terrible about something
5. send a telegram
6. leave your sunglasses at a restaurant
7. sit on a cactus

(Switch roles if working in pairs.)

8. spend one whole day doing nothing
9. lend (. . .) any money
10. sleep in a tent

11. make a birthday cake
12. build sand castles

13. win money at a racetrack
14. hang a picture on the wall

☐ **EXERCISE 16. Irregular verbs. (Chart 2-5)**

Directions: Write the simple past and the past participles.

1. sell _____ _____
2. tell _____ _____
3. hear _____ _____
4. hold _____ _____
5. feed _____ _____
6. read _____ _____
7. find _____ _____
8. buy _____ _____

9. think _____ _____
10. teach _____ _____
11. catch _____ _____
12. cut _____ _____
13. hit _____ _____
14. quit★ _____ _____
15. put _____ _____

───────────

★**Quit** can be used as a regular verb in British English: *quit, quitted, quitted.*

☐ **EXERCISE 17. Practicing irregular verbs. (Charts 2-5 and 4-2 → 4-4)**
   Directions: Ask questions beginning with "Have you ever . . . ?" and give answers.

   (Switch roles if working in pairs.)

1. teach a child to count to ten
2. hold a newborn baby
3. find any money on the sidewalk
4. cut your own hair
5. think about the meaning of life
6. hear strange noises at night
7. read *Tom Sawyer* by Mark Twain
8. feed pigeons in the park

9. tell a little white lie
10. quit smoking
11. buy a refrigerator
12. sell a car
13. hit another person with your fist
14. put off doing your homework
15. catch a fish

☐ **EXERCISE 18. Preview: SINCE vs. FOR. (Chart 4-5)**
   Directions: Complete the sentence "I have been here . . . ." Use **since** or **for** with the given expressions.

   I have been here . . .

1. __for__ two months.
2. __since__ September.
3. __since__ 1998.
4. __since__ last year.
5. __for__ two years.
6. __since__ last Friday.
7. __since__ 9:30.
8. __for__ three days.

9. __since__ the first of January.
10. __for__ almost four months.
11. __since__ the beginning of the term.
12. __since__ the semester started.
13. __for__ a couple of hours.
14. __for__ fifteen minutes.
15. __since__ yesterday.
16. __for__ about five weeks.

4-5 USING *SINCE* AND *FOR*

SINCE			
	(a) I *have been* here	since eight o'clock. since Tuesday. since May. since 1999. since January 3, 2001. since yesterday. since last month.	*Since* is followed by the mention of *a specific point in time:* an hour, a day, a month, a year, etc. *Since* expresses the idea that something began at a specific time in the past and continues to the present.
	(b) CORRECT: I *have lived* here since May.* 　　 CORRECT: I *have been* here since May. (c) INCORRECT: I *am living* here since May. (d) INCORRECT: I *live* here since May. (e) INCORRECT: I *lived* here since May. 　　 INCORRECT: I *was* here since May.		The *present perfect* is used in sentences with **since**. In (c): The present progressive is NOT used. In (d): The simple present is NOT used. In (e): The simple past is NOT used.
		MAIN CLAUSE (present perfect)　　 SINCE-CLAUSE (simple past) (f) I *have lived* here　　 since I *was* a child. (g) Al *has met* many people　　 since he *came* here.	*Since* may also introduce a time clause (i.e., a subject and verb may follow *since*). Notice in the examples: The present perfect is used in the main clause; the simple past is used in the *since*-clause.
FOR	(h) I *have been* here	for ten minutes. for two hours. for five days. for about three weeks. for almost six months. for many years. for a long time.	*For* is followed by the mention of a *length of time:* two minutes, three hours, four days, five weeks, etc. Note: If the noun ends in *-s (hours, days, weeks,* etc.), use *for* in the time expression, not *since*.
	(i) I *have lived* here *for two years.* I moved here two years ago, and I still live here. (j) I *lived* in Athens *for two years.* I don't live in Athens now.		In (i): The use of the present perfect in a sentence with *for* + *a length of time* means that the action began in the past and continues to the present. In (j): The use of the simple past means that the action began and ended in the past.

*ALSO CORRECT: *I have been living* here since May.* See Chart 4-7, p. 100, for a discussion of the present perfect progressive.

☐ EXERCISE 19. SINCE vs. FOR. (Chart 4-5)
　　Directions: Complete the sentences.

1. I've been in this building . . . . { since ___nine o'clock this morning.___
　　　　　　　　　　　　　　　　　　　　　　{ for ___27 minutes.___

2. We've been in class . . . . { since ___September___
　　　　　　　　　　　　　　　　　　　　　　{ for ___2 months___

3. I've been in this city . . . . { since ___last December___
　　　　　　　　　　　　　　　　　　　　　　{ for ___almost 11 months___

4. I've had a driver's license . . . . { since _____ September _____
                                                for _____ 2 month _____

5. I've had this book . . . . { since _____ yesterday _____
                                                  for _____ 1 day _____

☐ EXERCISE 20. SINCE vs. FOR. (Chart 4-5)

Directions: Answer the leader's questions. Only the leader's book is open. Work as a class or in groups.
Speaker A: Use *since* in your answer.
Speaker B: Use *for*.

Example:

LEADER *(book open):*   How long have you had this book?
SPEAKER A *(book closed):*   I've had this book *since* (the beginning of the term).
LEADER TO B *(book open):*   How long has *(Speaker A)* had this book?
SPEAKER B *(book closed):*   S/He has had this book *for* (five weeks).

1. How long have you been in *(this country/city)?*
2. How long have you been at *(this school)?*
3. How long have you been up today?
4. How long have you known (. . .)?
5. Where do you live? How long have you lived there?
6. How long have you had your wristwatch?
7. Who has a car/bicycle? How long have you had it?
8. How long have you been in this room today?
9. Who is wearing new clothes? What is new? How long have you had it/them?
10. Who is married? How long have you been married?

☐ EXERCISE 21. Sentences with SINCE-clauses. (Chart 4-5)

Directions: Complete the sentences with the words in parentheses. Put brackets around the *since*-clauses.

1. I *(know)* __have known__ Mark Miller [ever since* we *(be)* _____ were _____ in college.]

2. Pedro *(change)* _____ his major three times since he *(start)* _____ school.

3. Ever since I *(be)* _____ a child, I *(be)* _____ afraid of snakes.

4. I can't wait to get home to my own bed. I *(sleep, not)* _____ well since I *(leave)* _____ home three days ago.

_____

*Ever since has the same meaning as *since.*

5. Ever since Danny *(meet)* _____ Nicole, he *(be, not)* _____ able to think about anything or anyone else. He's in love.

6. Otto *(have)* _____ a lot of problems with his car ever since he *(buy)* _____ it. It's a lemon.

7. A: What *(you, eat)* _____ since you *(get)* _____ up this morning?

   B: I *(eat)* _____ a banana and some yogurt. That's all.

8. I'm eighteen. I have a job and am in school. My life is going okay now, but I *(have)* _____ a miserable home life when I *(be)* _____ a young child. Ever since I *(leave)* _____ home at the age of fifteen, I *(take)* _____ care of myself. I *(have)* _____ some hard times, but I *(learn)* _____ how to stand on my own two feet.*

☐ **EXERCISE 22. SINCE vs. FOR. (Chart 4-5)**
   Directions: Describe yourself, orally or in writing, using **since, for,** or **never** with the present perfect.

   Example: have *(a particular kind of watch)*
   → *I've had my Seiko quartz watch for two years.* OR
   → *I've had my Seiko quartz watch since my eighteenth birthday.*

   Example: smoke cigars/cigarettes/a pipe
   → *I've never smoked cigarettes.* OR
   → *I've smoked cigarettes since I was seventeen.*

   1. know *(a particular person)*

   2. live in *(this city)*

   3. study English

   4. be in this class/at this school/with this company

   5. have long hair/short hair/a mustache

   6. wear glasses/contact lenses

   7. have *(a particular article of clothing)*

   8. be interested in *(a particular subject)*

   9. be married

   10. have a driver's license

   _____

   *To "stand on one's own two feet" is an idiom meaning to be able to take care of oneself and be independent.

4-6 PRESENT PERFECT PROGRESSIVE

Al and Ann are in their car right now. They are driving home. It is now four o'clock. (a) They **have been driving** since two o'clock. (b) They **have been driving** for two hours. They will be home soon.	The PRESENT PERFECT PROGRESSIVE talks about *how long* an activity has been in progress before now. Note: Time expressions with *since*, as in (a), and *for*, as in (b), are frequently used with this tense. STATEMENT: ***have/has + been + -ing***
(c) How long **have** they **been driving**?	QUESTION FORM: ***have/has*** + *subject* + ***been + -ing***

COMPARE the present progressive and the present perfect progressive.

PRESENT PROGRESSIVE		
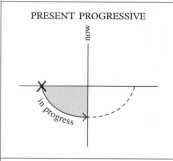	(d) Po **is sitting** in class right now.	The PRESENT PROGRESSIVE describes an activity that is in progress right now, as in (d). It does not discuss duration (length of time). INCORRECT: *Po has been sitting in class right now.*
PRESENT PERFECT PROGRESSIVE 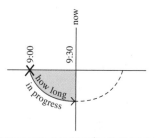	Po is sitting at his desk in class. He sat down at nine o'clock. It is now nine-thirty. (e) Po **has been sitting** in class **since** nine o'clock. (f) Po **has been sitting** in class **for** thirty minutes.	The PRESENT PERFECT PROGRESSIVE expresses the **duration** (length of time) of an activity that began in the past and is in progress right now. INCORRECT: *Po is sitting in class since nine o'clock.*

(g) CORRECT: I ***know*** Yoko. (h) INCORRECT: *I am knowing Yoko.* (i) CORRECT: I ***have known*** Yoko ***for*** two years. (j) INCORRECT: *I have been knowing Yoko for two years.*	Reminder: Non-action verbs (e.g., *know, like, own, belong*) are not used in any progressive tenses.* In (i): With non-action verbs, the present perfect is used with ***since*** or ***for*** to express the duration of a situation that began in the past and continues to the present.

*See Chart 1-6 (Non-Action Verbs), p. 17.

☐ **EXERCISE 23. Present progressive vs. present perfect progressive. (Chart 4-6)**

Directions: Complete the sentences. Use the present progressive or the present perfect progressive.

1. I *(sit)* __am sitting__ in class right now. I *(sit)* __have been sitting__ here since one o'clock.

2. Kate is standing at the corner. She *(wait)* __is waiting__ for the bus. She *(wait)* __has been waiting__ for the bus for twenty minutes.

3. Scott and Rebecca *(talk)* __are talking__ on the phone right now. They *(talk)* __have been talking__ on the phone for over an hour.

4. Right now we're in class. We *(do)* __are doing__ an exercise. We *(do)* __have been doing__ this exercise for a couple of minutes.

5. A: You look busy right now. What *(you, do)* __are you doing__ ?

   B: I *(work)* __am working__ on my physics experiment. It's a long and difficult experiment.

   A: How long *(you, work)* __have you been working__ on it?

   B: I started planning it last January. I *(work)* __have been working__ on it since then.

☐ **EXERCISE 24. Present perfect progressive. (Chart 4-6)**

Directions: Answer the questions. Only the teacher's book is open.

Example:
TEACHER: Where are you living?
RESPONSE: I'm living in an apartment on Fourth Avenue.
TEACHER: How long have you been living there?
RESPONSE: I've been living there since last September.

1. Right now you are sitting in class. How long have you been sitting here?

2. When did you first begin to study English? How long have you been studying English?

3. I began to teach English in *(year)*. How long have I been teaching English?

4. I began to work at this school in *(month or year)*. How long have I been working here?

5. What are we doing right now? How long have we been doing it?

6. (. . .), I see that you wear glasses. How long have you been wearing glasses?

7. Who drives? When did you first drive a car? How long have you been driving?

8. Who drinks coffee? How old were you when you started to drink coffee? How long have you been drinking coffee?

4-7 PRESENT PERFECT PROGRESSIVE vs. PRESENT PERFECT

PRESENT PERFECT PROGRESSIVE (a) Rita and Josh are talking on the phone. They ***have been talking*** on the phone for twenty minutes.	The PRESENT PERFECT PROGRESSIVE expresses the **duration of present** *activities* that are in progress, using action verbs, as in (a).
PRESENT PERFECT (b) Rita ***has talked*** to Josh on the phone many times (before now). (c) *INCORRECT: Rita has been talking to Josh on the phone many times.* (d) Rita ***has known*** Josh for two years. (e) *INCORRECT: Rita has been knowing Josh for two years.*	The PRESENT PERFECT expresses (1) repeated activities that occur at **unspecified times in the past**, as in (b), or (2) the **duration of present** *situations*, as in (d), using non-action verbs.
(f) I ***have been living*** here for six months. OR (g) I ***have lived*** here for six months. (h) Al ***has been wearing*** glasses since he was ten. OR Al ***has worn*** glasses since he was ten. (i) I'***ve been going*** to school ever since I was five years old. OR I'***ve gone*** to school ever since I was five years old.	For some (not all) verbs, duration can be expressed by either the present perfect or the present perfect progressive. (f) and (g) have essentially the same meaning, and both are correct. Often either tense can be used with verbs that express the **duration of usual or habitual activities/situations** (things that happen daily or regularly), e.g., *live, work, teach, smoke, wear glasses, play chess, go to school, read the same newspaper every morning, etc.*

☐ **EXERCISE 25. Present perfect vs. the present perfect progressive. (Chart 4-7)**
   Directions: Complete the sentences. Use the present perfect or the present perfect progressive. In some sentences, either form is possible.

   1. A: I'm tired. We *(walk)* ____have been walking____ for more than an hour.
      Let's stop and rest for a while.

      B: Okay.

   2. A: Is the post office far from here?

      B: Not at all. I *(walk)* ____have walked____ there many times.

3. A: Do you like it here?

   B: I (live) __have been living/have lived__ here for only a short while. I don't know yet.

4. A: I (read) __have read__ this chapter in my chemistry text three times, and I still don't understand it!

   B: Maybe I can help.

5. A: My eyes are getting tired. I (read) __have been reading__ for two hours. I think I'll take a break.

   B: Why don't we go for a walk?

6. A: Do you like the Edgewater Inn?

   B: Very much. I (stay) __'ve stayed__ there at least a dozen times. It's my favorite hotel.

7. A: The baby's crying. Shouldn't we do something?

   B: He's all right.

   A: Are you sure? He (cry) __has been crying__ for almost ten minutes.

   B: Okay. I'll go into his room and see if anything's wrong.

8. A: Who's your daughter's new teacher?

   B: Mrs. Jackson.

   A: She's one of the best teachers at the elementary school. She (teach) __has been teaching__ kindergarten for twenty years.

9. A: Ed (play) __has been playing__ tennis for ten years, but he (still) doesn't have a good backhand.

   B: Neither do I, and I (play) __'ve played__ tennis for twenty years.

10. A: Where does Mr. Alvarez work?

    B: At the power company. He (work) __has been working__ there for fifteen years. He likes his job.

    A: What about his neighbor, Mr. Perez?

    B: He's currently unemployed, but he'll find a new job soon.

    A: What kind of job experience does he have?

    B: He (work) __has worked__ for a small manufacturing firm, for the telephone company, and at two of the world's leading software companies. With all that work experience, he won't have any trouble finding another job.

4-8 USING *ALREADY, YET, STILL,* AND *ANYMORE*

ALREADY	(a) The mail came an hour ago. **The mail is *already* here.**	Idea of *already:* Something happened before now, before this time. *Position: midsentence.*★
YET	(b) I expected the mail an hour ago, but **it hasn't come *yet*.**	Idea of *yet:* Something did not happen before now (up to this time), but it may happen in the future. *Position: end of sentence.*
STILL	(c) It was cold yesterday. **It is *still* cold** today. **We *still* need to wear coats.** (d) I could play the piano when I was a child. **I can *still* play the piano.** (e) The mail didn't come an hour ago. **The mail *still* hasn't come.**	Idea of *still:* A situation continues to exist from past to present without change. *Position: midsentence.*★
ANYMORE	(f) I lived in Chicago two years ago, but then I moved to another city. **I don't live in Chicago *anymore*.**	Idea of *anymore:* A past situation does not continue to exist at present; a past situation has changed. ***Anymore*** has the same meaning as ***any longer.*** *Position: end of sentence.*

Note: ***Already*** is used in *affirmative* sentences.
Yet and ***anymore*** are used in *negative* sentences.
Still is used in either *affirmative or negative* sentences.

★See Chart 1-3, p. 9. A midsentence adverb
(1) precedes a simple present verb: *We **still need** to wear coats.*
(2) follows *am, is, are, was, were: It **is still** cold.*
(3) comes between a helping verb and a main verb: *Bob **has already arrived**.*
(4) precedes a negative helping verb: *Ann **still hasn't** come.*
(5) follows the subject in a question: *Have **you already** seen that movie?*

☐ **EXERCISE 26. ALREADY, YET, STILL, ANYMORE.** (Chart 4-8)
Directions: Complete the sentences with *already*, *yet*, *still*, or *anymore*.

1. It's 1:00 P.M. I'm hungry. I haven't eaten lunch _____yet_____ .

2. It's 1:00 P.M. I'm not hungry. I've _____already_____ eaten lunch.

3. Eric was hungry, so he ate a candy bar a few minutes ago. But he's _____still_____ hungry, so he's going to have another candy bar.

4. I used to eat lunch at the cafeteria every day, but now I bring my lunch to school in a paper bag instead. I don't eat at the cafeteria _____anymore_____ .

5. I don't have to study tonight. I've _____already_____ finished all my homework.

6. I started a letter to my parents yesterday, but I haven't finished it _____yet_____ . I'll finish it later today and put it in the mail.

7. I started a letter to my parents yesterday. I thought about finishing it last night before I went to bed, but I didn't. I _____ *still* _____ haven't finished it.*

8. A: Is Mary home _____ *yet* _____?

   B: No, but I'm expecting her soon.

9. A: Is Mary _____ *still* _____ in class?

   B: Yes, she is. Her class doesn't end until 11:30.

10. A: Has Rob found a new job _____ *yet* _____?

    B: No. He _____ *still* _____ works at the bookstore.

11. A: When is your sister going to come to visit you?

    B: She's _____ *already* _____ here. She got here yesterday.

12. A: Do you _____ *still* _____ live on Pine Avenue?

    B: No, I don't live there _____ *anymore* _____. I moved to another apartment closer to school.

☐ **EXERCISE 27. ALREADY, YET, STILL, ANYMORE. (Chart 4-8)**
   Directions: Complete the sentences with your own words.

   Example: I . . . not . . . because I've already . . . .
   → **I'm not** hungry **because I've already** eaten.   OR
   → **I'm not** going to go to the movie **because I've already** seen it.   OR
   → **I don't** have to take the English test **because I've already** taken it.

   1. I used to . . . , but . . . anymore.
   2. I can't . . . because I haven't . . . yet.
   3. Are . . . still . . . ?
   4. . . . because I've already . . . .
   5. I don't . . . anymore, but . . . still . . . .

☐ **EXERCISE 28. Verb tense review. (Chapters 1, 2, and 4)**
   Directions: Compare the different meanings of the verb tenses. Identify which sentences express duration.

   1. a. Rachel *is taking* English classes.
      b. Nadia *has been taking* English classes for two months.
   2. a. Ann *has been* in Jerusalem for two years. She likes it there.
      b. Sue *has been* in Jerusalem. She's also been in Paris. She's been in New York and Tokyo. She's been in lots of cities. She travels a lot.

---

*In negative sentences, *still* and *yet* express similar meanings. The meanings of *I haven't finished it yet* and *I still haven't finished it* are similar.

3. a. Jack **has visited** his aunt and uncle many times.
   b. Matt **has been visiting** his aunt and uncle for the last three days.

4. a. Jack **is talking** on the phone.
   b. Jack **talks** on the phone a lot.
   c. Jack **has been talking** to his boss on the phone for half an hour.
   d. Jack **has talked** to his boss on the phone lots of times.

5. a. Mr. Woods **walks** his dog in Forest Park every day.
   b. Mr. Woods **has walked** his dog in Forest Park many times.
   c. Mr. Woods **walked** his dog in Forest Park five times last week.
   d. Mr. Woods **is walking** his dog in Forest Park right now.
   e. Mr. Woods **has been walking** his dog in Forest Park since two o'clock.

☐ EXERCISE 29. Verb tenses. (Charts 4-2 → 4-8)
Directions: Make sentences about your life using the given time expressions. Use the simple past, present perfect, or present perfect progressive.

Example: for the last two weeks
   → *I've had a cold for the last two weeks.*

1. since I was a child
2. for a long time
3. two years ago
4. so far today
5. many times in my lifetime
6. never

7. since last Tuesday
8. for a number of years*
9. a week ago today
10. for the last ten minutes
11. already . . . , but . . . yet
12. still . . . , but . . . anymore

---

*a number of years = many years.

□ EXERCISE 30. Review of verb tenses. (Chapters 1 → 4)
   Directions: Complete the sentences with the words in parentheses.

1. A: *(you, have)* _____**Do you have**_____ any plans for vacation?
   B: Yes, I do. I *(plan)* _____**am planning**_____ to go to Toronto.
   A: *(you, be, ever)* __Have you ever been__ there before?
   B: Yes, I have. I *(be)* ___was___ in Toronto two months ago. My brother
      (live) ___lives___ there, so I *(go)* ___go___ there often.

2. A: Where's Jessica?
   B: She *(study)* ___is studying___ at the library.
   A: When *(she, get)* __is she going to get__ back home?
   B: In an hour or so. Probably around five o'clock.
   A: How long *(she, study)* __has she been studying__ at the
      library?
   B: Since two o'clock this afternoon.
   A: *(she, study)* __Does she study__ on Has she studied __ at the library every day?
   B: Not every day, but often.

3. A: Shhh. Irene *(talk)* ___is talking___ on the phone long-distance.
   B: Who *(she, talk)* ___is she talking___ to?
   A: Her brother. They *(talk)* __have been talking__ for almost an hour.
      I think her brother is in some kind of trouble.
   B: That's too bad. I hope it's nothing serious.

4. A: *(you, know)* __Do ya know__ Abdullah's new address?
   B: Not off the top of my head. But I *(have)* ___have___ it at home in my
      computer. When I *(get)* ___get___ home this evening, I *(call)*
      ___will call___ and *(give)* ___give___ you his address.
   A: Thanks. Or you could e-mail it to me.
   B: Okay. I *(do)* ___will do___ that.

5. A: Where's Juan? He *(be)* ___has been___ absent from class for the last three
      days. *(anyone, see)* __Has anyone seen__ him lately?
   B: I have. I *(see)* ___saw___ him yesterday. He has a bad cold, so he *(be)*
      ___has been___ home in bed since the weekend. He *(be, probably)*
      ___will probably be___ back in class tomorrow.

6. A: How long *(you, wear)* __have you worn__ glasses?
   B: Since I *(be)* ___was___ ten years old.
   A: *(you, be)* __Are you__ nearsighted or farsighted?
   B: Nearsighted.

7. A: Let's go to a restaurant tonight.

B: Okay. Where should we go?

A: *(you, like)* __Do you like__ Thai food?

B: I don't know. I *(eat, never)* __have never eaten__ any. What's it like?

A: It's delicious, but it can be pretty hot!

B: That's okay. I *(love)* __love__ really hot food.

A: There *(be)* __is__ a Thai restaurant downtown. I *(go)* __'ve gone__ _____ there a couple of times. The food is excellent.

B: Sounds good. I *(be, never)* __'ve never been__ to a Thai restaurant, so it *(be)* __will be__ a new experience for me. After we *(get)* __'ll get__ there, can you explain the menu to me?

A: Sure. And if I can't, our waiter or waitress can.

8. A: *(you, smoke)* __Do you smoke__ ?

B: Yes, I do.

A: How long *(you, smoke)* __have you smoked__ ?

B: Well, let me see. I *(smoke)* __'ve smoked__ since I *(be)* __was__ seventeen. So I *(smoke)* __have been smoking__ for almost four years.

A: Why *(you, start)* __did you start__ ?

B: Because I *(be)* __was__ a dumb, stupid kid.

A: *(you, want)* __Do you want__ to quit?

B: Yes. I *(plan)* __am planning__ to quit very soon. In fact, I *(decide)* __will decide__ to quit on my next birthday. My twenty-first birthday is two weeks from now. On that day, I *(intend)* __will intend__ to smoke my last cigarette.

A: That's terrific! You *(feel)* __may feel__ much better after you *(stop)* __will__ smoking.

B: *(you, smoke, ever)* __Have you ever smoked__ ?

A: No, I haven't. I *(smoke, never)* __I 've never smoked__ a cigarette in my life. When I *(be)* __was__ ten years old, I *(smoke)* __smoked__ one of my uncle's cigars. My sister and I *(steal)* __stealed__ a couple of his cigars and *(go)* __went__ behind the garage to smoke them. Both of us *(get)* __got__ sick. I *(have, not)* __haven't had__ anything to smoke since then.

B: That's smart.

☐ EXERCISE 31. Error analysis. (Charts 4-1 → 4-8)

Directions: Correct the errors. Most of the errors are in verb usage, but some are miscellaneous (e.g., capitalization, word order, spelling, agreement, etc.).

1. I have been ~~studied~~ ^{studying} ~~e~~nglish for eight year_s, but I still have a lot to learn.

2. I want to learn English since I am a child.

3. Our class has have three tests since the beggining of the term.

4. I have started the English classes since three weeks ago and I am learning some English since that time.

5. I have been thinking about how to improve my English ability since I came here, but I still don't find a good way.

6. All of us has learn many thing since we were children.

7. When I was at my sister's house, we had an argument. Since then I didn't talk to her for three days.

8. Since I was very young, I like animals.

9. I have been study english since three and a half month.

10. I like very much the English. Since I was young my father found an American girl to teach my brothers and me English, but when I move to another city my father hasn't find one for five years. Now I'm living here and studying in this English program.

11. I almost die in an automobile accident five year ago. Since that day my life changed completely.

12. In my country, women are soldiers in the army since the 1970s.

13. I meet Abdul in my first English class last June. He was friendly and kind. We are friends since that day.

14. My favorite place in the world is my hometown. I live there for twenty years.

15. My wife and I have been in Italy two weeks ago. We went there to ski.

16. My wife broke her leg while she was skiing in Italy. Now she's home, but she can't walk without help. A lot of our friends are visiting her since she has broken her leg.

17. I was busy every day since I arrived at this city.

18. I haven't to eaten any kind of chinese food for a week. I miss it a lot!

☐ EXERCISE 32. Verb tense review. (Chapters 1 → 4)
Directions: Complete the sentences with the words in parentheses.

Dear Adam,

Hi! Remember me? (Just a joke!) I *(write, not)* ___haven't written___₁ to you for at least six months, but that's not long enough for you to forget me! I think about writing to you often, but I *(be, not)* __haven't been__₂ a good correspondent for the last few months. You *(hear, not)* __haven't heard__₃ from me for such a long time because I *(be)* __'ve been | was__₄ really busy. For the last few months, I *(work)* __have worked__₅ full-time at a shoe store and *(go)* __gone__₆ to school at the local community college to study business and computers. When I *(write)* __wrote__₇ to you six months ago—last April, I think—I *(go)* __was going__₈ to the university full-time and *(study)* __studying__₉ anthropology. A lot of things *(happen)* __'ve happened__₁₀ since then.

some event

At the end of the spring semester last June, my grades (be) _____were_____
11

terrible. As a result, I (lose) _____lost_____ my scholarship and my parents'
12

support. I really (mess) _____messed_____ up when I (get) _____got_____ those
13   14

bad grades. When I (show) _____showed_____ my grade report to my parents, they
15

(refuse) _____refused_____ to help me with my living expenses at school anymore.
16

They (feel) _____felt_____ that I was wasting my time and their money, so they (tell)
17

_____told_____ me to get a job. So last June I (start) _____started_____ working
18   19

at a shoe store: Imperial Shoes at Southcenter Mall. I (work) _'ve worked! I've been_
20   working

there ever since.

It (be, not) _____isn't_____ a bad job, but it (be, not) _____isn't_____
21   22

wonderful either. Every day, I (fetch) _____fetch_____ shoes from the back room for
23

people to try on, boxes and boxes of shoes, all day long. I (meet) _____'ve met_____
24

some pretty weird people since I (start) _____started_____ this job. A couple of
25

weeks ago, a middle-aged man (come) _____came_____ into the store. He
26

(want) _____wanted_____ to try on some black leather loafers. I (bring)
27

_____brought_____ the loafers, and he (put) _____put_____ them on. While
28   29

he (walk) _____was walking_____ around to see if they fit okay, he (pull)
30

_____pulled_____ from his pocket a little white mouse with pink eyes and
31

(start) _____started_____ talking to it. He (look) _____looked_____ right at the
32   33

mouse and (say) _____said_____, "George, (you, like) _Do you like_
34   35

this pair of shoes?" When the mouse (twitch) _____twitched_____ its nose, the man
36

(say) _____said_____, "Yes, so do I." Then he (turn) _____turned_____ to me
37   38

and (say) _____said_____, "We'll take them." Can you believe that!?
39

Most of the people I meet are nice—and normal. My favorite customers *(be)*

_____ are _____ people who *(know)* _____ know _____ what they want when they
40   41

(enter) _____ enter _____ the store. They *(come)* _____ come _____ in, *(point)*
                42   43

_____ point _____ at one pair of shoes, politely *(tell)* _____ tell _____ me their
    44   45

size, *(try)* _____ try _____ the shoes on, and then *(buy)* _____ buy _____ them,
             46   47

just like that. They *(agonize, not)* _____ don't agonize _____ for a long time over
                upset and don't like 48

which pair to buy.

    I *(learn)* _____ learn _____ one important thing from working at the
                      49

shoe store: I *(want, not)* _____ don't want _____ to sell shoes as a career. I *(need)*
                        50

_____ need _____ a good education that *(prepare)* _____ prepares _____ me for a
    51   52

job that I can enjoy for the rest of my life. And even though I love studying anthropology,

I *(decide)* _____ 've decided _____ that a degree in business and computers will
                      53

provide the best career opportunities.

Now I *(work)* __'m working__ part-time at the shoe store and *(go)*
54

__going__ to school at the same time. I *(want, always)* __'ve always wanted__
55   56

to be completely independent and self-reliant, and now I *(be)* __am__ .
57

I *(have)* __have__ to pay every penny of my tuition and living expenses now.
58

Ever since I *(lose)* __lost__ my scholarship and *(make)* __made__
59   60

my parents mad, I *(be)* __'ve been__ completely on my own. I'm glad to
61

report that my grades at present *(be)* __are__ excellent, and right now I
62

(enjoy, really) __really enjoy__ my work with computers. In the
63

future, I *(continue)* __will continue__ to take courses in anthropology
64

whenever I can fit them into my schedule, and I *(study)* __'m going to__
65

anthropology on my own for the rest of my life, but I *(pursue)* __am going to__
66

a career in business. Maybe there is some way I can combine anthropology, business, and

computers. Who knows?

There. I *(tell)* __'ve told__ you everything I can think of that is at all
67

important in my life at the moment. I think I *(grow)* __'ve grown__ up a
68

lot during the last six months. I *(understand)* __understand__ that my education
69

is important. Losing my scholarship *(make)* __made__ my life more difficult,
70

but I *(believe)* __believe__ that I *(take, finally)* __'ve finally taken__
71   72

charge of my life. It's a good feeling.

Please write. I'd love to hear from you.

Jessica

☐ EXERCISE 33. Writing: verb tense review. (Chapters 1 → 4)

Directions: Think of a friend you haven't spoken or written to since the beginning of this term. Write this friend a letter about your activities from the start of this school term to the present time. Begin your letter as follows:

Dear (. . .),
    I'm sorry I haven't written for such a long time. Lots of things have happened since I last wrote to you.

☐ EXERCISE 34. Writing: verb tense review. (Chapters 1 → 4)

Directions: Write about one (or both) of the following topics.

1. Think of two or three important events that have occurred in your life in the past year or two. In a paragraph for each, briefly tell your reader about these events and give your opinions and/or predictions.

2. Think of two or three important events that have occurred in the world in the past year or two. In a paragraph for each, briefly tell your reader about these events and give your opinions and/or predictions.

4-9 PAST PERFECT

Situation: Jack left his apartment at 2:00. Ann arrived at his apartment at 2:15 and knocked on the door.

(a) When Ann arrived, Jack wasn't there. He **had left**.

The PAST PERFECT is used when the speaker is talking about two different events at two different times in the past; one event ends before the second event happens.

In (a): There are two events, and both happened in the past: *Jack left his apartment. Ann arrived at his apartment.* To show the time relationship between the two events, we use the past perfect *(had left)* to say that the first event (Jack leaving his apartment) was completed before the second event (Ann arriving at his apartment) occurred.

4-9 PAST PERFECT—(continued)

(b) Jack **had left** his apartment when Ann arrived.	FORM: **had** + *past participle*
(c) *He'd* left. *I'd* left. *They'd* left. Etc.	CONTRACTION: *I/you/she/he/it/we/they* + **'d**

COMPARE THE PRESENT PERFECT AND THE PAST PERFECT.

PRESENT PERFECT	(d) I am not hungry now. I **have** already **eaten**.	The PRESENT PERFECT expresses an activity that *occurred before now, at an unspecified time in the past*, as in (d).
before now — *now*		
PAST PERFECT	(e) I was not hungry at 1:00 P.M. I **had** already **eaten**.	The PAST PERFECT expresses an activity that *occurred before another time in the past.* In (e): I ate at noon. I was not hungry at 1:00 P.M. because I had already eaten before 1:00 P.M.
before 1:00 — *1:00 P.M.*		

COMPARE THE PAST PROGRESSIVE AND THE PAST PERFECT.

PAST PROGRESSIVE	(f) I **was eating** when Bob came.	The PAST PROGRESSIVE expresses an activity that was *in progress at a particular time in the past.* In (f): I began to eat at noon. Bob came at 12:10. My meal was in progress when Bob came.
began eating — *Bob came* / *eating in progress*		
PAST PERFECT	(g) I **had eaten** when Bob came.	The PAST PERFECT expresses an activity that was *completed before a particular time in the past.* In (g): I finished eating at noon. Bob came at 1:00 P.M. My meal was completed before Bob came.
finished eating — *Bob came*		

□ EXERCISE 35. Past perfect. (Chart 4-9)

Directions: Identify which action took place first (1st) in the past and which action took place second (2nd).

1. The tennis player **jumped** in the air for joy. She **had won** the match.

   a. ____1st____ The tennis player won the match.

   b. ____2nd____ The tennis player jumped in the air.

2. Before I went to bed, I **checked** the front door. My roommate **had** already **locked** it.

   a. ____2nd____ I checked the door.

   b. ____1st____ My roommate locked the door.

3. I **looked** for Bob, but he **had left** the building.

   a. _____ Bob left the building.

   b. _____ I looked for Bob.

4. I **laughed** when I saw my son. He **had poured** a bowl of noodles on top of his head.

   a. _____ I laughed.

   b. _____ My son poured a bowl of noodles on his head.

5. Oliver **arrived** at the theater on time, but he couldn't get in. He **had left** his ticket at home.

   a. _____ Oliver left his ticket at home.

   b. _____ Oliver arrived at the theater.

6. I **handed** Betsy the newspaper, but she didn't want it. She **had read** it during her lunch hour.

   a. _____ I handed Betsy the newspaper.

   b. _____ Betsy read the newspaper.

7. After Carl arrived in New York, he **called** his mother. He **had promised** to call her as soon as he got in.

    a. _____ Carl made a promise to his mother.

    b. _____ Carl called his mother.

8. Stella was alone in a strange city. She walked down the avenue slowly, looking in shop windows. Suddenly, she **turned** her head and **looked** behind her. Someone **had called** her name.

    a. _____ Stella turned her head and looked behind her.

    b. _____ Someone called her name.

☐ EXERCISE 36. Present perfect vs. past perfect. (Chart 4-9)
Directions: Complete the sentences with the present perfect or the past perfect form of the verb in parentheses.

1. A: Oh no! We're too late. The train *(leave, already)* _____has already left_____ .
   B: That's okay. We'll catch the next train to Athens.

2. Last Thursday, we went to the station to catch a train to Athens, but we were too late. The train *(leave, already)* _____had already left_____ .

3. A: Go back to sleep. It's only six o'clock in the morning.
   B: I'm not sleepy. I *(sleep, already)* _____ for eight hours. I'm going to get up.

4. I woke up at six this morning, but I couldn't get back to sleep. I wasn't sleepy. I *(sleep, already)* _____ for eight hours.

5. A: I'll introduce you to Professor Newton at the meeting tonight.
   B: You don't need to. I *(meet, already)* _____ him.

6. Jack offered to introduce me to Professor Newton, but it wasn't necessary. I *(meet, already)* _____ him.

7. A: Do you want to go to the movie tonight?
   B: What are you going to see?
   A: *Distant Drums.*
   B: I *(see, already)* _____ it. Thanks anyway.

8. I didn't go to the movie with Francisco last Tuesday night. I *(see, already)* _____ it.

9. A: Jane? Jane! Is that you? How are you? I haven't seen you for ages!

    B: Excuse me? Are you talking to me?

    A: Oh. You're not Jane. I'm sorry. It is clear that I *(make)* _____
        a mistake. Please excuse me.

10. Yesterday I approached a stranger who looked like Jane Moore and started talking to
    her. But she wasn't Jane. It was clear that I *(make)* _____ a
    mistake. I was really embarrassed.

☐ EXERCISE 37. Past progressive vs. past perfect. (Chart 4-9)
    Directions: Circle the correct completion.

1. Amanda didn't need to study the multiplication tables in fifth grade. She _____
   them.
   A. was learning   B. had already learned

2. I enjoyed visiting Tommy's class. It was an arithmetic class. The students _____
   their multiplication tables.
   A. were learning   B. had already learned

3. While I _____ up the mountain, I got tired. But I didn't stop until I reached the
   top.
   A. was walking   B. had walked

4. I was very tired when I got to the top of the mountain. I _____ a long distance.
   A. was walking   B. had walked

5. I knocked. No one answered. I turned the handle and pulled sharply on the door, but
   it did not open. Someone _____ it.
   A. was locking   B. had locked

6. "Where were you when the earthquake occurred?"
   "In my office. I _____ to my assistant. We were working on a report."
   A. was talking   B. had already talked

7. "Ahmed's house was destroyed in the earthquake."
   "I know! It's lucky that he and his family _____ for his parents' home before the
   earthquake struck."
   A. were leaving   B. had already left

8. We drove two hundred miles to see the circus in Kansas City. When we got there, we
   couldn't find the circus. It _____ town. We _____ all the way to Kansas City for
   nothing.
   A. was leaving . . . were driving   C. was leaving . . . had driven
   B. had left . . . had driven   D. had left . . . were driving

☐ EXERCISE 38. Present perfect, past progressive, and past perfect. (Chart 4-9)
Directions: Complete the sentences with the correct forms of the words in parentheses.
Use the present perfect, past progressive, or past perfect.

1. When I went to bed, I turned on the radio. While I *(sleep)* _____was sleeping_____ ,
somebody turned it off.

2. You're from Jakarta? I *(be, never)* _____ there. I'd like to go
there someday.

3. I started to tell Rodney the news, but he stopped me. He *(hear, already)* _____
_____ it.

4. When Gina went to bed, it was snowing. It *(snow, still)* _____
_____ when she woke up in the morning.

5. Rita called me on the phone to tell me the good news. She *(pass)* _____
her final exam in English.

6. I couldn't think. The people around me *(make)* _____ too
much noise. Finally, I gave up and left to try to find a quiet place to work.

7. Are you still waiting for David? *(he, come, not)* _____
yet? He's really late, isn't he?

8. Otto's back to work today, but was in the hospital last week. He *(be, never)*
_____ a patient in a hospital before. It was a new
experience for him.

9. A couple of weeks ago Mr. Fox, our office manager, surprised all of us. When he
walked into the office, he *(wear)* _____ a T-shirt and jeans.
Everyone stopped and stared. Mr. Fox is a conservative dresser. Before that time, he
(wear, never) _____ anything but a blue or gray suit.
And he *(wear, not)* _____ his jeans to the office since
that time. He wore them only that one time.

☐ EXERCISE 39. Verb tense review. (Chapters 1 → 4)
Directions: Circle the correct completion.

Example:
    I can't come with you. I need to stay here. I _____ for a phone call.
    A. wait   B. will wait   Ⓒ am waiting   D. have waited

1. I _____ my glasses three times so far this year. One time I dropped them on a
cement floor. Another time I sat on them. And this time I stepped on them.
    A. broke   B. was breaking   C. have broken   D. have been breaking

2. Kate reached to the floor and picked up her glasses. They were broken. She _____ on them.

    A. stepped   B. had stepped   C. was stepping D. has stepped

3. Sarah gets angry easily. She _____ a bad temper ever since she was a child.

    A. has   B. will have   C. had   D. has had

4. Now, whenever Sarah starts to lose her temper, she _____ a deep breath and _____ to ten.

    A. takes . . . counts   C. took . . . counted
    B. has taken . . . counted   D. is taking . . . counting

5. Nicky, please don't interrupt me. I _____ to Grandma on the phone. Go play with your trucks so we can finish our conversation.

    A. talk   B. have talked   C. am talking   D. have been talking

6. We _____ at a hotel in Miami when the hurricane hit southern Florida last month. As soon as the hurricane moved out of the area, we left and went back home.

    A. had stayed   B. stay   C. were staying D. stayed

7. Now listen carefully. When Aunt Martha _____ tomorrow, give her a big hug.

    A. arrives   B. will arrive   C. arrived   D. is going to arrive

8. My cousin _____ with me in my apartment for the last two weeks. I'm ready for him to leave, but he seems to want to stay forever. Maybe I should ask him to leave.

    A. is staying   B. stayed   C. was staying   D. has been staying

9. Mrs. Larsen discovered a bird in her apartment. It was in her living room. It _____ into her apartment through an open window.

    A. was flying   B. had flown   C. has flown   D. was flown

10. The phone rang, so I _____ it up and _____ hello.

    A. picked . . . had said   C. was picking . . . said
    B. picked . . . said   D. was picking . . . had said

☐ EXERCISE 40. Verb tense review. (Chapters 1 → 4)
    Directions: Circle the correct completion.

Example:
    I can't come with you. I need to stay here. I _____ for a phone call.
    A. wait   B. will wait   Ⓒ am waiting   D. have waited

1. My mother began to drive cars when she was fourteen. Now she is eighty-nine, and she still drives. She _____ cars for seventy-five years.

    A. was driving   B. drives   C. drove   D. has been driving

2. In every culture, people _____ jewelry since prehistoric times.

    A. wear   B. wore   C. have worn   D. had worn

3. It _____ when I left the house this morning, so I opened my umbrella.
   A. rained   B. had rained   C. is raining   D. was raining

4. Australian koala bears are interesting animals. They _____ practically their entire lives in trees without ever coming down to the ground.
   A. are spending   C. have spent
   B. have been spending   D. spend

5. The teacher is late today, so class hasn't begun yet. After she _____ here, class will begin.
   A. will get   B. is going to get   C. gets   D. is getting

6. It's raining hard. It _____ an hour ago and _____ yet.
   A. had started . . . doesn't stop   C. started . . . hasn't stopped
   B. has started . . . didn't stop   D. was starting . . . isn't stopping

7. Alex's bags are almost ready for his trip. He _____ for Syria later this afternoon. We'll say good-bye to him before he _____.
   A. left . . . went   C. is leaving . . . goes
   B. leaves . . . will go   D. has left . . . will go

8. I heard a slight noise, so I walked to the front door to investigate. I looked down at the floor and saw a piece of paper. Someone _____ a note under the door to my apartment.
   A. had pushed   B. is pushing   C. has pushed   D. pushed

9. I walked slowly through the market. People _____ all kinds of fruits and vegetables. I studied the prices carefully before I decided what to buy.
   A. have sold   B. sell   C. had sold   D. were selling

10. I really like my car. I _____ it for six years. It runs beautifully.
    A. have   B. have had   C. had   D. have been having

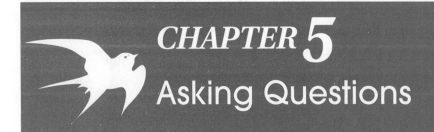

CHAPTER 5
Asking Questions

☐ EXERCISE 1. Preview: asking questions. (Chapter 5)

Directions: This exercise previews some of the grammar in this chapter. Create questions that fit the given answers. Discuss question forms.

Example: No, I _____ . I'm allergic to them.

→ QUESTION: *Do you like cats?*
ANSWER: *No, I don't. I'm allergic to them.*

1. Downtown.

2. No, I _____ .

3. Seven-thirty.

4. Two hours.

5. Because I overslept.

6. This one, not that one.

7. Yes, she _____ .

8. Mine.

9. My cousin.

10. Five blocks.

11. Once a week.

12. Answering your question.

5-1 YES/NO QUESTIONS AND SHORT ANSWERS

YES/NO QUESTION	SHORT ANSWER (+ LONG ANSWER)
(a) **Do** you **like** tea?	*Yes, I do.* (I like tea.) *No, I don't.* (I don't like tea.)
(b) **Did** Sue **call**?	*Yes, she did.* (Sue called.) *No, she didn't.* (Sue didn't call.)
(c) **Have** you **met** Al?	*Yes, I have.* (I have met Al.) *No, I haven't.* (I haven't met Al.)
(d) **Is** it **raining**?	*Yes, it is.* (It's raining.) *No, it isn't.* (It isn't raining.)
(e) **Will** Rob **be** here?	*Yes, he will.* (Rob will be here.) *No, he won't.* (Rob won't be here.)

A **yes/no question** is a question that can be answered by *yes* or *no*.

In an affirmative short answer (yes), a helping verb is NOT contracted with the subject.

In (c): INCORRECT: *Yes, I've.*
In (d): INCORRECT: *Yes, it's.*
In (e): INCORRECT: *Yes, he'll.*

The spoken emphasis in a short answer is on the verb.

☐ EXERCISE 2. Short answers to yes/no questions. (Chart 5-1)

Directions: In these dialogues, the long answer is given in parentheses. Look at the long answer, and then write the appropriate yes/no question and short answer to complete each dialogue. Do not use a negative verb in the question.

1. A: _Do you know my brother?_

   B: No, _I don't._ (I don't know your brother.)

2. A: _Does aspirin relive pain?_

   B: Yes, _it does_ (Aspirin relieves pain.)

3. A: _Do snakes have legs?_

   B: No, _they don't_ (Snakes don't have legs.)

4. A: _Can snakes move backward?_

   B: No, _they can't_ (Snakes can't move backward.)

5. A: _Is the U.S.A. in North America?_

   B: Yes, _it is_ (The United States is in North America.)

6. A: _Did you enjoy the movie?_

   B: Uh-huh, _I did_ (I enjoyed the movie.)

7. A: _Will you be at home tonight?_

   B: Huh-uh, _I won't_ (I won't be at home tonight.)

8. A: _Do you have a bicycle?_

   B: Yes, _I have_ (I have a bicycle.)*

9. A: _Has Paul left?_

   B: Yes, _he has_ (Paul has left.)

10. A: _Did he leave with Kate_

    B: Yes, _he did_ (He left with Kate.)

□ EXERCISE 3. Short answers to yes/no questions. (Chart 5-1)

Directions: Work in groups of three.

Speaker A: Whisper the cue to Speaker B. Your book is open.

Speaker B: Ask a yes/no question using the information Speaker A gave you. Your book is closed.

Speaker C: Give a short answer to the question. Your book is closed.

Example: (. . .) is wearing jeans today.

SPEAKER A *(book open):* Rosa is wearing jeans today. *(whispered)*

SPEAKER B *(book closed):* Is Rosa wearing jeans today?

SPEAKER C *(book closed):* Yes, she is.

1. (. . .) has curly hair.

2. (. . .) doesn't have a mustache.

3. (. . .) is sitting down.

4. Isn't talking to (. . .)

Switch roles.

5. (. . .) and (. . .) were in class yesterday.

6. This exercise is easy.

7. That book belongs to (. . .)

8. An ostrich can't fly.

Switch roles.

9. (. . .) is wearing earrings.

10. This book has an index.

11. (. . .)'s grammar book isn't open.

12. Giraffes don't eat meat.

*In American English, a form of *do* is usually used when *have* is the main verb:

   Do you have a car?

In British English, a form of *do* with main verb *have* is not necessary:

   Have you a car?

5-2 YES/NO QUESTIONS AND INFORMATION QUESTIONS

A yes/no question = a question that can be answered by "yes" or "no."
    A: *Does Ann live in Montreal?*
    B: *Yes, she does.* OR *No, she doesn't.*

An information question = a question that asks for information by using a question word: ***where, when, why, who, whom, what, which, whose, how.***
    A: *Where does Ann live?*
    B: *In Montreal.*

(QUESTION WORD)	HELPING VERB	SUBJECT	MAIN VERB	(REST OF SENTENCE)	The same subject-verb word order is used in both yes/no and information questions.
(a)	***Does***	*Ann*	***live***	in Montreal?	HELPING VERB + SUBJECT + MAIN VERB
(b) Where	***does***	*Ann*	***live?***		
(c)	***Is***	*Sara*	***studying***	at the library?	(a) is a yes/no question.
(d) Where	***is***	*Sara*	***studying?***		(b) is an information question.
(e)	***Will***	*you*	***graduate***	next year?	In (i) and (j): Main verb ***be*** in simple present and simple past (***am, is, are, was, were***) precedes the subject. It has the same position as a helping verb.
(f) When	***will***	*you*	***graduate?***		
(g)	***Did***	*they*	***see***	Jack?	
(h) Who(m)★	***did***	*they*	***see?***		
(i)	***Is***	*Heidi*		at home?	
(j) Where	***is***	*Heidi?*			
(k)		*Who*	***came***	to dinner?	When the question word (e.g., ***who*** or ***what***) is the subject of the question, usual question word order is not used. No form of ***do*** is used. Notice (k) and (l).
(l)		*What*	***happened***	yesterday?	

★See Chart 5-4, p. 125, for a discussion of ***who(m)***.

☐ EXERCISE 4. Yes/no and information questions. (Chart 5-2)
    Directions: Review the patterns of yes/no and information questions.
    Speaker A: Create a yes/no question.
    Speaker B: Create an information question using ***where.***

    Example: I live there.
    SPEAKER A: Do you live there?
    SPEAKER B: Where do you live?

  1. She lives there.

  2. The students live there.

  3. Bob lived there.

  4. Mary is living there.

  5. I was living there.

  6. They are going to live there.

  7. John will live there.

  8. The students can live there.

  9. Jim has lived there.

10. Tom has been living there.

5-3 WHERE, WHY, WHEN, AND WHAT TIME

QUESTION	ANSWER	
(a) **Where** did you go?	Paris.	**Where** asks about *place*.
(b) **Why** did you stay home?	Because I didn't feel well.★	**Why** asks about *reason*.
(c) **What time** did he come?	Seven-thirty. Around five o'clock. A quarter past ten.	A question with **what time** asks about *time on a clock*.
(d) **When** did he come?	Seven-thirty. Last night. Two days ago. Monday morning. In 1998.	A question with **when** can be answered by any time expression, as in the sample answers in (d).

★See Chart 8-6, p. 239, for the use of *because*. "Because I didn't feel well" is an adverb clause. It is not a complete sentence. In this example, it is the short answer to a question.

☐ EXERCISE 5. Information questions. (Charts 5-2 and 5-3)
   Directions: Create information questions. Use **where, why, when,** or **what time**.

1. A: _____When are you going to go downtown?_____
   B: Tomorrow. (I'm going to go downtown tomorrow.)

2. A: _____
   B: At Lincoln Elementary School. (My children go to school at Lincoln Elementary School.)

3. A: _____
   B: At 1:10. (Class begins at 1:10.)

4. A: _____
   B: Four years ago. (I met the Smiths four years ago.)

5. A: _____
   B: It's waiting for a mouse. (The cat is staring at the hole in the wall because it's waiting for a mouse.)

EXERCISE 6. Yes/no and information questions. (Charts 5-2 and 5-3)

Directions: Work in pairs to create dialogues. Switch roles after item 6.

Speaker A: Ask a question that will produce the given answer.

Speaker B: Give the short answer, and then give a long answer.

Example: After midnight.

SPEAKER A: What time did you go to bed last night?

SPEAKER B: After midnight. I went to bed after midnight last night.

1. The day before yesterday.
2. Yes, I do.
3. Because I wanted to.
4. At 8:30.
5. Yes, he is.
6. At a grocery store.

7. Tomorrow afternoon.
8. Viet Nam.
9. No, I can't.
10. Because the weather is . . . today.
11. Yeah, sure. Why not?
12. I don't know. Maybe.

□ EXERCISE 7. Questions with WHY. (Chart 5-3)

Directions: Work in pairs to create dialogues. Switch roles after item 4.

Speaker A: Say the sentence in the book.

Speaker B: Ask "Why?" or "Why not?" and then ask the full *why*-question.

Speaker A: Make up an answer to the question.

Example: I can't go with you tomorrow.

SPEAKER A: I can't go with you tomorrow.

SPEAKER B: Why not? Why can't you go with me tomorrow?

SPEAKER A: Because I have to study for a test.

1. I ate two breakfasts this morning.
2. I don't like to ride on airplanes.
3. I'm going to sell my guitar.
4. I didn't go to bed last night.

5. I'm happy today.
6. I had to call the police last night.
7. I can't explain it to you.
8. I'm not speaking to my cousin.

5-4 QUESTIONS WITH *WHO, WHO(M),* AND *WHAT*

QUESTION	ANSWER	
(a) **Who** came? *s*	**Someone** came. *s*	In (a): **Who** is used as the subject (**s**) of a question. In (b): **Who(m)** is used as the object (**o**) in a question. **Whom** is used in formal English. In everyday spoken English, **who** is usually used instead of **whom**: FORMAL: Whom did you see? INFORMAL: Who did you see?
(b) **Who(m)** did *you* see? *o*	*I* saw **someone**. *s* *o*	
(c) **What** happened? *s*	**Something** happened. *s*	**What** can be used as either the subject or the object in a question. Notice in (a) and (c): When **who** or **what** is used as the subject of a question, usual question word order is not used; no form of **do** is used: CORRECT: Who came? *INCORRECT: Who did come?*
(d) **What** did *you* see? *o*	*I* saw **something**. *s* *o*	

□ EXERCISE 8. Questions with WHO, WHO(M), and WHAT. (Chart 5-4)
　　　Directions: Create questions with **who, who(m),** and **what.** Write "**s**" if the question word is the subject. Write "**o**" if the question word is the object.

QUESTION	ANSWER
1. ᔆ Who knows?	ᔆ **Someone** knows.
2. ᴼ Who(m) did you ask?	ᴼ I asked **someone.**
3. _____	**Someone** knocked on the door.
4. _____	Sara met **someone.**
5. _____	Mike learned **something.**
6. _____	**Something** changed Ann's mind.
7. _____	Ann is talking about **someone.***

□ EXERCISE 9. Questions with WHO, WHO(M), and WHAT. (Chart 5-4)
　　　Directions: Create questions. Use **who, whom,** or **what.**

　1. A: What did you see? _____

　　 B: An accident. (I saw an accident.)

　2. A: _____

　　 B: An accident. (Mary saw an accident.)

WHO　　　　　　　　　**WHAT**

　3. A: _____

　　 B: Mary. (Mary saw an accident.)

　4. A: _____

　　 B: John. (Mary saw John.)

WHO　　　　　**WHO(M)**

————————

*A preposition may come at the beginning of a question in very formal English:
　　　About whom (NOT **who**) *is Ann talking?*
In everyday English, a preposition usually does not come at the beginning of a question.

5. A: _____
   B: Mary. (Mary saw John.)

6. A: _____
   B: An accident. (An accident happened.)

7. A: _____
   B. A new coat. (Alice bought a new coat.)

8. A: _____
   B: Alice. (Alice bought a new coat.)

9. A: _____
   B: A map of the world. (I'm looking at a map of the world.)

10. A: _____
    B: Jane. (I'm looking at Jane.)

11. A: _____
    B: The secretary. (I talked to the secretary.)

12. A: _____
    B: His problems. (Tom talked about his problems.)

13. A: _____
    B: The board. (The teacher looked at the board.)

14. A: _____
    B: The teacher. (The teacher looked at the board.)

15. A: _____
    B: The students. (The teacher looked at the students.)

16. A: _____
    B: An amphibian. (A frog is an amphibian.)

17. A: _____
    B: An animal that can live on land or in water. (An amphibian is an animal that can live on land or in water.)

18. A: _____
    B: Mostly insects. (Frogs eat mostly insects.)

☐ EXERCISE 10. Questions with WHO, WHO(M), and WHAT. (Chart 5-4)
Directions: Work in pairs.
Speaker A: Complete each question with *who, whom,* or *what.*
Speaker B: Answer the question.

Example: . . . are you currently reading?
SPEAKER A: What are you currently reading?
SPEAKER B: A novel about a cowboy.

1. . . . do you like to read?
2. . . . do you like to spend a lot of time with?
3. . . . is your idea of the perfect vacation?
4. . . . do you like to spend your vacations with?
5. . . . are the most important people in your life?

Switch roles.
6. . . . was the most memorable event of your childhood?
7. . . . stresses you out?
8. . . . do you need that you don't have?
9. . . . would you most like to invite to dinner? The person can be living or dead.
10. . . . has had the most influence on you in your life?

5-5 SPOKEN AND WRITTEN CONTRACTIONS WITH QUESTION WORDS

		SPOKEN ONLY		*Is, are, did,* and *will* are usually contracted with question words in speaking. These contractions are usually NOT written.
is	(a)	"*When's* he coming?" "*Why's* she late?"		
are	(b)	"*What're* these?" "*Who're* they?"		
did	(c)	"*Who'd* you see?" "*What'd* you do?"		
will	(d)	"*Where'll* you be?" "*When'll* they be here?"		
		SPOKEN	WRITTEN	
is	(e)	"*Where's* Ed?" "*What's* that?" "*Who's* he?"	(f) Where's Ed? What's that? Who's he?	Only contractions with *is* and *where, what,* or *who* are commonly used in writing.★

★Contractions are used in informal writing, such as letters to friends or e-mails, but are generally not appropriate in more formal writing, such as in magazine articles or reference books.

☐ EXERCISE 11. Spoken contractions with question words. (Chart 5-5)
Directions: Listen to your teacher say the following questions in contracted speech, and practice saying them yourself.

1. Where is my book?
2. What is in that drawer?
3. Why is Anita absent?
4. Who is that man?

5. Who are those men?
6. Where are you going?
7. What are you doing?
8. Where did Bob go last night?
9. What did you say?

10. Why did you say that?
11. Who did you see at the party?
12. Where will you be?
13. When will you arrive?
14. Who will meet you at the airport?

□ EXERCISE 12. Information questions. (Charts 5-2 → 5-5)
Directions: Create any appropriate question for the given answer.

Example: Larry.
→ *Who is the fax from?*
Who(m) did you go to the movie with?
Etc.

1. Yesterday.
2. A new pair of shoes.
3. Mr. Soto.
4. Six-thirty.
5. To the zoo.

6. Because I was tired.
7. A sandwich.
8. I don't know.
9. Tomorrow.
10. My brother.

□ EXERCISE 13. Asking for the meaning of a word. (Chart 5-4)
Directions: Ask your classmates for the meaning of each *italicized* word in the sentences below. Refer to a dictionary as necessary. Work in groups or as a class.

Example: It's raining. *Perhaps* we should take a taxi.
STUDENT A: **What does** "perhaps" **mean?**
STUDENT B: "Perhaps" means "maybe."

1. Water is *essential* to all forms of life on earth.

2. Why do soap bubbles *float?*

3. I think Carol's *mad.*

4. Some fish *bury* themselves in sand on the ocean bottom and live their entire lives there.

5. Mr. Chan gently put his hand *beneath* the baby's head.

6. I *grabbed* my briefcase and started running for the bus.

7. We walked hand in hand through the *orchard.*★

8. Mark and Olivia went to Hawaii on their *honeymoon.*

9. I'm not very good at *small talk,* so I avoid social situations like cocktail parties.

10. Mr. Weatherbee liked to have *hedges* between his house and his neighbors' houses. He planted the bushes close together so that people couldn't see through them.

★To ask for the meaning of a noun, two question forms are common. For example, using the noun "pocket": **What does** "pocket" **mean?** OR **What is** a pocket?/**What are** pockets?

5-6 USING *WHAT* + A FORM OF *DO*

QUESTION	ANSWER	*What* + a form of *do* is used to ask questions about activities. Examples of forms of *do*: *am doing, will do, are going to do, did,* etc.
(a) *What **does** Bob **do** every morning?*	He *goes to class.*	
(b) *What **did** you **do** yesterday?*	I *went downtown.*	
(c) *What **is** Anna **doing** (right now)?*	She*'s studying.*	
(d) *What **are** you **going to do** tomorrow?*	I*'m going to go to the beach.*	
(e) *What **do** you **want to do** tonight?*	I *want to go to a movie.*	
(f) *What **would** you **like to do** tomorrow?*	I *would like to visit Jim.*	
(g) *What **will** you **do** tomorrow?*	I*'ll go downtown.*	
(h) *What **should** I **do** about my headache?*	You *should take an aspirin.*	

☐ **EXERCISE 14. Using WHAT + a form of DO.** (Chart 5-6)

Directions: Create questions. Use ***what*** + a form of ***do***.

1. A: _____What are you doing_____ right now?

   B: I'm studying.

2. A: _____ last night?

   B: I studied.

3. A: _____ tomorrow?

   B: I'm going to visit my relatives.

4. A: _____ tomorrow?

   B: I want to go to the beach.

5. A: _____ this evening?

   B: I would like to go to a movie.

6. A: _____ tomorrow?

   B: I'm planning to stay home and relax most of the day.

7. A: _____ in class every day?

   B: I study English.

8. A: _____ (for a living)?★

   B: I'm a teacher.

_____

★*What do you do?* has a special meaning. It means: *What is your occupation, your job?* Another way of asking the same question: *What do you do for a living?*

9. A: _____ when he stopped you for speeding?

   B: He (the police officer) gave me a ticket.

10. A: _____ in the winter?

    B: It (a bear) hibernates.

11. A: I have the hiccups. _____ ?

    B: You should drink a glass of water.

12. A: _____ ?

    B: He (Mr. Rice) is a businessman. He works for General Electric.

    A: _____ ?

    B: She (Mrs. Rice) designs websites. She works for an Internet company.

☐ EXERCISE 15. Using WHAT + a form of DO and verb tense review. (Chart 5-6)
Directions: Work in pairs. Ask a classmate a question. Use ***what + do***.

Example: tomorrow
SPEAKER A: What are you going to do tomorrow? / What do you want to do tomorrow? /
            What would you like to do tomorrow? / Etc.
SPEAKER B: *(Answer the question.)*

Switch roles.

1. last night
2. right now
3. next Saturday
4. this afternoon
5. tonight
6. every morning

7. this morning
8. last weekend
9. on weekends
10. after class yesterday
11. after class today
12. since you arrived in this city

5-7 USING *WHAT KIND OF*

QUESTION	ANSWER	

(a) **What kind of** *shoes* did you buy?	Boots.
	Sandals.
	Tennis shoes.
	Loafers.
	Running shoes.
	High heels.
	Etc.
		What kind of asks for information about a specific type (a specific kind) in a general category.
		
		In (a):
		general category = shoes
		specific kinds = boots
		                   sandals
		                   tennis shoes
		                   etc.

(b) **What kind of** *fruit* do you like best?	Apples.
	Bananas.
	Oranges.
	Grapefruit.
	Grapes.
	Strawberries.
	Etc.
		In (b):
		general category = fruit
		specific kinds = apples
		                   bananas
		                   oranges
		                   etc.

☐ EXERCISE 16. Using WHAT KIND OF. (Chart 5-7)
Directions: Complete each question. Give other possible answers to the question.

1. A: What kind of _____shoes_____ are you wearing?

   B: Boots. (*Other possible answers:* _____loafers/running shoes/etc._____)

2. A: What kind of _____meat_____ do you eat most often?

   B: Beef. (*Other possible answers:* _____chicken/lamb/pork/etc._____)

3. A: What kind of _____ do you like best?

   B: Rock 'n roll. (*Other possible answers:* _____)

4. A: What kind of _____ would you like to have?

   B: A Mercedes-Benz. (*Other possible answers:* _____)

5. A: What kind of _____ do you like to read?

   B: Science fiction. (*Other possible answers:* _____)

6. A: What kind of _____ do you have?

   B: _____ . (*Other possible answers:* _____)

7. A: What kind of _____ do you like best?

   B: _____ . (*Other possible answers:* _____)

8. A: What kind of _____ is (. . .) wearing?

   B: _____ . (*Other possible answers:* _____)

☐ **EXERCISE 17. Using WHAT KIND OF.** (Chart 5-7)
Directions: Find classmates who own the following things. Ask them questions using **what kind of**.

Example: a camera
SPEAKER A: Do you have a camera?
SPEAKER B: Yes.*
SPEAKER A: What kind of camera do you have?
SPEAKER B: I have a 35-millimeter Kodak camera.

1. a camera	6. a computer
2. a TV	7. a watch
3. a bicycle	8. a dog
4. a car	9. a cell phone
5. a refrigerator	10. (*use your own words*)

5-8 USING *WHICH*

(a) TOM: May I borrow a pen from you?
ANN: Sure. I have two pens. This pen has black ink. That pen has red ink.
    Which pen do you want? OR
    Which one do you want? OR
    Which do you want?
	In (a): Ann uses **which** (not **what**) because she wants Tom to choose.
	Which is used when the speaker wants someone to make a choice, when the speaker is offering alternatives: *this one or that one; these or those.*

(b) SUE: I like these earrings, and I like those, too. BOB: **Which (earrings/ones)** are you going to buy? SUE: I think I'll get these.	**Which** can be used with either singular or plural nouns.
(c) JIM: Here's a photo of my daughter's class. KIM: Very nice. **Which one** is your daughter?	**Which** can be used to ask about people as well as things.
(d) SUE: My aunt gave me some money for my birthday. I'm going to take it with me to the mall. BOB: **What** are you going to buy with it? SUE: I haven't decided yet.	In (d): The question doesn't involve choosing from a particular group of items, so Bob uses **what**, not **which**.

---

*If the answer is "no," ask another question from the list.

Directions: Complete the questions with **which** or **what**.

1. A: This hat comes in brown and in gray. _____Which_____ color do you think your husband would prefer?
   B: Gray, I think.

2. A: I've never been to Mrs. Hall's house. _____What_____ color is it?
   B: Gray.

3. A: I have two dictionaries. _____ one do you want?
   B: The Arabic–English dictionary, not the English–English one.

4. A: May I help you?
   B: Please.
   A: _____ are you looking for?
   B: An Arabic–English dictionary.
   A: Right over there in the reference section.
   B: Thanks.

5. A: _____ did you get on your last test?
   B: I don't want to tell you. It was an awful grade.

6. A: If I need only half an onion, _____ half should I use and
   _____ half should I save?
   B: Save the root half. It lasts longer.

☐ EXERCISE 19. WHICH vs. WHAT. (Chart 5-8)

Directions: Create questions. Use **which** or **what**.

1. A: I have two books. ___Which book/Which one/Which do you want?___
   B: That one. (I want that book.)

2: A: ___What did you buy when you went shopping?___
   B: A book. (I bought a book when I went shopping.)

3. A: Could I borrow your pen for a minute?
   B: Sure. I have two. _____
   A: That one. (I would like that one.)

4. A: _____
   B: A pen. (Chris borrowed a pen from me.)

5. A: _____
   B: Two pieces of hard candy. (I have two pieces of hard candy in my hand.) Would you like one?
   A: Yes. Thanks.
   B: _____
   A: The yellow one. (I'd like the yellow one.)

6. A: Do you like this tie?

   B: Yes.

   A: Do you like that tie?

   B: It's okay.

   A: _____

   B: This one. (I'm going to buy this one.)

7. A: Tony and I went shopping. I got some new shoes.

   B: _____

   A: A tie. (Tony got a tie.)

8. A: Did you enjoy your trip to Europe?

   B: Yes, I did. Very much.

   A: _____

   B: Poland, Germany, Czechoslovakia, and Italy. (I visited Poland, Germany, Czechoslovakia, and Italy.)★

   A: _____

   B: Poland. (I enjoyed visiting Poland the most.)

5-9 USING *WHOSE*

QUESTION	ANSWER	*Whose* asks about possession.★ Notice in (a): The speaker of the question may omit the noun *(book)* if the meaning is clear to the listener.
(a) **Whose (book)** is this? (b) **Whose (books)** are those? (c) **Whose car** did you borrow?	It's John's (book). They're mine (OR my books). I borrowed Karen's (car).	
COMPARE (d) **Who's** that? (e) **Whose** is that?	Mary Smith. Mary's.	**Who's** and **whose** have the same pronunciation. **Who's** = a contraction of **who is**. **Whose** = asks about possession.

★See Charts 6-11, p. 173, and 6-12, p. 176, for ways of expressing possession.

★The difference between *what country* and *which country* is often very small.

☐ EXERCISE 20. Using WHOSE. (Chart 5-9)
    Directions: Create questions with **whose** or **who**. The things near Susan belong to her.
    The things near Eric belong to him. Point to the things and people in the pictures when
    you ask some of the questions.

SUSAN   ERIC

1. A: _____Whose basketball is_____ this?
   B: Susan's. (It's Susan's basketball.)

2. A: _____Who is_____ this?
   B: Susan. (This is Susan.)

3. A: _____ that?
   B: Eric's. (It's Eric's notebook.)

4. A: _____ these?
   B: Eric's. (They're Eric's tapes.)

5. A: _____ that?
   B: Eric. (That is Eric.)

6. A: _____ those?
   B: Susan's. (They're Susan's clothes.)

7. A: _____ that?
   B: Susan's. (It's Susan's coat.)

8. A: _____ in a gym?
   B: Susan. (Susan is in a gym.)

9. A: _____ sitting down?

   B: Eric. (Eric is sitting down.)

10. A: _____ longer?

    B: Eric's. (Eric's hair is longer than Susan's.)

□ **EXERCISE 21. Using WHOSE. (Chart 5-9)**

Directions: Ask and answer questions about possession. Follow the pattern in the examples. Talk about things in the classroom.

Example: pen

SPEAKER A: Is this your pen? / Is this (pen) yours?

SPEAKER B: No, it isn't.

SPEAKER A: Whose is it?

SPEAKER B: It's Ali's.

Example: pens

SPEAKER A: Are these Yoko's (pens)? / Are these (pens) Yoko's?

SPEAKER B: No, they aren't.

SPEAKER A: Whose are they?

SPEAKER B: They're mine.

1. dictionary	5. bookbag	9. purse
2. books	6. briefcase	10. calculator
3. notebook	7. glasses	11. things
4. papers	8. backpack	12. stuff★

□ **EXERCISE 22. Review: information questions. (Charts 5-2 → 5-9)**

Directions: Work in pairs. Create questions for the given answers. Use any appropriate question word.

Example: I'm reading.

SPEAKER A: What are you doing?

SPEAKER B: I'm reading.

	Switch roles.
1. They're mine.	7. Jazz.
2. I'm going to study.	8. Because I didn't feel good.
3. A Toyota.	9. This one, not that one.
4. Mr. (. . .).	10. (. . .)'s.
5. It's (. . .)'s.	11. A couple of days ago.
6. It means "small."	12. India.

★*Stuff* is used in informal spoken English to mean miscellaneous things. For example, when a speaker says, "This is my stuff," the speaker may be referring to pens, pencils, books, papers, notebooks, clothes, etc. (Note: *stuff* is a noncount noun; it never has a final *-s.*)

□ **EXERCISE 23. Asking questions.** (Charts 5-1 → 5-9)

Directions: Work in pairs.

Speaker A: Choose any one of the possible answers below and ask a question that would produce that answer.

Speaker B: Decide which answer Speaker A has in mind and answer his/her question. Pay special attention to the form of Speaker A's question. Correct any errors.

Alternate asking questions. (First Speaker A asks a question and Speaker B answers. Next Speaker B asks a question and Speaker A answers.)

Example:

SPEAKER A: What is Maria's favorite color?

SPEAKER B: (Speaker B reviews the list of possible answers below and chooses the appropriate one.) Pink.

Possible answers:

Sure! Thanks!	Probably.
Call the insurance company.	The teacher's.
Next week.	Not that one. The other one.
A rat.	A Panasonic or a Sony.
Mr. (. . .).	Pink.
Answering your questions.	No, a friend of mine gave them to me a few days ago.
Cheese.	Historical fiction.
Mine.	Study, and then watch a movie.
Eight-thirty.	On the Internet.
Her husband.	

5-10 USING *HOW*

QUESTION	ANSWER	
(a) **How** did you get here?	I drove./By car. I took a taxi./By taxi. I took a bus./By bus. I flew./By plane. I took a train./By train. I walked./On foot.	**How** has many uses. One use of **how** is to ask about means (ways) of transportation.
(b) **How old** are you? (c) **How tall** is he? (d) **How big** is your apartment? (e) **How sleepy** are you? (f) **How hungry** are you? (g) **How soon** will you be ready? (h) **How well** does he speak English? (i) **How quickly** can you get here?	Twenty-one. About six feet. It has three rooms. Very sleepy. I'm starving. In five minutes. Very well. I can get there in 30 minutes.	**How** is often used with adjectives (e.g., *old, big*) and adverbs (e.g., *well, quickly*).

☐ **EXERCISE 24. Using HOW.** (Chart 5-10)

Directions: Create questions with ***how***.

1. A: ___How old is your daughter?___
   B: Ten. (My daughter is ten years old.)

2. A: _____
   B: Very important. (Education is very important.)

3. A: _____
   B: By bus. (I get to school by bus.)

4. A: _____
   B: Very, very deep. (The ocean is very, very deep.)

5. A: _____
   B: By plane. (I'm going to get to Denver by plane.)

6. A: _____
   B: Not very. (The test wasn't very difficult.)

7. A: _____
   B: It's 29,028 feet high. (Mt. Everest is 29,028 feet high.)★

8. A: _____
   B: I walked. (I walked to school today.)

5-11 USING *HOW OFTEN*

QUESTION	ANSWER	*How often* asks about frequency.
(a) ***How often*** do you go shopping?	Every day. Once a week. About twice a week. Every other day or so.★ Three times a month.	
(b) ***How many times a day*** do you eat? ***How many times a week*** do you go shopping? ***How many times a month*** do you go to the post office? ***How many times a year*** do you take a vacation?	Three or four. Two. Once. Once or twice.	Other ways of asking ***how often***: ***how many times*** ⎰ a day a week a month a year

★*Every other day* means "Monday yes, Tuesday no, Wednesday yes, Thursday no," etc. *Or so* means "approximately."

_____

★29,028 feet = 8,848 meters.

□ **EXERCISE 25. Using HOW OFTEN.** (Chart 5-11)

Directions: Work in pairs.

Speaker A: Ask a question with ***how often*** or ***how many times a day/week/month/year***.

Speaker B: Answer the question. (Possible answers are suggested in the list of frequency expressions.)

Example: eat lunch at the cafeteria

SPEAKER A: How often do you eat lunch at the cafeteria?

SPEAKER B: About twice a week.

FREQUENCY EXPRESSIONS		
a lot	*every*	
*occasionally**★*	*every other*	
once in a while	*once a*	
not very often	*twice a*	*day/week/month/year*
hardly ever	*three times a*	
almost never	*ten times a*	
never		

Switch roles.

1. play cards
2. get on the Internet
3. go out to eat
4. cook your own dinner
5. read a newspaper
6. get your hair cut
7. buy a toothbrush
8. go to a laundromat
9. go swimming
10. be late for class
11. attend a wedding
12. see a falling star

5-12 USING *HOW FAR*

(a) ***It is*** 289 miles ***from*** St. Louis ***to*** Chicago.* (b) ***It is*** 289 miles { ***from*** St. Louis ***to*** Chicago. ***from*** Chicago ***to*** St. Louis. ***to*** Chicago ***from*** St. Louis. ***to*** St. Louis ***from*** Chicago.	The most common way of expressing distance: ***It is*** + *distance* + ***from/to*** + ***to/from*** In (b): All four expressions with ***from*** and ***to*** have the same meaning.
(c) A: ***How far is it*** from St. Louis to Chicago? B: 289 miles. (d) A: ***How far do you*** live from school? B: Four blocks.	***How far*** is used to ask questions about distance.
(e) ***How many miles*** is it from St. Louis to Chicago? (f) ***How many kilometers*** is it to Montreal from here? (g) ***How many blocks*** is it to the post office?	Other ways to ask ***how far:*** *how many miles* *how many kilometers* *how many blocks*

*1 mile = 1.60 kilometers.
  1 kilometer = 00.614 mile.

★Notice: *Occasionally* is spelled with *two* "c"s but only *one* "s."

Directions: Create questions.

1. A: _How far is it to Chicago from New Orleans?_

   B: 919 miles. (It's 919 miles to Chicago from New Orleans.)

2. A: _____

   B: 257 kilometers. (It's 257 kilometers from Montreal to Quebec.)

3. A: _____

   B: Six blocks. (It's six blocks to the post office.)

4. A: I had a terrible day yesterday.

   B: What happened?

   A: I ran out of gas while I was driving to work.

   B: _____ before you ran out of gas?

   A: To the junction of I-90 and 480. (I got to the junction of I-90 and 480.) Luckily, there was a gas station about half a mile down the road.

□ EXERCISE 27. Using HOW FAR. (Chart 5-12)
Directions: Bring road maps of your geographical area to class. In small groups, look at a map of your area and ask each other questions with **how far**.

5-13   LENGTH OF TIME: *IT* + *TAKE* AND *HOW LONG*

IT + *TAKE* + (SOMEONE) + LENGTH + INFINITIVE OF TIME			*It* + *take* is often used with time words and an infinitive to express **length of time**, as in (a) and (b). An infinitive = *to* + *the simple form of a verb.*★ In (a): *to cook* is an infinitive.
(a) *It* takes		20 minutes *to cook* rice.	
(b) *It* took	Al	two hours *to drive* to work.	

(c) *How long* does it take to cook rice? —20 minutes. (d) *How long* did it take Al to drive to work today? —Two hours. (e) *How long* did you study last night? —Four hours. (f) *How long* will you be in Hong Kong? —Ten days.	*How long* asks about **length of time**.
(g) *How many days* will you be in Hong Kong?	Other ways of asking *how long*: *how many* + { minutes hours days weeks months years }

*See Chart 13-3, p. 373.

☐ **EXERCISE 28. Length of time. (Chart 5-13)**
Directions: Create sentences using *it* + *take* to express length of time.

1. I drove to Madrid. *(Length of time: three days)*
   → *It took me three days to drive to Madrid.*
2. I walk to class. *(Length of time: twenty minutes)*
3. Gino finished the test. *(Length of time: an hour and a half)*
4. We will drive to the airport. *(Length of time: forty-five minutes)*
5. Alan hitchhiked to Alaska. *(Length of time: two weeks)*
6. I wash my clothes at the laundromat. *(Length of time: two hours)*

☐ **EXERCISE 29. Length of time. (Chart 5-13)**
Directions: Use *it* + *take*.

1. How long does it take you to . . .
   a. eat breakfast? → *It takes me ten minutes to eat breakfast.*
   b. get to class?
   c. write a short paragraph in English?
   d. read a 400-page novel?
2. Generally speaking, how long does it take to . . .
   a. fly from *(name of a city)* to *(name of a city)?*
   b. get from here to your hometown?
   c. get used to living in a foreign country?
   d. commute from *(name of a local place)* to *(name of a local place)* during rush hour?

☐ **EXERCISE 30. Length of time. (Chart 5-13)**
Directions: Create questions using *how long*.

1. A: _____How long did it take you to drive to New York?_____
   B: Five days. (It took me five days to drive to New York.)

2. A: _____
   B: A week. (Mr. McNally will be in the hospital for a week.)

3. A: _____
   B: A long time. (It takes a long time to learn a second language.)

4. A: _____
   B: Six months. (I've been living here for six months.)

5. A: _____
   B: Six years. (I lived in Istanbul for six years.)

6. A: _____
   B: A couple of years. (I've known Nho Pham for a couple of years.)

7. A: _____
   B: Since 1999. (He's been living in Canada since 1999.)

8. A: _____
   For 21 to 30 days, according to psychologists. (A person has to do something consistently for 21 to 30 days before it becomes a habit.)

□ **EXERCISE 31. Length of time.** (Chart 5-13)

> *Directions:* Work in groups of three. Only Speaker A's book is open.
> Speaker A: Complete the sentence with your own words.
> Speaker B: Ask a question about Speaker A's sentence, using **how long**.
> Speaker C: Answer the question. Give both a short answer and a long answer.

Example: It takes me . . . to . . . .
SPEAKER A: It takes me twenty minutes to walk to class from my apartment.
SPEAKER B: How long does it take (Ana) to walk to class from her apartment?
SPEAKER C: Twenty minutes. It takes her twenty minutes to walk to class from her apartment.

1. It took me . . . to get to school today.
2. It usually . . . me . . . to get dressed in the morning.
3. It . . . to fly from . . . to . . . .
4. It . . . 45 minutes to an hour to . . . .

Switch roles.   *Switch roles.*
5. It . . . to change the sheets on a bed.   9. It . . . to walk from . . . to . . .
6. It usually takes me . . . to eat . . . .   10. It takes . . . drive . . . .
7. It took me . . . this morning.   11. It used to take . . . to . . . .
8. It takes only a few minutes to . . . .   12. In class, it takes us approximately . . . to . . . .

5-14 MORE QUESTIONS WITH *HOW*

QUESTION	ANSWER	
(a) **How do you spell** "coming"? (b) **How do you say** "yes" in Japanese? (c) **How do you say/pronounce** this word?	C-O-M-I-N-G. Hai. _____	To answer (a): Spell the word. To answer (b): Say the word. To answer (c): Pronounce the word.
(d) **How are you getting along?** (e) **How are you doing?** (f) **How's it going?**	Great. Fine. Okay. So-so.	In (d), (e), and (f): How is your life? Is your life okay? Do you have any problems? Note: (f) is also used in greetings: *Hi, Bob. How's it going?*
(g) **How do you feel?** **How are you feeling?**	Terrific! Wonderful! Great! Fine. Okay. So-so. A bit under the weather. Not so good. Terrible!/Lousy./Awful!	The questions in (g) ask about health or about general emotional state.
(h) **How do you do?**	How do you do?	**How do you do?** is used by both speakers when they are introduced to each other in a somewhat formal situation.*

> *A: *Dr. Erickson, I'd like to introduce you to a friend of mine, Rick Brown. Rick, this is my biology professor, Dr. Erickson.*
> B: ***How do you do,*** *Mr. Brown?*
> C: ***How do you do,*** *Dr. Erickson? I'm pleased to meet you.*

☐ EXERCISE 32. More questions with HOW. (Chart 5-14)

Directions: Close your books. Divide into two teams. Ask a student on the other team how to spell the word your teacher says. (Alternatively, work in pairs, switching roles after item 9.)

Example: country

SPEAKER A: How do you spell "country"?

SPEAKER B: C-O-N-T-R-Y

SPEAKER A: No, that isn't right. The correct spelling is C-O-U-N-T-R-Y. OR
Yes, that's right.

1. together	7. different	13. beginning
2. purple	8. foreign	14. intelligent
3. daughter	9. studying	15. writing
4. planned	10. bought	16. occasionally
5. rained	11. people	17. family
6. neighbor	12. beautiful	18. Mississippi

☐ EXERCISE 33. More questions with HOW. (Chart 5-14)

Directions: Ask your classmates how to say these words in their native languages.

Example: yes

SPEAKER A: How do you say "yes" in Japanese?

SPEAKER B: Hai.

1. Yes.
2. No.
3. Thank you.
4. I love you.

☐ EXERCISE 34. More questions with HOW. (Chart 5-14)

Directions: Ask your classmates how to pronounce these words. Work in groups or as a class.

Example:

SPEAKER A: How do you pronounce the number 9?

SPEAKER B: *(Speaker B pronounces the word.)*

SPEAKER A: Good. OR No, I don't think that's right.

LIST A.	(1)	(2)	(3)	(4)	(5)	(6)	(7)	(8)	(9)	(10)
	beat	bit	bet	bite	bait	bat	but	boot	boat	bought

LIST B.	(1)	(2)	(3)	(4)	(5)	(6)	(7)	(8)	(9)	(10)
	zoos	Sue's	shoes	chews	choose	chose	those	toes	doze	dose

☐ EXERCISE 35. Review of HOW. (Charts 5-10 → 5-14)

Directions: Complete the questions.

1. A: _____How often_____ do you get a haircut?
   B: About every six weeks, I think/guess.

2. A: _____ does it take to get a haircut at Bertha's Beauty Boutique?
   B: Half an hour.

3. A: _____ is it from the earth to the moon?
   B: Approximately 239,000 miles or 385,000 kilometers.

4. A: _____ times a day do you brush your teeth?
   B: At least three.

5. A: _____ does a snake shed its skin?
   B: From once a year to more than six times a year, depending on the kind of snake.

6. A: _____ is it from your desk to the door?
   B: I'd say about four regular steps or two giant steps.

7. A: _____ times does the numeral 9 appear in the numerals from 1 to 100?
   B: 20 times.

8. A: _____ does a bird's heart beat?
   B: It depends on size. A big bird's heart beats more than 300 times a minute. A small bird like a hummingbird has a normal heart beat of more than 600 beats a minute.

9. A: _____ volcanoes erupt every year?
   B: About 50. But that's just on Earth.

10. A: _____ 's it going?
    B: Okay, I guess. What about you? What's new with you?
    A: Nothin' much.

11. A: Could you carry this box of books for me?
    B: I'd like to, but I have a bad back. _____ is it?
    A: Pretty heavy. That's okay. I'll ask Jack to carry it.

12. A: You blow on your hands to warm them. You blow on your soup to cool it. Imagine that! Hot and cold from the same mouth. _____ do you explain that?
    B: I don't know. _____ do you explain it?

□ **EXERCISE 36. Review of HOW.** (Charts 5-10 → 5-14)

　　Directions: Create questions for the given answers. Use **how** in each question.

　　Example: It's very important.
　　　　　　→ *How important is good health?*

　　　1. Very expensive.
　　　2. I took a taxi.
　　　3. Four hours.
　　　4. He's nineteen.
　　　5. In five minutes.
　　　6. With a knife.
　　　7. Every day.
　　　8. Three blocks.
　　　9. Fine.
　　10. With two "t"s.
　　11. It gets below zero.
　　12. Excellent.

□ **EXERCISE 37. Review of questions.** (Charts 5-1 → 5-14)

　　Directions: Complete the dialogue with questions. Use any appropriate question words. Work in pairs or as a class.

　　A: ___*What are you going to do*___ this weekend?
　　　　　　　　　　　　　1

　　B: I'm going to go to a baseball game.

　　A: There are two games this weekend. _____?
　　　　　　　　　　　　　　　　　　　　　　　　　2

　　B: The one on Sunday.

A: _____ yesterday?
                    3

B: No, I didn't. I didn't know there was a game yesterday. _____?
                                                                              4

A: Yes, I did, and I really enjoyed it.

B: _____ to the game alone?
                    5

A: No.

B: _____ with you?
                    6

A: Linda Rivera. _____ to Sunday's game with?
                              7

B: A guy I work with named Bob Woo. He's a real fan.

A: _____ to the stadium from your apartment?
                    8

B: No, I can't. It's too far.

A: _____ ?
                    9

B: Six miles.

A: _____ get there?
                    10

B: By bus.

A: _____ get there?
                    11

B: Just twenty minutes.

A: _____ start Sunday?
                    12

B: One o'clock.

A: I wish I could join you. _____ to a baseball game?
                                              13

B: About once a month. How about you?

A: I go to a baseball game as often as I can.

B: _____ to baseball games?
                    14

A: Because it's a wonderful game, and it's so much fun to be there and watch it in person.

B: _____ when you go to a game?
                    15

A: I yell, enjoy the sunshine, eat peanuts, and drink soda.

B: That's exactly what I do, too!

☐ **EXERCISE 38. Review of questions. (Charts 5-1 → 5-14)**

Directions: Create questions for the given answers.

Example: I'm reading.
SPEAKER A: What are you doing?
SPEAKER B: I'm reading.

1. It means "big."
2. Three days ago.
3. Once a week.
4. Okay.
5. By bus.
6. Mine.
7. Nonfiction.
8. B-E-A-U-T-I-F-U-L.
9. The park.
10. Because I . . . .
11. 100 (miles/kilometers).
12. I'm going to study.
13. A bit under the weather.
14. How do you do?
15. Two hours.
16. Six o'clock.

17. Mary.
18. Blue.
19. Cold and wet.
20. The one on the red chair.
21. Chris's.
22. With two "r"s.
23. Andy and Ed.
24. Five blocks.
25. 1989.
26. Biochemistry.
27. Making questions.
28. Saudi Arabia.
    In the Middle East.
    Oil.
    Riyadh.

☐ **EXERCISE 39. Review of questions. (Charts 5-1 → 5-14)**

Directions: Work in pairs. Create dialogues from the given words.

Example: . . . usually get up?
SPEAKER A: What time do you usually get up?
SPEAKER B: 6:30.

1. . . . fruit . . . like best?
2. . . . is south of . . . ?
3. . . . times a week do you . . . ?
4. . . . do tomorrow?
5. . . . is it from . . . to . . . ?
6. . . . in this city?

Switch roles.

7. . . . is sitting . . . ?
8. . . . should I . . . ?
9. . . . do for a living?
10. . . . spell "happened"?
11. . . . take to get to . . . from the airport?
12. . . . getting along in your English classes?

□ EXERCISE 40. Review of questions. (Charts 5-1 → 5-14)

Directions: In small groups (or by yourself), make up questions about some or all of the following topics. What would you like to know about these topics? Share your questions with your classmates. Maybe some of them can answer some of your questions.

Example: tigers

Questions: How long do tigers usually live? Where do they live? What do they eat? Do they kill and eat people? How big is a tiger? Is it bigger than a lion? Can a tiger climb a tree? Do tigers live alone or in groups? How many tigers are there in the world today? How many tigers were there one hundred years ago?

Topics:

1. world geography
2. the universe
3. the weather

4. dinosaurs
5. birds
6. (a topic of your own choosing)

5-15 USING *HOW ABOUT* AND *WHAT ABOUT*

(a) A: We need one more player.
  B: ***How about (what about) Jack?*** Let's ask him if he wants to play.
(b) A: What time should we meet?
  B: ***How about (what about) three o'clock?***
	How about and ***what about*** have the same meaning and usage. They are used to make suggestions or offers.
	How about and ***what about*** are followed by a noun (or pronoun) or the *-ing* form of a verb.

(c) A: What should we do this afternoon?
  B: ***How about going*** to the zoo?
(d) A: ***What about asking*** Sally over for dinner next Sunday?
  B: Okay. Good idea.
	Note: ***How about*** and ***what about*** are frequently used in informal spoken English, but are usually not used in writing.

(e) A: I'm tired. ***How about you?***
  B: Yes, I'm tired too.
(f) A: Are you hungry?
  B: No. ***What about you?***
  A: I'm a little hungry.
	How about you? and ***What about you?*** are used to ask a question that refers to the information or question that immediately preceded it. In (e): *How about you?* = *Are you tired?* In (f): *What about you?* = *Are you hungry?*

□ EXERCISE 41. HOW ABOUT and WHAT ABOUT. (Chart 5-15)

Directions: Complete the dialogues with your own words.

1. A: _____What time do you want to meet for dinner_____ ?

   B: How about _____nine or nine-thirty_____ ?

   A: That's too late for me. How about _____eight_____ ?

   B: Okay.

2. A: _____ ?

   B: No, Tuesday's not good for me.

   A: Then what about _____ ?

   B: Okay. That's fine.

3. A: There's room in the car for one more person. Do you think _____

would like to go to _____ with us?

B: _____ can't go with us because _____ .

A: Then how about _____ ?

B: _____ .

4. A: Do you like fish?

B: Yes, very much. How about _____ ?

A: Yes, I like fish a lot. In fact, I think I'll order fish for dinner tonight. That sounds

good. What about _____ ?

B: _____ .

□ EXERCISE 42. HOW ABOUT and WHAT ABOUT. (Chart 5-15)

Directions: Complete the dialogues by using ***How about you?*** or ***What about you?*** and
an appropriate response.

Example:

SPEAKER A: What are you going to do over vacation?

SPEAKER B: I'm staying here. *What about (How about) you?*

SPEAKER A: *I'm going to Texas to visit my sister.*

1. A: Did you like the movie?
   B: It was okay, I guess . . . . .
   A: . . . .

2. A: Are you going to the company picnic?
   B: I haven't decided yet . . . . .
   A: . . . .

3. A: Do you like living in this city?
   B: Sort of . . . . .
   A: . . . .

4. A: What are you going to have?
   B: Well, I'm not really hungry. I think I might have just a salad . . . . .
   A: . . . .

5. A: Where are you planning to go to school next year?
   B: A small college in California . . . . .
   A: . . . .

6. A: Are you married?
   B: . . . .
   A: . . . .

☐ EXERCISE 43. HOW ABOUT and WHAT ABOUT. (Chart 5-15)

Directions: Work in pairs.

Speaker A: Read the cue. Your book is open.

Speaker B: Respond by asking a question with **how about** or **what about**. Your book is closed.

Speaker A: Respond to Speaker B's suggestion.

Example:

SPEAKER A: I'm looking for a good book to read. Do you have any suggestions?

SPEAKER B: How about (What about) *Tom Sawyer* by Mark Twain? That's a good book.

SPEAKER A: I've already read it. / Okay. Do you have a copy I could borrow? / Etc.

1. I'm glad we're having dinner together this evening, (. . .). What time should we get together?

2. I can't figure out what to give my sister for her birthday.

3. I'm hungry, but I'm not sure what I want to eat.

4. We have a whole week of vacation. Where should we go?

Switch roles.

5. I need to talk to you on the phone this evening. What time should I call you?

6. Where should we go for dinner tonight?

7. I've already asked (. . .) and (. . .) to my party. Who else should I ask?

8. Some friends are coming to visit me this weekend. They said they wanted to see some of the interesting places in the city. I'm wondering where I should take them.

☐ EXERCISE 44. HOW ABOUT and WHAT ABOUT. (Chart 5-15)

Directions: Work in pairs.

Speaker A: The given questions are conversation openers. Glance at a question quickly, then look up—directly into the eyes of Speaker B—and initiate the conversation. Your book is open.

Speaker B: Answer Speaker A's question. Then ask "How about you?" or "What about you?" to continue the conversation. Your book is closed.

Speaker A: Answer the question. Then continue the conversation by asking related questions.

Example: What kind of books do you like to read?

SPEAKER A: What kind of books do you like to read?

SPEAKER B: Mostly nonfiction. I like books about nature or history. How about you?

SPEAKER A: I like fiction. I read a lot of novels. Mysteries are my favorite. What about you? Do you ever read mysteries?

SPEAKER B: No, not really. But I like to read poetry. How about you? Do you ever read poetry?

SPEAKER A: Etc.

1. How long have you been living in *(this city or country)*?

2. What are you going to do after class today?

3. What kind of movies do you like to watch?

Switch roles.

4. Do you come from a large family?

5. What kind of sports do you enjoy?

6. Do you speak a lot of English outside of class?

5-16 TAG QUESTIONS

AFFIRMATIVE (+)	NEGATIVE (−)	A tag question is a question that is added onto the end of a sentence. An auxiliary verb is used in a tag question.
(a) *You **know** Bob Wilson,*	***don't** you?*	
(b) *Marie **is** from Paris,*	***isn't** she?*	When the main verb is affirmative, the tag question is negative.
(c) *Jerry **can play** the piano,*	***can't** he?*	
NEGATIVE (−)	**AFFIRMATIVE (+)**	When the main verb is negative, the tag question is affirmative.
(d) *You **don't know** Jack Smith,*	***do** you?*	
(e) *Marie **isn't** from Athens,*	***is** she?*	
(f) *Jerry **can't speak** Arabic,*	***can** he?*	

In using a tag question, a speaker gives his idea while asking a question at the same time. In (g) and (h) below: I (the speaker) use a tag question because I expect you (the listener) to tell me that my information or my idea is correct.
  As with other kinds of questions, a speaker usually uses a rising intonation at the end of a tag question.★

THE SPEAKER'S IDEA	THE SPEAKER'S QUESTION	EXPECTED ANSWER
(g) I think that you know Bob Wilson.	You **know** Bob Wilson, **don't** you?	**Yes**, I **do**.
(h) I think that you don't know Jack Smith.	You **don't know** Jack Smith, **do** you?	**No**, I **don't**.

COMPARE	
(i) A: Do you know Tom Lee? *(a yes/no question)* B: Yes, I do. OR No, I don't.	In (i): The speaker has no idea. The speaker is simply looking for information.
(j) A: You know Tom Lee, don't you? *(a tag question)* B: Yes, I do.	In (j): The speaker believes that the listener knows Tom Lee. The speaker wants to make sure that his idea is correct.

★Sometimes a falling intonation is used with tag questions. For example:
    A: It's a beautiful day today, *isn't it? (voice falling rather than rising)*
    B: Yes, indeed. The weather's perfect.
A speaker uses falling intonation for a tag question when he is making an observation, commenting on something rather than making sure his information is correct. In the example, the speaker is making a comment about the weather to invite conversation.
    Other examples: *That was a good movie, wasn't it? Mr. Smith is a good teacher, isn't he? It's really hot today, isn't it?*

☐ EXERCISE 45. Tag questions. (Chart 5-16)
  Directions: Add tag questions and give the expected answers.

  1. A: You are a student, _____ aren't you _____ ?

     B: _____ Yes, I am _____ .

  2. A: Ahmed came to class yesterday, _____ ?

     B: _____ .

3. A: Pedro was in class too, _____ ?

    B: _____ .

4. A: Anna will be at the meeting tomorrow, _____ ?

    B: _____ .

5. A: You can speak Spanish, _____ ?

    B: _____ .

6. A: Our teacher didn't give us a homework assignment, _____ ?

    B: _____ .

7. A: You haven't eaten dinner yet, _____ ?

    B: _____ .

8. A: All birds lay eggs, _____ ?

    B: _____ .

☐ EXERCISE 46. Use of auxiliary verbs in tag questions. (Chart 5-16)
Directions: Add tag questions.

1. Mr. Adams was born in England, _____wasn't he_____ ?
2. Flies can fly upside down, _____ ?
3. Po lives with his brother, _____ ?
4. Mike isn't married, _____ ?
5. You would rather have a roommate than live alone, _____ ?
6. Janet has a car, _____ ?
7. She's had her car for several years, _____ ?
8. She has to get a new license plate for her car, _____ ?
9. If you want to get to work on time, you should leave pretty soon, _____ ?
10. Ms. Boxlight will be here tomorrow, _____ ?
11. You didn't forget to finish your homework, _____ ?
12. This is your pen,* _____ ?

_____

*When **this** or **that** is used in the first part of the sentence, **it** is used in the tag question: *This is your book, isn't it?*
When **these** or **those** is used in the first part of the sentence, **they** is used in the tag question: *These are your shoes, aren't they?*

13. That is Ivana's dictionary, _____ ?

14. Those are your gloves, _____ ?

15. The average lifespan of a horse is more than 40 years, _____ ?

And sea turtles can live to be more than 200, _____ ?

ONLY 40? YOU'RE JUST A YOUNGSTER.

☐ **EXERCISE 47. Tag questions. (Chart 5-16)**

Directions: Ask and answer tag questions.

Speaker A: Ask a tag question about someone in the room. Ask the person directly or direct the question to another classmate, as you prefer.

Speaker B: Answer.

Example: You think that someone in this room lives in an apartment.

SPEAKER A: (Maria), you live in an apartment, don't you?

SPEAKER B: Yes, I do. OR No, I don't.

Example: You think that someone in this room doesn't own a car.

SPEAKER A: (Maria), (Ali) doesn't own a car, does he?

SPEAKER B: No, he doesn't. OR Yes, he does. OR I don't know.

You think that someone in this room . . .

1. was in class yesterday.
2. didn't come to class a few days ago.
3. isn't married.
4. is from (country).
5. can't speak (language).
6. likes to play (name of a sport).
7. will be in class tomorrow.
8. can whistle.
9. knows (name of a person).
10. has met (name of a person).
11. wore jeans to class yesterday.
12. has brown eyes.

☐ **EXERCISE 48. Summary: creating and roleplaying dialogues. (Chapter 5)**
   Directions: Work in pairs. Together create a long dialogue for one of the following situations. Present your dialogue to the class. The beginning of the dialogue is given.

1. SITUATION: The dialogue takes place on the telephone.
               Speaker A: You are a travel agent.
               Speaker B: You want to take a trip.

   DIALOGUE: *A: Hello. Worldwide Travel Agency. May I help you?*
              B: Yes. I need to make arrangements to go to . . . .
              A: Etc.

2. SITUATION: The dialogue takes place at a police station.
               Speaker A: You are a police officer.
               Speaker B: You are the suspect of a crime.

   DIALOGUE: *A: Where were you at eleven o'clock on Tuesday night, the 16th of last month?*
              B: I'm not sure I remember. Why do you want to know, Officer?
              A: Etc.

3. SITUATION: The dialogue takes place in an office.
               Speaker A: You are the owner of a small company.
               Speaker B: You are interviewing for a job in Speaker A's company.

   DIALOGUE: *A: Come in, come in. I'm (. . .). Glad to meet you.*
              B: How do you? I'm (. . .). I'm pleased to meet you.
              A: Have a seat, (. . .).
              B: Thank you.
              A: So you're interested in working at (make up the name of a company)?
              B: Yes, I am.
              A: Etc.

CHAPTER 6
Nouns and Pronouns

CONTENTS

□ **EXERCISE 1. Preview: grammar terms.** (Chapter 6)

Directions: This exercise previews grammar terms used in this chapter. Identify the *italicized* word in each sentence as a NOUN, ADJECTIVE, PREPOSITION, or PRONOUN.

1. Eric is wearing a new *shirt* today.   *shirt*   <u>noun</u>

2. Algeria is *in* North Africa.   *in*   <u>preposition</u>

3. Steve is in Asia. *He* is traveling.   *he*   <u>pronoun</u>

4. I'm *thirsty*.   *thirsty*   <u>adjective</u>

5. We have class in this *room* every day.   *room*   _____

6. I know my *way* to Joanna's house.   *way*   _____

7. The *happy* children squealed with joy.   *happy*   _____

8. I walked to class *with* Maria.   *with*   _____

9. Hawaii has eight principal *islands*.   *islands*   _____

10. The *hungry* man stuffed his mouth with rice.   *hungry*   _____

11. Tokyo is the capital of *Japan*.   *Japan*   _____

12. Athens is a *beautiful* city.   *beautiful*   _____

13. My history book is *under* my desk.   *under*   _____

14. Do you like classical *music?*   *music*   _____

15. I can't find my keys. Have you seen *them?*   *them*   _____

6-1 PRONUNCIATION OF FINAL -S/-ES

Final **-s/-es** has three different pronunciations: /s/, /z/, and /əz/.

(a)	seats = seat/s/ maps = map/s/ lakes = lake/s/	/s/ is the sound of "s" in "bus." Final **-s** is pronounced /s/ after voiceless sounds. Examples of voiceless★ sounds: /t/, /p/, /k/.
(b)	seeds = seed/z/ stars = star/z/ holes = hole/z/ laws = law/z/	/z/ is the sound of "z" in "buzz." Final **-s** is pronounced /z/ after voiced sounds. Examples of voiced★ sounds: /d/, /r/, /l/, /m/, /b/, and all vowel sounds.
(c)	dishes = dish/əz/ matches = match/əz/ classes = class/əz/ sizes = size/əz/ pages = page/əz/ judges = judge/əz/	/əz/ adds a whole syllable to a word. Final **-s/-es** is pronounced /əz/ after *-sh, -ch, -s, -z, -ge/-dge* sounds.

★See Chart 2-4, p. 28, for more information about voiceless and voiced sounds.

□ EXERCISE 2. Pronunciation of final -S/-ES. (Chart 6-1)
Directions: Write the correct pronunciations and practice saying the words.

1. names = name/ z /
2. clocks = clock/ s /
3. eyes = eye/   /
4. heads = head/   /
5. boats = boat/   /
6. ribs = rib/   /
7. lips = lip/   /

8. hills = hill/   /
9. cars = car/   /
10. ways = way/   /
11. months = month/   /
12. eyelashes = eyelash/   /
13. itches = itch/   /

14. glasses = glass/   /
15. prices = price/   /
16. prizes = prize/   /
17. faxes = fax/   /
18. bridges = bridge/   /
19. cages = cage/   /

□ EXERCISE 3. Preview: plural nouns. (Chart 6-2)
Directions: These sentences have many mistakes in the use of nouns. <u>Underline</u> each noun. Write the correct plural form if necessary. Do not change any of the other words in the sentences.

1. <u>Chicago</u> has busy ~~street~~ *streets* and ~~highway~~ *highways*.

2. Box have six side.

3. Big city have many problem.

4. Banana grow in hot, humid area.

5. Insect don't have nose.

6. Lamb are the offspring of sheep.

7. Library keep book on shelf.

8. Parent support their child.

9. Indonesia has several active volcano.

10. Baboon are big monkey. They have large head and

sharp tooth. They eat leaf, root, insect, and egg.

6-2 PLURAL FORMS OF NOUNS

SINGULAR	PLURAL	
(a) one bird one street one rose	two *birds* two *streets* two *roses*	To make most nouns plural, add *-s*.
(b) one dish one match one class one box	two *dishes* two *matches* two *classes* two *boxes*	Add *-es* to nouns ending in *-sh*, *-ch*, *-ss*, and *-x*.
(c) one baby one city (d) one toy one key	two *babies* two *cities* two *toys* two *keys*	If a noun ends in a consonant + *-y*, change the *y* to *i* and add *-es*, as in (c). If *-y* is preceded by a vowel, add only *-s*, as in (d).
(e) one knife one shelf	two *knives* two *shelves*	If a noun ends in *-fe* or *-f*, change the ending to *-ves*. (Exceptions: *beliefs, chiefs, roofs, cuffs, cliffs.*)

(f) one tomato
one zoo
one zero
	two *tomatoes*
	two *zoos*
	two *zeroes/zeros*
		The plural form of nouns that end in *-o* is sometimes *-oes* and sometimes *-os*.
		   -oes: *tomatoes, potatoes, heroes, echoes*
		   -os: *zoos, radios, studios, pianos, solos, sopranos, photos, autos, videos*
		   -oes or *-os*: *zeroes/zeros; volcanoes/volcanos, tornadoes/tornados, mosquitoes/mosquitos*

(g) one child one foot one goose one man one mouse one tooth one woman ————	two *children* two *feet* two *geese* two *men* two *mice* two *teeth* two *women* two *people*	Some nouns have irregular plural forms. (Note: The singular form of *people* can be *person, woman, man, child*. For example, one man and one child = two people.)
(h) one deer one fish one sheep one offspring one species	two *deer* two *fish* two *sheep* two *offspring* two *species*	The plural form of some nouns is the same as the singular form.
(i) one bacterium one cactus one crisis one phenomenon	two *bacteria* two *cacti* two *crises* two *phenomena*	Some nouns that English has borrowed from other languages have foreign plurals.

☐ EXERCISE 4. Plural nouns. (Chart 6-2)
   Directions: Write the plural forms of the nouns.

1. one potato, two ____*potatoes*____

2. a library, many _____

3. one child, two _____

4. a leaf, a lot of _____

5. a wish, many _____

6. one fish, two _____

7. an opinion, many _____

8. a mouse, several _____

9. a sandwich, some _____

10. a man, many _____

11. one woman, two _____

12. a flash, three _____

13. one tomato, a few _____

14. one tooth, two _____

15. one half, two _____

16. a tax, a lot of _____

17. a possibility, several _____

18. a thief, many _____

19. a hero, many _____

20. a goose, a lot of _____

21. an attorney, a few _____

22. a butterfly, several _____

23. one category, two _____

24. a mosquito, a lot of _____

25. one sheep, two _____

26. a wolf, some _____

27. one stitch, two _____

28. one foot, three _____

29. one piano, two _____

30. a belief, many _____

6-3 SUBJECTS, VERBS, AND OBJECTS

(a) The $\overset{s}{\text{sun}}$ $\overset{v}{\text{shines}}$.
    (noun) (verb)
 	
 (b) $\overset{s}{\textbf{Plants}}$ $\overset{v}{\textbf{grow}}$.
   (noun) (verb)
	An English sentence has a SUBJECT (**s**) and a VERB (**v**).
	
	 The SUBJECT is a **noun**. In (a): *sun* is a noun; it is the subject of the verb *shines*.

(c) $\overset{s}{\textbf{Plants}}$ $\overset{v}{\textbf{need}}$ $\overset{o}{\textbf{water}}$.
   (noun) (verb) (noun)
 	
 (d) $\overset{s}{\textbf{Bob}}$ $\overset{v}{\textbf{is reading}}$ a $\overset{o}{\textbf{book}}$.
   (noun) (verb)   (noun)
	Sometimes a VERB is followed by an OBJECT (**o**).
	
	 The OBJECT of a verb is a **noun**. In (c): *water* is the object of the verb *need*.

□ EXERCISE 5. Subjects, verbs, and objects. (Chart 6-3)
   Directions: Identify the subject (**s**) and verb (**v**) of each sentence. Also find the object (**o**) of the verb if the sentence has an object.

                       s   v   o

1. The carpenter built a table.

                  s   v

2. Birds fly.

3. Cows eat grass.

4. My dog barked.

5. The dog chased the cat.

6. Steam rises.

7. Accidents happen.

8. Most birds build nests.

9. Our guests arrived.

10. Teachers assign homework.

11. My roommate opened the window.

12. Jack raised his hand.

13. Irene is watching her sister's children.

□ EXERCISE 6. Nouns and verbs. (Charts 6-2 and 6-3)
   Directions: Some words can be used both as a noun and as a verb. If the word in *italics* is used as a noun, circle **n.** If the word in *italics* is used as a verb, circle **v.** (**n.** = **noun** and **v.** = **verb**)

1. **n.** (**v.**) People *smile* when they're happy.

2. (**n.**) **v.** Mary has a nice *smile* when she's happy.

3. **n.** **v.** Emily does good *work*.

4. **n.** **v.** Emily and Mike *work* at the cafeteria.

5. **n.** **v.** People usually *store* milk in the refrigerator.

6. **n.** **v.** We went to the *store* to buy some milk.

7. **n.** **v.** The child wrote her *name* on the wall with a crayon.

8. **n.** **v.** People often *name* their children after relatives.

9. **n.** **v.** Airplanes *land* on runways at the airport.

10. **n.** **v.** The ship reached *land* after seventeen days at sea.

11. **n.** **v.** I took a *train* from New York to Boston last week.

12. **n.** **v.** I *train* my dogs to sit on command.

13. **n.** **v.** Alex *visits* his aunt every week.

14. **n.** **v.** Alex's aunt enjoys his *visits* every week.

☐ EXERCISE 7. Nouns and verbs. (Charts 6-2 and 6-3)

> *Directions:* Use each word in **two** different sentences. Use the word as a noun (**n.**) in the first sentence and as a verb (**v.**) in the second sentence. Consult your dictionary if necessary to find out the different uses and meanings of a word.

> *Example:* watch
>> → n. *I am wearing a **watch**.*
>> v. *I **watched** TV after dinner last night.*

1. rain	4. phone	7. water
2. paint	5. shop	8. circle
3. tie	6. face	9. fly

Other common words that are used as both nouns and verbs are listed below. Choose several from the list to make additional sentences. Use your dictionary if necessary.

center/centre★	garden	question	snow
date	mail	rock	star
experience	mind	season	tip
e-mail	place	sense	trip
fear	plant	shape	value
fish	promise	smoke	

6-4 OBJECTS OF PREPOSITIONS

$\quad$ S $\quad$ V $\quad\quad$ O $\quad$ **PREP** $\quad$ **O OF PREP** (a) Ann put her books **on** *the* **desk**. $\qquad\qquad\qquad\qquad\qquad$ (noun) $\quad$ S $\quad$ V $\quad$ **PREP** $\quad$ **O OF PREP** (b) A leaf fell **to** *the* **ground**. $\qquad\qquad\qquad$ (noun)	Many English sentences have prepositional phrases. In (a): *on the desk* is a prepositional phrase. A prepositional phrase consists of a PREPOSITION (**PREP**) and an OBJECT OF A PREPOSITION (**O OF PREP**). The object of a preposition is a NOUN.

REFERENCE LIST OF PREPOSITIONS

about	*before*	*despite*	*of*	*to*
above	*behind*	*down*	*off*	*toward(s)*
across	*below*	*during*	*on*	*under*
after	*beneath*	*for*	*out*	*until*
against	*beside*	*from*	*over*	*up*
along	*besides*	*in*	*since*	*upon*
among	*between*	*into*	*through*	*with*
around	*beyond*	*like*	*throughout*	*within*
at	*by*	*near*	*till*	*without*

★American English: *center;* British English: *centre.*

Nouns and Pronouns **161**

☐ **EXERCISE 8. Subjects, verbs, and objects. (Charts 6-3 and 6-4)**
Directions: Identify the subjects, verbs, and objects. Also identify the preposition (**PREP**) and the noun that is used as the object of the preposition (**O OF PREP**).

              S   V   O   PREP O of PREP
1. Sara saw a picture on the wall.

2. Sara looked at the pictures.

3. Emily waited for her friend at a restaurant.

4. The sun rises in the east.

5. Sue lost her ring in the sand at the beach.

6. The moon usually disappears from view during the day.

7. Eric talked to his friend on the phone for thirty minutes.

8. Children throughout the world play with dolls.

9. Astronauts walked on the moon in 1969.

10. A woman in a blue suit sat beside me until the end of the meeting.

☐ **EXERCISE 9. Prepositions of place. (Chart 6-4)**
Directions: Review prepositions of place* by using the following phrases in sentences. Demonstrate the meaning of the preposition by some action. Work in pairs, in small groups, or as a class.

Example: above my head
→ *I'm holding my hand above my head.* (The speaker demonstrates this action.)

1. across the room	11. below the window
2. against the wall	12. beside my book
3. among my books and papers	13. near the door
4. between two pages of my book	14. far from the door
5. around my wrist	15. off my desk
6. at my desk	16. out the window
7. on my desk	17. under my desk
8. in the room	18. through the door
9. into the room	19. throughout the room
10. behind me	20. toward(s) the door

---

*Prepositions of place are also called "prepositions of location."

6-5 PREPOSITIONS OF TIME

IN	(a) Please be on time *in* the future. (b) I usually watch TV *in* the evening.	*in* + the past, the present, the future* *in* + the morning, the afternoon, the evening
	(c) I was born *in* October. (d) I was born *in* 1985. (e) I was born *in* the twentieth century. (f) The weather is hot *in* (the) summer.	*in* + { a month a year a century a season
ON	(g) I was born *on* October 31, 1985. (h) I went to a movie *on* Thursday. (i) I have class *on* Thursday morning(s).	*on* + a date *on* + a weekday *on* + a weekday morning(s), afternoon(s), evening(s)
AT	(j) We sleep at night. I was asleep *at* midnight. (k) I fell asleep *at* 9:30 (nine-thirty). (l) He's busy *at* present. Please call again.	*at* + noon, night, midnight *at* + "clock time" *at* + present, the moment, the present time

*Possible in British English: *in future (Please be on time in future.)*.

☐ EXERCISE 10. Prepositions of time. (Chart 6-5)

Directions: Complete the sentences with *in, at,* or *on*. All the sentences contain time expressions.

1. We don't know what will happen ___in___ the future.

2. History is the study of events that occurred _____ the past.

3. Newspapers report events that happen _____ the present.

4. Last year I was a junior in high school. _____ present, I am a senior in high school.

5. I am a student _____ the present time, but I will graduate next month.

6. Ms. Walker can't come to the phone right now. She's in a meeting _____ the moment.

7. I usually take a walk _____ the morning before I go to work.

8. Frank likes to take a nap _____ the afternoon.

9. Our family enjoys spending time together _____ the evening.

10. Our children always stay home _____ night.

11. I ate lunch _____ noon.

12. I got home _____ midnight.

13. I moved to this city _____ September.

14. I moved here _____ 2001.

15. I moved here _____ September 2001.

16. I moved here _____ September 3.

17. I moved here _____ September 3, 2001.

18. I moved here _____ the fall.

19. I work _____ the morning. _____ the afternoon, I have an English class.

20. _____ Wednesday, I work all day. _____ Thursday, I have an English class.

21. _____ Thursday afternoon, I have an English class.

22. My plane was supposed to leave _____ 7:07 P.M., but it didn't take off until 8:30.

☐ EXERCISE 11. Prepositions of time. (Chart 6-5)
Directions: Supply the appropriate preposition and create a sentence.

Example: _____ the moment
→ **at** the moment
We're doing an exercise on prepositions **at the moment**.

1. _____ the future	7. _____ January 1, 1999
2. _____ present	8. _____ the twenty-first century
3. _____ the winter	9. _____ the evening
4. _____ January	10. _____ night
5. _____ January 1	11. _____ Saturday morning(s)
6. _____ 1999	12. _____ six o'clock _____ the morning

6-6 WORD ORDER: PLACE AND TIME

S V PLACE TIME (a) Ann moved *to Paris* *in 1998.* We went *to a movie* *yesterday.*	In a typical English sentence, "place" comes before "time," as in (a). *INCORRECT: Ann moved in 1998 to Paris.*
S V O P T (b) We bought a house in Miami in 1995.	S-V-O-P-T = Subject-Verb-Object-Place-Time S-V-O-P-T = a basic English sentence structure.
TIME S V PLACE (c) *In 1998,* Ann moved *to Paris.* (d) *Yesterday* we went *to a movie.*	Expressions of time can also come at the beginning of a sentence, as in (c) and (d). A time phrase at the beginning of a sentence is often followed by a comma, as in (c).

☐ EXERCISE 12. Word order: place and time. (Chart 6-6)
Directions: Create sentences from the given words. Add prepositions as necessary.

Example: Bangkok / we / February / went
→ *We went to Bangkok in February.*   OR   *In February, we went to Bangkok.*

1. his uncle's bakery / Alex / Saturday mornings / works

2. the evening / often take / the park / a walk / I

3. arrived / the morning / the airport / my plane / six-thirty

6-7 SUBJECT–VERB AGREEMENT

(a) SINGULAR SINGULAR The sun shine**s**. (b) PLURAL PLURAL *Bird***s** *sing*.	A singular subject takes a singular verb, as in (a). A plural subject takes a plural verb, as in (b). Notice: *verb* + **-s** = singular (*shines*) *noun* + **-s** = plural (*birds*)
(c) SINGULAR SINGULAR *My brother* **lives** in Jakarta. (d) PLURAL PLURAL *My brother **and** sister* **live** in Jakarta.	Two subjects connected by **and** take a plural verb, as in (d).
(e) The **glasses** over there under the window by the sink **are** clean. (f) The **information** in those magazines about Vietnamese culture and customs **is** very interesting.	Sometimes phrases come between a subject and a verb. These phrases do not affect the agreement of the subject and verb.
(g) V S *There **is** a **book*** on the desk. (h) V S *There **are** some **books*** on the desk.	**There** + **be** + *subject* expresses that something exists in a particular place. The verb agrees with the noun that follows **be**.
(i) **Every student is** sitting down. (j) **Everybody/Everyone hopes** for peace.	**Every** is a singular word. It is used with a singular, not plural, noun. *INCORRECT: Every students . . . .* Subjects with **every** take singular verbs, as in (i) and (j).
(k) **People** in my country **are** friendly.	**People** is a plural noun and takes a plural verb.

☐ EXERCISE 13. Subject–verb agreement. (Chart 6-7)

Directions: Underline and identify the subject (**s**) and the verb (**v**). Correct errors in agreement.

             s   v
1. Earthquakes occurs every day of the year.

2. Candles burn slowly. OK (*no error*)

3. My mother speak Spanish.

4. My aunt and uncle speak Spanish.

5. Oscar speaks Spanish and English.

6. The students in this class speaks English very well.

7. Every students in my class speak English well.

8. There are five student from Korea in Mr. Brown's class.

9. There's a vacant apartment in my building.

10. Does people in the United States like Chinese food?

11. The people in Brazil speaks Portuguese.

12. There is many different kinds of fish in the ocean.

13. The neighbors in the apartment next to mine is very friendly and helpful.

14. Every students in this room have a grammar book.

6-8 USING ADJECTIVES TO DESCRIBE NOUNS

ADJ NOUN (a) Bob is reading a ***good*** book.	Words that describe nouns are called *adjectives*. In (a): ***good*** is an adjective; it describes the book.
(b) The ***tall*** *woman* wore a ***new*** *dress*. (c) The ***short*** *woman* wore an ***old*** *dress*. (d) The ***young*** *woman* wore a ***short*** *dress*.	We say that adjectives "modify" nouns. "Modify" means "change a little." An adjective changes the meaning of a noun by giving more information about it.
(e) Roses are ***beautiful*** *flowers*. *INCORRECT: Roses are beautifuls flowers.*	Adjectives are neither singular nor plural. They do NOT have a plural form.
(f) He wore a ***white*** *shirt*. *INCORRECT: He wore a shirt white.* (g) Roses *are* ***beautiful***. (h) His shirt *was* ***white***.	Adjectives usually come immediately before nouns, as in (f). Adjectives can also follow main verb ***be***, as in (g) and (h).

☐ EXERCISE 14. Adjectives. (Chart 6-8)
    Directions: <u>Underline</u> and identify the adjectives (**ADJ**) in the sentences.

                   ADJ
1. The students wrote <u>long</u> compositions.

2. Deserts are dry.

3. Crocodiles have big teeth.

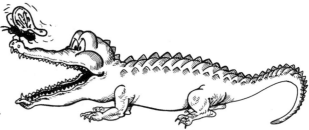

4. Knives are sharp.

5. Dark places frighten small children.

6. The audience laughed at the funny joke.

7. Sensible people wear comfortable shoes.

8. Steve cleaned the shelves of the refrigerator with soapy water.

9. The local police searched the stolen car for illegal drugs.

10. Before the development of agriculture, primitive people gathered wild plants for food.

□ EXERCISE 15. Using adjectives with nouns. (Chart 6-8)

Directions: Add adjectives to the sentences. Choose **two** of the three adjectives in each item to add to the given sentence.

Example: *hard, heavy, strong*   A man lifted the box.
       → *A strong man lifted the heavy box.*

1. *beautiful, safe, red*   Roses are flowers.

2. *dark, cold, dry*   Rain fell from the clouds.

3. *empty, wet, hot*   The waiter poured coffee into my cup.

4. *easy, blue, young*   The girl in the dress was looking for a telephone.

5. *quiet, sharp, soft*   Annie sleeps on a bed in a room.

6. *fresh, clear, hungry*   Mrs. Fox gave the children some fruit.

7. *dirty, modern, delicious*   After we finished our dinner, Frank helped me with the dishes.

8. *round, inexperienced, right*   When Tom was getting a haircut, the barber accidentally cut Tom's ear with the scissors.

□ EXERCISE 16. Adjectives and nouns. (Chart 6-8)

Directions: Don't look at the passage in Part II on the next page. First write the words asked for in Part I. Don't use the same word twice. Then turn the page and use the words to complete Part II.

PART I. Write:

1. an adjective   ___old_____

2. a name   _____

3. a plural noun   _____

4. a plural noun   _____

5. a singular noun   _____

6. an adjective   _____

7. an adjective   _____

8. a preposition of place   _____

9. an adjective   _____

10. a plural noun   _____

PART II. Write the words on your list in the blanks. Some of your completions might be a little odd and funny. Read your completed passage aloud in a group or to the rest of the class.

One day a/an _____old_____ girl was walking in the city. Her name was
　　　　　　　　1

_____. She was carrying a package for her grandmother. It
　　　　　　　2

contained some _____, some _____, and
　　　　　　　　　　　3　　　　　　　　　　　　　　　　　　　　　4

a/an _____, among other things.
　　　　　　　5

　　　As she was walking down the street, a/an _____ thief stole
　　　　　　　　　　　　　　　　　　　　　　　　　　　　　　　　6

her package. The _____ girl pulled out her cell phone and called
　　　　　　　　　　　　　7

the police, who caught the thief _____ a nearby building and
　　　　　　　　　　　　　　　　　　8

returned her package to her. She took it immediately to her _____
　　　　　　　　　　　　　　　　　　　　　　　　　　　　　　　　　　　9

grandmother, who was glad to get the package because she really needed some new

_____.
　　　　　10

6-9 USING NOUNS AS ADJECTIVES

(a) I have a ***flower*** garden. (b) The ***shoe*** store also sells socks. (c) INCORRECT: a flowers garden (d) INCORRECT: the shoes store	Sometimes words that are usually used as nouns are used as adjectives. For example, *flower* is usually a noun, but in (a) it is used as an adjective to modify *garden*. When a noun is used as an adjective, it is singular in form, NOT plural.

☐ EXERCISE 17. Using nouns as adjectives. (Chart 6-9)
　　Directions: <u>Underline</u> and identify the nouns (N). Use a noun in the first sentence as an adjective in the second sentence.

　　　　　　　　N　　　　　　　N
　　1. This <u>book</u> is about <u>grammar</u>. It's a _____grammar book*_____.

　　2. My garden has vegetables. It is a _____.

　　3. The program is on television. It's a _____.

　　4. The soup has beans. It is _____.

————————

*When one noun modifies another noun, the spoken stress is usually on the first noun: a ***grammar*** book.

5. We made plans for our vacation. We made _____.

6. I read a lot of articles in newspapers. I read a lot of _____.

7. The factory makes automobiles. It's an _____.

8. The lesson concerned history. It was a _____.

9. The villages are in the mountains. They are _____.

10. Flags fly from poles. Many government buildings have _____.

☐ **EXERCISE 18. Using nouns as adjectives. (Chart 6-9)**
   Directions: Add **-s** to the *italicized* nouns if necessary.

   1. *Computer*ₛ cannot think. They need human operators.

   2. *Computer* operators are essential in today's business world. OK *(no change)*

   3. *Airplane* allow us to travel to all parts of the world.

   4. *Airplane* seats are narrow and uncomfortable.

   5. This school has several *language* programs.

   6. This school teaches several *language*.

   7. *Bicycle* have two tires. *Automobile* have four tires.

   8. *Bicycle* tires are considerably smaller and cheaper than *automobile* tires.

☐ **EXERCISE 19. Review: nouns. (Charts 6-1 → 6-9)**
   Directions: These sentences contain many mistakes in noun usage. Make the nouns
   PLURAL whenever possible and appropriate. Do not change any other words.

   1. Birdₛ are interesting.

   2. There are around 8,600 kind of bird in the world.

   3. Bird hatch from egg. Baby bird stay in their
      nest for several week or month. Their parent
      feed them until they can fly.

   4. People eat chicken egg. Some animal eat
      bird egg.

5. Fox and snake are natural enemy of bird. They eat bird and their egg.

6. Some bird eat only seed and plant. Other bird eat mainly insect and earthworm.

7. Weed are unwanted plant. They prevent farm crop or garden flower from growing properly. Bird help farmer by eating weed seed and harmful insect.

8. Rat, rabbit, and mouse can cause huge loss on farm by eating stored crop. Certain big bird like hawk help farmer by hunting these animal.

9. The feather of certain kind of bird are used in pillow and mattress. The soft feather from goose are often used for pillow and quilt. Goose feather are also used in winter jacket.

10. The wing feather from goose were used as pen from the sixth century to the nineteenth century, when steel pen were invented.

□ EXERCISE 20. Review: nouns. (Charts 6-1 → 6-9)
Directions: Find the nouns. Make them plural if necessary.

(1)   Whales
        ~~Whale~~ look like fish, but they aren't fish. They are mammal. Mouse, tiger,

(2)   and human being are other example of mammal. Whale are intelligent animal like

(3)   dog and chimpanzee. Even though they live in sea, ocean, and river, whale are

(4)   not fish. Fish lay egg and do not feed their offspring. Mammal give birth to live

(5)   offspring and feed them.

(6)   There are many kind of whale. Most whale are huge creature. The largest

(7)   whale are called blue whale. They can grow to 100 foot (30 meter) in length and

(8)   can weigh 150 ton (135,000 kilogram). Blue whale are much larger than elephant

(9)   and larger than any of the now extinct dinosaur. The heart of an adult blue whale

RELATIVE SIZES OF A BLUE WHALE
AND AN AFRICAN ELEPHANT

(10)   is about the size of a compact car. Its main blood vessel, the aorta, is large

(11)   enough for a person to crawl through.

(12)   Human being have hunted and killed whale since ancient times. Aside from

(13)   people, whale have no natural enemy. Today many people are trying to stop the

(14)   the hunting of whale.

6-10 PERSONAL PRONOUNS: SUBJECTS AND OBJECTS

PERSONAL PRONOUNS				
SUBJECT PRONOUNS: *I*	*we*	*you*	*he, she, it*	*they*
OBJECT PRONOUNS: *me*	*us*	*you*	*him, her, it*	*them*

(a) **Kate** is married. **She** has two children. ⌃_____⌃	A pronoun refers to a noun. In (a): **she** is a pronoun; it refers to **Kate**. In (b): **her** is a pronoun; it refers to **Kate**. **She** is a subject pronoun; **her** is an object pronoun.
(b) **Kate** is my friend. I know **her** well. ⌃_____⌃	
(c) Mike has **a new blue bicycle**. He bought **it** yesterday.	A pronoun can refer to a single noun (e.g., *Kate*) or to a noun phrase. In (c): **it** refers to the whole noun phrase *a new blue bicycle*.
(d) |Eric and **I**| are good friends. (e) Ann met |Eric and **me**| at the museum. (f) Ann walked between |Eric and **me**.|	Guidelines for using pronouns following **and**: If the pronoun is used as part of the subject, use a subject pronoun, as in (d). If it is part of the object, use an object pronoun, as in (e) and (f). *INCORRECT: Eric and me are good friends.* *INCORRECT: Ann met Eric and I at the museum.*

SINGULAR PRONOUNS:	*I*	*me*	*you*	*he, she, it*	*him, her*
PLURAL PRONOUNS:	*we*	*us*	*you*	*they*	*them*

(g) **Mike** is in class. **He** is taking a test. (h) The **students** are in class. **They** are taking a test. (i) **Kate and Tom** are married. **They** have two children.	*Singular* = one. *Plural* = more than one. Singular pronouns refer to singular nouns, plural pronouns to plural nouns, as in the examples.

☐ EXERCISE 21. Personal pronouns: subjects and objects. (Chart 6-10)
　　Directions: Circle the correct words in *italics*.

1. Nick ate dinner with   *I,* (*me.*)

2. Nick ate dinner with Betsy and   *I, me.*

3. *I, Me*   had dinner with Nick last night.

4. Betsy and   *I, me*   had dinner with Nick last night.

5. Please take this food and give   *it, them*   to the dog.

6. Please take these food scraps and give   *it, them*   to the dog.

7. My brother drove Emily and   *I, me*   to the store. He didn't come in. He waited for
　　we, us   in the car. *We, Us*   hurried.

8. A: I want to get tickets for the soccer game.
　　B: You'd better get   *it, them*   right away. *It, They*   *is, are*   selling fast.

9. Ms. Lee wrote a note on my test paper. *She, Her*   wanted to talk to   *I, me*   after class.

10. Between you and   *I, me,*   I think Ivan made a bad decision to quit his job.
　　He, Him   and   *I, me*   see things differently.

☐ EXERCISE 22. Personal pronouns. (Chart 6-10)
　　Directions: Complete the sentences with **she, he, it, her, him, they,** or **them**.

1. I have a grammar book. _____It_____ is black.

2. Tom borrowed my books. _____He_____ returned _____them_____ yesterday.

3. Susan is wearing some new earrings. _____ look good on _____ .

4. Table tennis (also called ping-pong) began in England in the late 1800s. Today
　　_____ is an international sport. My brother and I played _____ a
　　lot when we were teenagers. I beat
　　_____ sometimes, but
　　_____ was a better player and
　　usually won.

5. Don't look directly at the sun. Don't look at _____ directly even if you are wearing sunglasses. The intensity of its light can injure your eyes.

6. Do bees sleep at night? Or do _____ work in the hive all night long? You never see _____ after dark. What do _____ do after night falls?

7. The apples were rotten, so the children didn't eat _____ even though _____ were really hungry.

8. The scent of perfume rises. According to one expert, you should put _____ on the soles of your feet.

9. Even though clean, safe water is fundamental to human health, an estimated 800 million people in the world are still without _____. Unsafe water causes illnesses. _____ contributes to high numbers of deaths in children under five years of age.

10. Magazines are popular. I enjoy reading _____. _____ have news about recent events and discoveries. Recently, I read about "micromachines." _____ are human-made machines that are smaller than a grain of sand. One scientist called _____ "the greatest scientific invention of our time."

6-11 POSSESSIVE NOUNS

SINGULAR:	(a) I know the **student's** name.	An apostrophe (') and an **-s** are used with nouns to show possession.
PLURAL:	(b) I know the **students'** names.	
PLURAL:	(c) I know the **children's** names.	

Singular	(d) the student my baby a man	→ the **student's** name → my **baby's** name → a **man's** name	SINGULAR POSSESSIVE NOUN: *noun* + *apostrophe* (') + **-s**	
	(e) James	→ **James'/James's** name	A singular noun that ends in *-s* has two possible possessive forms: *James'* OR *James's*.	
Plural	(f) the students my babies	→ the **students'** names → my **babies'** names	PLURAL POSSESSIVE NOUN: *noun* + **-s** + *apostrophe* (')	
	(g) men the children	→ **men's** names → the **children's** names	IRREGULAR PLURAL POSSESSIVE NOUN: *noun* + *apostrophe* (') + **-s** (An irregular plural noun is a plural noun that does not end in **-s**: *children, men, people, women*. See Chart 6-2, p. 158.)	

COMPARE (h) **Tom's** here. (i) **Tom's** brother is here.	In (h): **Tom's** is not a possessive. It is a contraction of *Tom is*, used in informal writing. In (i): **Tom's** is a possessive.

□ EXERCISE 23. Possessive nouns. (Chart 6-11)

    Directions: Use the correct possessive form of the nouns in *italics* to complete the sentences.

1. *student*   One student asked several questions. I answered the ___student's___ questions.

2. *students*   Many students had questions after the lecture. I answered the ___students'___ questions.

3. *daughter*   We have one child, a girl. Our _____ bedroom is near ours.

4. *daughters*   We have two children, both girls. They share a bedroom. Our _____ bedroom is next to ours.

5. *man*   Robert is a _____ name.

6. *woman*   Heidi is a _____ name.

7. *men*   Robert and Thomas are _____ names.

8. *women*   Emily and Colette are _____ names.

9. *people*   It's important to be sensitive to other _____ feelings.

10. *person*   I always look straight into a _____ eyes during a conversation.

11. *earth*   The _____ surface is about seventy percent water.

12. *elephant*   An _____ skin is gray and wrinkled.

13. *teachers*   We have class in this building, but all of the _____ offices are in another building.

14. *teacher*   My grammar _____ husband is an engineer.

15. *enemy*   Two soldiers, each faceless and nameless to the other, fought to the death on the muddy river bank. At the end, the victor could not help but admire his _____ courage.

16. *enemies*   Through the years in public office, he made many political enemies. He made a list of his _____ names so that he could get revenge when he achieved political power.

17. *Chris*   Did you add _____ name to the invitation list?

□ EXERCISE 24. Possessive nouns. (Chart 6-11)

    Directions: These sentences contain mistakes in the punctuation of possessive nouns. Add apostrophes in the right places.

1. A king's chair is called a throne.

2. Kings' chairs are called thrones.

3. Babies toys are often brightly colored.

4. It's important to make sure your babys toys are safe for babies to play with.

5. Someone called, but because of the static on the cell phone, I couldn't understand the callers words.

6. A receptionists job is to write down callers names and take messages.

7. Newspapers aren't interested in yesterdays news. They want to report todays events.

8. Each flight has at least two pilots. The pilots seats are in a small area called the cockpit.

9. Rainforests cover five percent of the earths surface but have fifty percent of the different species of plants.

10. Mosquitoes wings move incredibly fast.

11. A mosquitos wings move about one thousand times per second. Its wing movement is the sound we hear when a mosquito is humming in our ears.

12. Elephants like to roll in mud. The mud protects the animals skin from insects and the sun.

13. When we were walking in the woods, we saw an animals footprints on the muddy path.

☐ EXERCISE 25. Review of nouns + -S/-ES. (Charts 6-1 → 6-11)
Directions: Add *-s/-es* if necessary. Add apostrophes to possessive nouns as appropriate.

    Butterflies
1. ~~Butterfly~~ are beautiful.

    David's
2. Nick is ~~David~~ brother.

3. Most leaf are green.

4. My mother apartment is small.

5. Potato are good for us.

6. Do bird have tooth?

7. Tom last name is Miller.

8. Two thief stole Mr. Lee car.

9. Mountain are high, and valley are low.

10. A good toy holds a child interest for a long time.

11. Children toy need to be strong and safe.

12. All of the actor name are listed on page six of your program.

13. Teacher are interested in young people idea.

14. Almost all monkey have opposable thumb on not only their hand but also their foot.

   People have thumb only on their hand.

6-12 POSSESSIVE PRONOUNS AND ADJECTIVES

This pen belongs to me. (a) It's **mine**. (b) It is **my** pen.	(a) and (b) have the same meaning; they both show possession. **Mine** is a *possessive pronoun;* **my** is a *possessive adjective*.

POSSESSIVE PRONOUNS	POSSESSIVE ADJECTIVES	
(c) I have **mine**.	I have **my** pen.	A **possessive pronoun** is used alone, without a noun following it. A **possessive adjective** is used only with a noun following it. *INCORRECT: I have mine pen.* *INCORRECT: I have my.*
(d) You have **yours**.	You have **your** pen.	
(e) She has **hers**.	She has **her** pen.	
(f) He has **his**.	He has **his** pen.	
(g) We have **ours**.	We have **our** pens.	
(h) You have **yours**.	You have **your** pen.	
(i) They have **theirs**.	They have **their** pens.	
(j) ————————	I have a book. **Its** *cover* is black.	

COMPARE *its* vs. *it's:* (k) Sue gave me a book. I don't remember *its* title. (l) Sue gave me a book. *It's* a novel.	In (k): *its* (NO apostrophe) is a possessive adjective modifying the noun *title*. In (l): *It's* (with an apostrophe) is a contraction of *it + is*.

COMPARE *their* vs. *there* vs. *they're:* (m) The students have *their* books. (n) My books are over *there*. (o) Where are the students? *They're* in class.	*Their, there,* and *they're* have the same pronunciation, but not the same meaning. *their* = possessive adjective, as in (m). *there* = an expression of place, as in (n). *they're* = *they are*, as in (o).

☐ **EXERCISE 26. Possessive pronouns and adjectives. (Chart 6-12)**
   Directions: Circle the correct words in *italics*.

   1. Alice called (her,) hers   friend.

   2. Tom wrote a letter to   *his, he's*   mother.

   3. Children should obey   *his, their*   parents.

   4. A: Excuse me. Is this   *my, mine*   dictionary or *your, yours?*

      B: This one is   *my, mine.*   *Your, Yours*   is on *your, yours* desk.

   5. The bird cleaned   *its, it's*   feathers with   *its, it's*   beak.

   6. A: What kind of bird is that?

      B: *Its, It's*   a crow.

   7. Paula had to drive my car to work.
      Hers, Her had a flat tire.

   8. Julie fell off her bicycle and broke   *hers, her*   arm.

   9. Fruit should be a part of   *your, yours*   daily diet.
      It, They   is, are good for   *you, your.*

   10. a. Adam and Amanda are married.   *They, Them* live in an apartment building.

       b. *Their, There, They're*   apartment is on the fifth floor.

       c. We live in the same building. *Our, Ours* apartment has one bedroom, but
           their, theirs   has two.

       d. *Their, There, They're*   sitting
           their, there, they're   now because
           their, there, they're   waiting for a
           phone call from   *their, there, they're*
           son.

   11. Alice is a good friend of   *me, mine.*★

   12. I met a friend of   *you, yours*   yesterday.

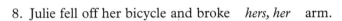

★*A friend of* + possessive pronoun (e.g., *a friend of mine*) is a common expression.

6-13 REFLEXIVE PRONOUNS

myself	(a) *I saw **myself** in the mirror.*	Reflexive pronouns end in **-self/-selves**. They are used when the subject (e.g., *I*) and the object (e.g., *myself*) are the same person. The action of the verb is pointed back to the subject of the sentence. *INCORRECT: I saw me in the mirror.*
yourself	(b) *You (one person) saw **yourself**.*	
herself	(c) *She saw **herself**.*	
himself	(d) *He saw **himself**.*	
itself	(e) *It (e.g., the kitten) saw **itself**.*	
ourselves	(f) *We saw **ourselves**.*	
yourselves	(g) *You (plural) saw **yourselves**.*	
themselves	(h) *They saw **themselves**.*	

(i) *Greg lives **by himself**.*	**By** + *a reflexive pronoun* = alone. In (i): Greg lives alone, without family or roommates.
(j) *I sat **by myself** on the park bench.*	

(k) I ***enjoyed myself*** at the fair.	*Enjoy* and a few other verbs are commonly followed by a reflexive pronoun. See the list below.

COMMON EXPRESSIONS WITH REFLEXIVE PRONOUNS

believe in yourself	*help yourself*	*pinch yourself*	*teach yourself*
blame yourself	*hurt yourself*	*be proud of yourself*	*tell yourself*
cut yourself	*give yourself (something)*	*take care of yourself*	*work for yourself*
enjoy yourself	*introduce yourself*	*talk to yourself*	*wish yourself (luck)*
feel sorry for yourself	*kill yourself*		

☐ EXERCISE 27. Reflexive pronouns. (Chart 6-13)

Directions: Using a mirror in the classroom, describe who is looking at whom.

Example: (. . .) holds the mirror and looks into it.

TEACHER: What is Spyros doing?

SPEAKER A: He is looking at **himself** in the mirror.

TEACHER: What are you doing, Spyros?

SPYROS: I am looking at **myself** in the mirror.

TEACHER: Tell Spyros what he is doing.

SPEAKER B: Spyros, you are looking at **yourself** in the mirror

Example: (. . .) and (. . .) hold the mirror and look into it.

TEACHER: What are (Min Sok) and (Ivonne) doing? Etc.

□ EXERCISE 28. Reflexive pronouns. (Chart 6-13)

Directions: Complete the sentences with reflexive pronouns.

1. Are you okay, Heidi? Did you hurt _____ **yourself** _____ ?

2. David was really embarrassed when he had to go to the job interview with a bandage on his face. He had cut _____ while he was shaving.

3. Do you ever talk to _____ ? Most people talk to _____ sometimes.

4. It is important for all of us to have confidence in our own abilities. We need to believe in _____ .

5. Sara is self-employed. She doesn't have a boss. She works for _____ .

6. Steve, who is on the wrestling team, wishes _____ good luck before each match.

7. There's plenty of food on the table. Would all of you please simply help _____ to the food?

8. Brian, don't blame _____ for the accident. It wasn't your fault. You did everything you could to avoid it.

9. I couldn't believe my good luck! I had to pinch _____ to make sure I wasn't dreaming.

10. A newborn puppy can't take care of _____ .

11. I know Nicole and Paul have had some bad luck, but it's time for them to stop feeling sorry for _____ and get on with their lives.

12. Jane and I ran into someone she knew. I'd never met this person before. I waited for Jane to introduce me, but she forgot her manners. I finally introduced _____ to Jane's friend.

□ EXERCISE 29. Reflexive pronouns. (Chart 6-13)

Directions: Complete the sentences with any appropriate expression from the list in Chart 6-13 and reflexive pronouns. Use any appropriate verb tense.

1. The accident was my fault. I caused it. I was responsible. In other words, I _____ **blamed myself** _____ for the accident.

2. Be careful with that sharp knife! You _____ if you're not careful.

3. It was the first day of class. I sat next to another student and started a conversation about the class and the classroom. After we had talked for a few minutes, I said, "Hi. My name is Rita Woo." In other words, I _____ to the other student.

4. When I walked into the room, I heard Joe's voice. I looked around, but the only person I saw and heard was Joe. In other words, Joe _____ _____ when I walked into the room.

5. My wife and I have our own business. We don't have a boss. In other words, we

_____ .

6. Mr. and Mrs. Hall own their own business. No one taught them how to be small business managers. In other words, they _____ everything they needed to know about running a small business.

7. Mr. Baker committed suicide. In other words, he _____ .

8. I climbed to the top of the diving tower and walked to the end of the diving board. Before I dived into the pool, I said "Good luck!" to myself. In other words, I _____ luck.

9. Rebecca is home in bed because she has the flu. She's resting and drinking plenty of fluids. She is being careful about her health. In other words, she _____ _____ .

10. Sometimes we have problems in our lives. Sometimes we fail. But we shouldn't get discouraged and sad. We need to have faith that we can solve our problems and succeed. If we _____ , we can accomplish our goals.

11. When I failed to get the new job, I was sad and depressed. I was full of self-pity. In other words, I _____ because I didn't get the job.

12. In a cafeteria, people walk through a section of the restaurant and pick up their food. They are not served by waiters. In other words, in a cafeteria people _____ to the food they want.

Directions: Create sentences with reflexive pronouns. Use imaginary situations.

Example: wish myself
→ *Last week I took my first lesson in skydiving. Before I jumped out of the airplane, I wished myself good luck.*

1. talk to himself
2. hurt myself
3. enjoy themselves
4. take care of herself

5. cut himself
6. wish yourself
7. be proud of yourselves
8. blame ourselves

9. feel sorry for myself
10. introduce herself
11. believe in yourself
12. pinch myself

6-14 SINGULAR FORMS OF *OTHER: ANOTHER* vs. *THE OTHER*

ANOTHER

(a) There is a large bowl of apples on the table. Paul is going to eat one apple. If he is still hungry after that, he can eat **another** apple. There are many apples to choose from.	**Another** means "one more out of a group of similar items, one in addition to the one(s) already mentioned." **Another** is a combination of *an + other*, written as one word.

THE OTHER

(b) There are two apples on the table. Paul is going to eat one of them. Sara is going to eat **the other** apple.	**The other** means "the last one in a specific group, the only one that remains from a given number of similar items."
(c) Paul ate one apple. Then he ate { **another** apple. / **another** one. / **another**.	**Another** and **the other** can be used as adjectives in front of a noun (e.g., *apple*) or in front of the word *one*.
(d) Paul ate one apple. Sara ate { **the other** apple. / **the other** one. / **the other**.	**Another** and **the other** can also be used alone as pronouns.

☐ **EXERCISE 31. Singular forms of OTHER. (Chart 6-14)**
   Directions: Complete the sentences with *another* or *the other*.

1. There are two birds in Drawing A. One is an eagle. _____The other_____ is a chicken.

DRAWING A   DRAWING B

2. There are three birds in Drawing B. One is an eagle.

   a. _____ one is a chicken.

   b. _____ bird is a crow.

3. There are many kinds of birds in the world. One kind is an eagle.

   a. _____ kind is a chicken.

   b. _____ kind is a crow.

   c. _____ kind is a sea gull.

   d. What is the name of _____ kind of bird in the world?

4. I have two brothers. One is named Nick. _____ is named Matt.

5. There are five names on this list. One is Adam. _____ is Greg.

   _____ is Nick.

   _____ one of the names is Eric.

   _____ name on the list (the last of the five) is Jessica.

People I need to call

✓ Adam
  Greg
  Eric
  Nick
  Jessica

6. It rained yesterday, and from the look of those dark clouds, we're going to have _____ rainstorm today.

7. Nicole and Michelle are identical twins. The best way to tell them apart is by looking at their ears. One of them has pierced ears, and _____ doesn't.

8. Of the fifty states in the United States, forty-nine are located on the North American continent. Where is _____ located?

9. France borders on several countries. One is Spain. _____ is Italy.

OTHER(S)

one
apple
other
apples

other
apples

others etc.

There are many apples in Paul's kitchen. Paul is holding one apple.
 	
(a) There are ***other*** *apples* in a bowl.
     (adjective) + (noun)
 	
(b) There are ***other*** *ones* on a plate.
     (adjective) + (ones)
 	
(c) There are ***others*** on a chair.
       (pronoun)
	Other(*s*) (without ***the***) means "several more out of a group of similar items, several in addition to the one(s) already mentioned." The adjective ***other*** (without an ***-s***) can be used with a plural noun (e.g., *apples*) or with the word *ones*.
	
	Others (with an ***-s***) is a plural pronoun; it is not used with a noun.
	In (c): ***others*** = ***other apples***.

THE OTHER(S)

one
apple

the
other
apples

There are four apples on the table. Paul is going to take one of them.
 	
(d) Sara is going to take ***the other*** *apples*.
          (adjective) + (noun)
 	
(e) Sara is going to take ***the other*** *ones*.
          (adjective) + (ones)
 	
(f) Sara is going to take ***the others***.
          (pronoun)
	The other(*s*) means "the last ones in a specific group, the remains from a given number of similar items."
	
	The other (without an ***-s***) can be used as an adjective in front of a noun or the word *ones*, as in (d) and (e).
	
	The others (with an ***-s***) is a plural pronoun; it is not used with a noun.
	In (f): ***the others*** = ***the other apples***.

☐ **EXERCISE 32. Forms of OTHER. (Charts 6-14 and 6-15)**
Directions: Perform the following actions.

1. Hold two pens. Use a form of *other* to describe the second pen.
   → *I'm holding two pens. One is mine, and the other belongs to Ahmed.*
2. Hold three pens. Use a form of *other* to describe the second and third pens.
3. Hold up your two hands. One of them is your right hand. Tell us about your left hand, using a form of *other*.
4. Hold up your right hand. One of the five fingers is your thumb. Using forms of *other*, tell us about your index finger (or forefinger), then your middle finger, then your ring finger, and then your little finger, the last of the five fingers on your right hand.
5. Write two names on the board. Use a form of *other* in your description of these names.
6. Write five names on the board and tell us about them, using forms of *other* in your descriptions. Begin with "One of the names on the board is . . . ."

☐ **EXERCISE 33. Plural forms of OTHER. (Chart 6-15)**
Directions: Complete the sentences with **other(s)** or **the other(s)**.

1. There are many kinds of animals in the world. The elephant is one kind. Some
   _____others_____ are tigers, horses, and whales.

2. There are many kinds of animals in the world. The elephant is one kind. Some
   _____ kinds are tigers, horses, and whales.

3. There are three colors in the U.S. flag. One of the colors is red. _____
   are white and blue.

4. There are three colors in the U.S. flag. One of the colors is red. _____
   colors are white and blue.

5. There are four birds in the picture. One is an eagle, and another one is a crow.
   _____ birds in the picture are chickens.

6. There are four birds in the picture. One is an eagle, and another one is a crow.
   _____ are chickens.

7. There are four seasons. Spring and summer are two. _____ are fall and winter.

8. Spring and summer are two of the four seasons. _____ seasons are fall and winter.

9. There are many kinds of geometric figures. Some are circles. _____ figures are squares. Still _____ are rectangular.

10. There are four geometric figures in the above drawing. One is a square. _____ figures are a rectangle, a circle, and a triangle.

11. Of the four geometric figures in the drawing, only the circle has curved lines. _____ have straight lines.

12. Birds have different eating habits. Some birds eat insects.
    a. _____ birds get their food chiefly from plants.
    b. _____ eat only fish.
    c. _____ hunt small animals like mice and rabbits.
    d. _____ birds prefer dead and rotting flesh.

13. A: There were ten questions on the test. Seven of them were easy. _____ three were really hard.

    B: Any question is easy if you know the answer. Seven of the questions were easy for you because you had studied for them. _____ were hard because you hadn't studied for them.

14. Many people like to get up very early in the morning. _____ like to sleep until noon.

15. A: What do you do when you're feeling lonely?

    B: I go someplace where I can be around _____ people. Even if they are strangers, I feel better when there are _____ around me. How about you?

    A: That doesn't work for me. For example, if I'm feeling lonely and I go to a movie by myself, I look at all _____ people who are there with their friends and family, and I start to feel even lonelier. So I try to find _____ things to do to keep myself busy. If I'm busy, I don't feel lonely.

6-16 SUMMARY OF FORMS OF *OTHER*

	ADJECTIVE	PRONOUN	Notice that the word **others** (*other* + *final* **-s**) is used only as a plural pronoun.
SINGULAR PLURAL	another apple other apples	another other**s**	
SINGULAR PLURAL	the other apple the other apples	the other the other**s**	

☐ **EXERCISE 34. Forms of OTHER. (Charts 6-12 → 6-16)**
    Directions: Complete the sentences with correct forms of *other:* **another, other, others, the other, the others**.

1. Jake has only two suits, a blue one and a gray one. His wife wants him to buy

    _____*another*_____ one.

2. Jake has two suits. One is blue, and _____ is gray.

3. Some suits are blue. _____ are gray.

4. Some suits have two buttons. _____ suits have three buttons.

5. Some people keep dogs as pets. _____ have cats. Still

    _____ people have fish or birds as pets. Can you name

    _____ kinds of animals that people keep for pets?

6. When I was a kid, I had two pets. One was a black dog. _____

    was an orange cat.

7. When I walked into the classroom on the first day, the room was empty. I sat down at

    a desk and wondered if I was in the right room. Soon _____

    student came and took a seat. Then a few _____ followed, and

    the room slowly began to fill.

8. My boyfriend gave me a ring. I tried to put it on my ring finger, but it didn't fit. So I

    had to put it on _____ finger.

9. People have two thumbs. One is on the right hand. _____ is on

    the left hand.

10. There are five letters in the word "fresh." One of the letters is a vowel. _____

    _____ are consonants.

11. Smith is a common last name in English. _____ common names

    are Johnson, Jones, Miller, Anderson, Moore, and Brown.

☐ **EXERCISE 35. Forms of OTHER.** (Charts 6-12 → 6-16)
   Directions: Complete the sentences with your own words. Use a form of ***other*** in the blank. If you write the completed sentences, underline the forms of ***other***.

   Example: I have . . . books on my desk. One is . . . , and _____ is/are . . . .
       → *I have three books on my desk. One is a grammar book, and* <u>*the others*</u> *are my dictionary and a science book.*

   1. I have two favorite colors. One is . . . , and _____ is . . . .

   2. Some students walk to school. _____ . . . .

   3. Ted drank . . . , but he was still thirsty, so . . . _____ one.

   4. I speak . . . languages. One is . . . , and _____ is/are . . . .

   5. Some people . . . , and _____ . . . .

   6. I have . . . sisters, brothers, and/or cousins. One is . . . , and _____ is/are . . . .

   7. One of my teachers is . . . . _____ is/are . . . .

   8. . . . and . . . are two common names in my country. _____ are . . . .

   9. . . . of the students in my class are from . . . . _____ students are from . . . .

   10. There are many popular sports in the world. One is . . . . _____ is . . . .
       _____ are . . . .

☐ **EXERCISE 36. Error analysis: summary review of nouns and pronouns.** (Chapter 6)
   Directions: Correct the errors.

   1. The fairy godmother told the boy to make three ~~wish.~~ ^wishes

   2. I had some black beans soup for lunch. They were very good.

   3. The highways in my country are excellents.

   4. My mother and father work in Milan. Their teacher's.

   5. Today many womens are miner, pilot, and doctor.

   6. My wife likes all kind of flower.

   7. We often read story in class and try to understand all the new word. I can't remember
       all of it.

8. There are two pool at the park. One is for childs. The another is for adults only.

9. My brother has an apple's trees orchard.

10. The windows in our classroom is dirty.

11. In addition to the news about the flood, I heard some others importants news this morning.

12. The population of my hometown in 1975 were about 50,000. Today they are more than 150,000.

13. I don't like my apartment. Its in a bad neighborhood. Is trash on both side of the street. I'm going to move to other neighborhood.

14. Every people needs an education. With a good education, people can improve they're live.

15. Alice when was a child lived in a very little town in the north of Brazil. Today is a very big city with many building and larges highways.

CHAPTER 7
Modal Auxiliaries

<table>
<tr><td colspan="2">CONTENTS</td></tr>
</table>

□ EXERCISE 1. Preview: modal auxiliaries. (Chapter 7)
    Directions: Complete the sentences with *to,* if possible. If not, write Ø. Discuss the meanings of the helping verbs in *italics*.

A: I've made a terrible mistake! I put the wrong numbers in my report. My report

    shows that the company made lots of money, but the truth is we lost money. What am

    I going to do!? *Should* I ___Ø___ tell the boss about the accounting error?
                      1

B: Of course! You *have* ___to___ tell her. That error *could* _____ get the company
                    2   3

    in big trouble.

A: I know that I *ought* _____ be honest about it, but I'm afraid she'll get angry. She
                    4

    might _____ fire me. *Would* you _____ go with me to see her?
          5   6

B: I think you *had better* _____ do this yourself. You *can* _____ do it.
                    7   8

    I'm sure the boss *will* _____ understand. You*'ve got* _____ be brave.
                    9   10

A: No, you *must* _____ go with me. I *can't* _____ face her alone.
                11   12

7-1 THE FORM OF MODAL AUXILIARIES

The verbs listed below are called "modal auxiliaries." They are helping verbs that express a wide range of meanings (ability, permission, possibility, necessity, etc.). Most of the modals have more than one meaning.

AUXILIARY + THE SIMPLE FORM OF A VERB		*Can, could, may, might, should, had better, must, will,* and *would* are immediately followed by the simple form of a verb.
can	(a) Olga *can speak* English.	• They are not followed by *to*.
could	(b) He *couldn't come* to class.	INCORRECT: *Olga can to speak English.*
may	(c) It *may rain* tomorrow.	• The main verb does not have a final *-s*.
might	(d) It *might rain* tomorrow.	INCORRECT: *Olga can speaks English.*
should	(e) Mary *should study* harder.	• The main verb is not in a past form.
had better	(f) I *had better study* tonight.	INCORRECT: *Olga can spoke English.*
must	(g) Joe *must see* a doctor today.	• The main verb is not in its *-ing* form.
will	(h) I *will be* in class tomorrow.	INCORRECT: *Olga can speaking English.*
would	(i) *Would* you please *close* the door?	
AUXILIARY + *TO* + THE SIMPLE FORM OF A VERB		*To* + *the simple form* is used with these auxiliaries: *have to, have got to,* and *ought to.*
have to	(j) I *have to study* tonight.	
have got to	(k) I *have got to study* tonight.	
ought to	(l) Kate *ought to study* harder.	

☐ **EXERCISE 2. The form of modal auxiliaries. (Chart 7-1)**
Directions: Add *to* where necessary. If no *to* is necessary, write **Ø**.

1. I have ___ **to** ___ go downtown tomorrow.

2. Tom must ___ **Ø** ___ see his dentist.

3. Could you please _____ open the window?

4. May I _____ borrow your pen?

5. A good book can _____ be a friend for life.

6. I ought _____ go to the post office this afternoon.

7. Jimmy is yawning and rubbing his eyes. He must _____ be sleepy.

8. I have got _____ go to the post office this afternoon.

9. Shouldn't you _____ save a little money for a rainy day?

10. Poor Edward. He has _____ go to the hospital for an operation.

11. Alex! Stop! You must not _____ run into the street when there's traffic!

□ EXERCISE 3. Error analysis: the form of modal auxiliaries. (Chart 7-1)
    Directions: Correct the errors.

1. Can you ~~to~~ help me, please?

2. I must studying for an exam tomorrow.

3. We couldn't went to the party last night.

4. I am have to improve my English as soon as possible.

5. You shouldn't to spend all your free time at the computer.

6. My mother can't speaking English, but she can speaks several other language.

7-2 EXPRESSING ABILITY: *CAN* AND *COULD*

(a) Bob *can play* the piano. (b) You *can buy* a screwdriver at a hardware store. (c) I *can meet* you at Ted's tomorrow afternoon.	*Can* expresses *ability* in the present or future.
(d) I $\begin{cases} \textbf{\textit{can't}} \\ \textbf{\textit{cannot}} \\ \textbf{\textit{can not}} \end{cases}$ understand that sentence.	The negative form of *can* may be written *can't*, *cannot*, or *can not*.
(e) Our son *could walk* when he was one year old.	The past form of *can* is *could*.
(f) He *couldn't walk* when he was six months old.	The negative of *could*: *couldn't* or *could not*.

□ EXERCISE 4. Expressing ability: CAN and CAN'T. (Chart 7-2)
    Directions: Complete the sentences with *can* and *can't*.

1. A cat _____can_____ climb trees, but it _____can't_____ fly.

2. A fish __can not__ walk, but it _____can_____ swim.

3. A dog _____can_____ bark, but it __can not__ sing.

4. A tiny baby _____can_____ cry, but it __can not__ talk.

5. You _____can_____ store water in a glass jar, but you __can not__

    store it in a paper bag.

6. You __can not__ drive from the Philippines to Australia, but you

    _____can_____ drive from Italy to Austria.

☐ **EXERCISE 5. Expressing ability: CAN and CAN'T. (Chart 7-2)**
Directions: Interview a classmate about each item in the list below, then make a report (written or oral) about your classmate's abilities.

Example: read pages that are upside down?
SPEAKER A: (Jose), can you read pages that are upside down?
SPEAKER B: Yes, I can. Here, I'll show you. OR
           No, I can't. OR
           I don't know. I'll try. Turn your book upside down, and I'll try to read it.

1. speak more than two languages?

2. play chess?

3. drive a stick-shift car?

4. read upside down?

5. play any musical instrument?

6. do card tricks?

7. pat the top of your head up and down with one hand and rub your stomach in a circular motion with the other hand at the same time?

Switch roles.
8. fold a piece of paper in half more than six times?

9. draw well—for example, draw a picture of me?

10. cook?

11. walk on your hands?

12. play tennis?

13. program a computer?

14. write legibly with both your right hand and your left hand?

☐ **EXERCISE 6. Expressing past ability: COULD and COULDN'T. (Chart 7-2)**
Directions: Complete the sentences with **could** or **couldn't** and your own words.

Example: A year ago I . . . , but now I can.
    → *A year ago I couldn't speak English well, but now I can.*

1. When I was a baby, I . . . , but now I can.

2. When I was a child, I . . . , but now I can't.

3. When I was thirteen, I . . . , but I couldn't do that when I was three.

4. Five years ago, I . . . , but now I can't.

5. In the past, I . . . , but now I can.

7-3 EXPRESSING POSSIBILITY: *MAY* AND *MIGHT*
EXPRESSING PERMISSION: *MAY* AND *CAN*

(a) It *may rain* tomorrow. (b) It *might rain* tomorrow. (c) A: Why isn't John in class? B: I don't know. He { *may* / *might* } be sick today.	*May* and *might* express *possibility* in the present or future. They have the same meaning. There is no difference in meaning between (a) and (b).
(d) It *may not rain* tomorrow. (e) It *might not rain* tomorrow.	Negative: *may not* and *might not*. (Do not contract *may* and *might* with *not*.)

(f) *Maybe* it will rain tomorrow.
 COMPARE
 (g) *Maybe* John is sick. *(adverb)*
 (h) John *may be* sick. *(verb)*
	In (f) and (g): *maybe* (spelled as one word) is an adverb. It means "possibly." It comes at the beginning of a sentence.
	     INCORRECT: It will maybe rain tomorrow.
	 In (h): *may be* (two words) is a verb form: the auxiliary *may* + *the main verb* *be*.
	     INCORRECT: John maybe sick.

(i) Yes, children, you *may have* a cookie after dinner. (j) Okay, kids, you *can have* a cookie after dinner.	*May* is also used to give *permission*, as in (i). Often *can* is used to give *permission*, too, as in (j). (i) and (j) have the same meaning, but *may* is more formal than *can*.
(k) You *may not have* a cookie. You *can't have* a cookie.	*May not* and *cannot* (*can't*) are used to deny permission (i.e., to say "no").

☐ EXERCISE 7. Expressing possibility: MAY, MIGHT, and MAYBE. (Chart 7-3)

Directions: Answer the questions. Include at least three possibilities in the answer to each question, using *may, might,* and *maybe* as in the example.

Example: What are you going to do tomorrow?

→ I don't know. I *may* go downtown. Or I *might* go to the laundromat. Maybe I'll study all day. Who knows?

1. What are you going to do tomorrow night?

2. What's the weather going to be like tomorrow?

3. What is (. . .) going to do tonight?

4. I'm taking something out of my briefcase/ purse/pocket/wallet. It's small, and I'm holding it in my fist. What is it?

5. What does (. . .) have in her purse?

6. What does (. . .) have in his pants pockets?

7. (. . .) isn't in class today. Where is he/she?

8. You have another class after this one. What are you going to do in that class?

9. Look at the picture. What is the man's occupation? What is the woman's occupation?

☐ **EXERCISE 8. Ability, possibility, and permission: CAN, MAY, and MIGHT.**
　　　　　　 (Charts 7-2 and 7-3)

Directions: Complete the sentences with **can**, **may**, or **might**. Use the negative as
appropriate. Identify the meaning expressed by the modals: ability, possibility, or permission.

1. I _____*can*_____ play only one musical instrument: the piano. I _____*can't*_____
   play a guitar. *(meaning expressed by modals: ability)*

2. Tommy, you _____*may/can*_____ stay up until eight tonight, but you
   _____*may not/cannot*_____ stay up past that time.
   (meaning expressed by modals: permission)

3. A: What are you going to do this evening?
   B: I don't know. I _____*may/might*_____ stay home, or I _____*may/might*_____
   　　go over to Anita's house. *(meaning expressed by modals: possibility)*

4. A: What are you going to order?
   B: I don't know.* I _____*may*_____ have the tofu pasta.

5. A: Would you like some more food?
   B: No thanks. I _____*might*_____ eat another bite. I'm full.

6. A: Is it okay if I have a piece of candy, Mom?
   B: No, but you _____*may*_____ have an orange.

7. A: Which of these oranges is sweet? I like only sweet oranges.
   B: How should I know? I _____*can*_____ tell if an orange is sweet
   　　just by looking at it. _____*Can*_____ you? Here. Try this one. It
   _____*may*_____ be sweet enough for you. If it isn't, put some
   　　sugar on it.

8. May I have everyone's attention? The test is about to begin. If you need to leave the
   room during the examination, please raise your hand. You _____*may　not*_____
   leave the room without permission. Are there any questions? No? Then you
   _____*may*_____ open your test booklets and begin.

9. A: What channel is the news special on tonight?
   B: I'm not sure. It _____*may*_____ be on Channel Seven. Try that
   　　one first.

───────────

*In informal spoken English, "I don't know" is often pronounced "I dunno."

7-4 USING *COULD* TO EXPRESS POSSIBILITY

(a) A: Why isn't Greg in class? B: I don't know. He *could be* sick. (b) Look at those dark clouds. It *could start* raining any minute.	*Could* can mean *past ability.* (See Chart 7-2, p. 191.) But that is not its only meaning. Another meaning of *could* is *possibility.* In (a): "He *could* be sick" has the same meaning as "He *may/might* be sick," i.e., "It is possible that he is sick." In (a): *could* expresses a **present** possibility. In (b): *could* expresses a **future** possibility.

☐ **EXERCISE 9. Meanings of COULD. (Charts 7-2 and 7-4)**

Directions: What is the meaning of *could* in the following? Does *could* express past, present, or future time?

1. I *could be* home late tonight. Don't wait for me for dinner.
   → *could be = may/might be. It expresses future time.*

2. Thirty years ago, when he was a small child, David *could speak* Arabic fluently. Now he's forgotten a lot.
   → *could speak = was able to speak. It expresses past time.*

3. A: Where's Alicia?
   B: I don't know. She *could be* at the mall.

4. When I was a child, we *could swim* in the Duckfoot River, but now it's too polluted. Today even the fish get sick.

5. A: What's this?
   B: I don't know. It looks like a glass bottle, but it *could be* a flower vase.

6. Let's leave for the airport now. Yuki's plane *could arrive* early, and we want to be there when she arrives.

7. When I was a kid, I *could jump* rope really well.

☐ **EXERCISE 10. Expressing possibility: COULD, MAY, and MIGHT. (Charts 7-3 and 7-4)**
   Directions: Listen to the clues with books closed. Make guesses using **could, may,** and **might**.

   Example: is made of metal and you keep it in a pocket
   TEACHER: I'm thinking of something that is made of metal. I keep it in my pocket. What
               could it be?
   STUDENTS: It could be a pen. It could be some keys. It might be a paper clip. It may be
               a small pocket knife. It could be a coin.
   TEACHER: (. . .) was right! I was thinking of the keys in my pocket.

   1. has wheels and a motor
   2. is made of plastic and can be found in my purse/pocket
   3. is brown, is made of leather, and is in this room
   4. is flat and rectangular
   5. is white, hard, and in this room
   6. is played with a ball on a large field
   7. has *(three)* stories* and is made of *(brick)*
   8. has four legs and is found on a farm
   9. is green and we can see it out that window
   10. is sweet and you can eat it

☐ **EXERCISE 11. Expressing possibility: COULD. (Chart 7-4)**
   Directions: Listen with books closed. Suggest possible courses of actions using **could**.
   Work in pairs, in groups, or as a class.

   Example: (. . .) has to go to work early tomorrow. His car is completely out of gas. His
               bicycle is broken.
               → *He could take the bus to work.*
                  He could take a gas can to a gas station, fill it up, and carry it home to his car.
                  He could try to fix his bicycle.
                  He could get up very early and walk to work.
                  Etc.

   1. (. . .) walked to school today. Now she wants to go home. It's raining hard. She
      doesn't have an umbrella. She doesn't want her hair to get wet.

   2. (. . .) and (. . .) want to get some exercise. They have a date to play tennis this
      morning, but the tennis court is covered with snow.

   (Switch roles if working in pairs.)

   3. (. . .) just bought a new camera. He has it at home now. He has the instruction
      manual. It is written in Japanese. He can't read Japanese. He doesn't know how to
      operate the camera.

   4. (. . .) likes to travel around the world. He is twenty-two years old. Today he is alone
      in *(name of a city)*. He needs to eat, and he needs to find a place to stay overnight.
      But while he was asleep on the train last night, someone stole his wallet. He has no
      money.

   ———————————
   *American English: *story, stories*; British English: *storey, storeys* (floors in a house).
   American and British English: *story, stories* = *tales*.

□ **EXERCISE 12. COULD, MAY, MIGHT, and WILL PROBABLY.** (Charts 3-4 and 7-2 → 7-4)
Directions: Complete the sentences with your own words.

Example: I could _____ today. (. . .) could _____ too, but we'll probably _____ .
→ ***I could*** *skip class and go to a movie* ***today***. *Pedro* ***could*** *come along* ***too, but***
we'll probably *go to class just like we're supposed to.*

1. Tonight I could _____ . Or I might _____ . Of course, I may _____ .
   But I'll probably _____ .

2. Next year, I might _____ . But I could _____ . I may _____ . But I'll
   probably _____ .

3. My friend (. . .) may _____ this weekend, but I'm not sure. He/She might
   _____ . He/She could also _____ . But he/she'll probably _____ .

4. One hundred years from now, _____ may _____ . _____ could _____ .
   _____ will probably _____ .

7-5 POLITE QUESTIONS: *MAY I, COULD I, CAN I*

POLITE QUESTION	POSSIBLE ANSWERS	People use ***may I, could I,*** ★ and ***can***
(a) ***May I*** please borrow your pen? (b) ***Could I*** please borrow your pen? (c) ***Can I*** please borrow your pen?	Yes. Yes. Of course. Yes. Certainly. Of course. Certainly. Sure. (informal) Okay. (informal) Uh-huh. (meaning "yes") I'm sorry, but I need to use it myself.	***I*** to ask polite questions. The questions ask for someone's permission or agreement. (a), (b), and (c) have basically the same meaning. Note: ***can I*** is less formal than ***may I*** and ***could I***. ***Please*** can come at the end of the question: *May I borrow your pen, please?* ***Please*** can be omitted from the question: *May I borrow your pen?*

★In a polite question, ***could*** is NOT the past form of ***can***.

□ **EXERCISE 13. Polite questions: MAY I, COULD I, and CAN I.** (Chart 7-5)
Directions: Following are some phone conversations. Complete the dialogues. Use ***may I,***
could I, or ***can I*** + a verb from the list. NOTE: The caller is Speaker B.

help	leave	speak/talk	take

1. A: Hello?
   B: Hello. Is Ahmed there?
   A: Yes, he is.
   B: ___May I talk___ to him?
   A: Just a minute. I'll get him.

2. A: Hello. Mr. Black's office.

   B: _May I speak_ to Mr. Black?

   A: May I ask who is calling?

   B: Susan Abbott.

   A: Just a moment, Ms. Abbott. I'll connect you.

3. A: Hello?

   B: Hi. This is Bob. _May I talk_ to Pedro?

   A: Sure. Hang on. Can
                       Could

4. A: Good afternoon. Dr. Wu's office. _May I help_ you?

   B: Yes. I'd like to make an appointment with Dr. Wu.

   A: Fine. Is Friday morning at ten all right?

   B: Yes. Thank you.

   A: Your name?

5. A: Hello?

   B: Hello. _Could I speak_ to Emily?

   A: She's not at home right now. _Would ya like to leave_ a message?

   B: No thanks. I'll call later.

6. A: Hello?

   B: Hello. _Can I talk_ to Maria?

   A: She's not here right now.

   B: Oh. _Could I leave_ a message?

   A: Certainly. Just a minute. I have to get a pen.

7. A: Hello?

   B: Hello. _May I talk_ to Jack?

   A: Who?

   B: Jack. Jack Butler.

   A: There's no one here by that name. I'm afraid you have the wrong number.

   B: Is this 221-3892?

   A: No, it's not.

   B: Oh. I'm sorry.

   A: That's okay.

□ **EXERCISE 14. Polite questions: MAY I, COULD I, and CAN I. (Chart 7-5)**

Directions: Ask and answer polite questions. Use *may I, could I,* or *can I*. Listen to the cues with books closed. Work in groups or as a class. (Alternatively, work in pairs, creating somewhat longer dialogues that you then role-play for the rest of the class.)

Example: (. . .), you want to see (. . .)'s grammar book for a minute.

SPEAKER A: May/Could/Can I (please) see your grammar book for a minute?
SPEAKER B: Of course. / Sure. / Etc.
SPEAKER A: Thank you. / Thanks. I forgot to bring mine to class today.

1. (. . .), you want to see (. . .)'s dictionary for a minute.

2. (. . .), you are at (. . .)'s house. You want to use the phone.

3. (. . .), you are at a restaurant. (. . .) is your waiter/waitress. You have finished your meal. You want the check.

4. (. . .), you run into (. . .) on the street. (. . .) is carrying some heavy packages. What are you going to say to him/her?

5. (. . .), you are speaking to (. . .), who is one of your teachers. You want to leave class early today.

6. (. . .), you want to use (. . .)'s calculator during the algebra test. (. . .) needs to use it himself/herself.

7. (. . .), you are in a store with your good friend (. . .). Your bill is *(a certain amount of money)*. You have only *(a lesser amount of money)*. What are you going to say to your friend?

7-6 POLITE QUESTIONS: *WOULD YOU, COULD YOU, WILL YOU, CAN YOU*

POLITE QUESTION	POSSIBLE ANSWERS	People use *would you, could you, will you,* and *can you* to ask polite questions. The questions ask for someone's help or cooperation. (a), (b), (c), and (d) have basically the same meaning. The use of *can,* as in (d), is less formal than the others.
(a) *Would you* please open the door?	Yes.	
(b) *Could you* please open the door?	Yes. Of course.	
(c) *Will you* please open the door?	Certainly. I'd be happy to.	
(d) *Can you* please open the door?	Of course. I'd be glad to.	
	Sure. (informal)	Note: *May* is NOT used when *you* is the subject of a polite question.
	Okay. (informal)	*INCORRECT: May you please open the door?*
	Uh-huh. (meaning "yes")	
	I'm sorry. I'd like to help, but my hands are full.	

☐ EXERCISE 15. Polite questions: WOULD/COULD/WILL/CAN YOU. (Chart 7-6)
Directions: Complete the dialogues. Use a polite question with ***would you/could you,
will you/can you*** in each. Use the expressions in the list or your own words.

---

answer the phone for me   tell me where the nearest post office is
open the window   turn it down
pick some up   turn the volume up
say that again

---

1.   TEACHER: It's getting hot in here.   *Would/Could/Will/Can you*
         please open the window?
      STUDENT: *Of course, I'd be happy to. / Sure. / Etc.*
      TEACHER: *Thank you. / Thanks.*
      STUDENT: You're welcome.

2.   FRIEND A: The phone is ringing, but my hands are full. _____
     Would you please answer the phone for me?
      FRIEND B: Yes, of course.
      FRIEND A: Thank you
      FRIEND B: No problem.

3. ROOMMATE A: I'm trying to study, but the radio is too loud. _____
     Could you turn it down, please?
   ROOMMATE B: Certainly, I'd be happy to.
   ROOMMATE A: Thank you
   ROOMMATE B: That's okay. No problem.

4.   SISTER: I'm trying to listen to the news on television, but I can't hear it.
     Will you please turn the volume up?
      BROTHER: Sure
       SISTER: Thanks
      BROTHER: Don't mention it.

5.   HUSBAND: Honey, I'm out of razor blades. When you go to the store, _____
     Will / Would you please pick some up?
        WIFE: Okay
     HUSBAND: Thanks
        WIFE: Anything else?

when you ask someone to do sth use would, will

6.   PERSON A: Hi.

        PERSON B: Hi. Walabaxitinpundoozit?

        PERSON A: Excuse me? _Would you say that again ?_

        PERSON B: Walabaxitinpundoozit.

        PERSON A: I'm sorry, but I don't understand.

7.   STRANGER A: Pardon me. I'm a stranger here. _Would you please tell me where the nearest post office is ?_

        STRANGER B: _I'm sorry. I'd like to help, but I don't know._

        STRANGER A: Well, thanks anyway. I'll ask someone else.

☐ **EXERCISE 16. Summary: polite questions. (Charts 7-5 and 7-6)**

     Directions: Work in pairs. Create a dialogue for one or more of the following situations. The beginning of each dialogue is given. Role-play a dialogue for the rest of the class.

     Example:

SITUATION: You're in a restaurant. You want the waiter to refill your coffee cup. You catch the waiter's eye and raise your hand slightly. He approaches your table.

DIALOGUE: *Yes? What can I do for you?*

SPEAKER A: Yes? What can I do for you?

SPEAKER B: Could I please have some more coffee?

SPEAKER A: Of course. Right away. Could I get you anything else?

SPEAKER B: No thanks. Oh, on second thought, yes. Would you bring some cream too?

SPEAKER A: Certainly.

SPEAKER B: Thanks.

1. SITUATION: You've been waiting in line at a busy bakery. Finally, the person in front of you is being waited on, and the clerk turns toward you.

     DIALOGUE: *Next!*

2. SITUATION: You are at work. You feel sick. Your head is pounding, and you have a slight fever. You really want to go home. You see your boss, Mr. Jenkins, passing by your desk.

     DIALOGUE: *Mr. Jenkins?*

3. SITUATION: Your cousin, Willy, is in the next room listening to music. You are talking on the telephone. The music is getting louder and louder. Finally, you can no longer hear your conversation over the phone. You put the phone down and turn toward the door to the next room.

     DIALOGUE: *Willy!*

4. SITUATION: The person next to you on the plane has finished reading his newspaper. You would like to read it.

     DIALOGUE: *Excuse me.*

5. SITUATION: You see a car on the side of the road with the hood raised and an older man standing next to it. He looks tired and concerned. You pull over and get out of your car to walk over to him.

     DIALOGUE: *Do you need some help, sir?*

7-7 EXPRESSING ADVICE: *SHOULD* AND *OUGHT TO*

(a) My clothes are dirty I $\begin{Bmatrix} \textit{\textbf{should}} \\ \textit{\textbf{ought to}} \end{Bmatrix}$ wash them.
 	
 (b) INCORRECT: *I should to wash them.*
 	
 (c) INCORRECT: *I ought washing them.*
	Should and *ought to* have the same meaning. They mean: "This is a good idea. This is good advice."
	 FORMS:
	       should + simple form of a verb (no *to*)
	       ought + *to* + simple form of a verb

(d) You need your sleep. You *should not* (*shouldn't*) stay up late.	NEGATIVE: *should* + *not* = *shouldn't* (*Ought to* is usually not used in the negative.)
(e) A: I'm going to be late. What *should I do?* B: Run.	QUESTION: *should* + subject + main verb (*Ought to* is usually not used in questions.)

(f) A: I'm tired today.
     B: You *should/ought to* go home and take a nap.
 	
 (g) A: I'm tired today.
     B: *Maybe* you *should/ought to* go home and take a nap.
	The use of *maybe* with *should* and *ought to* "softens" advice. COMPARE:
	 In (f): Speaker B is giving definite advice. He is stating clearly that he believes going home for a nap is a good idea and is the solution to Speaker A's problem.
	 In (g): Speaker B is making a suggestion: going home for a nap is one possible way to solve Speaker A's problem.

☐ EXERCISE 17. Expressing advice: SHOULD and OUGHT TO. (Chart 7-7)

Directions: Work in pairs.

Speaker A: State the problem.

Speaker B: Give advice using *should* or *ought to*. Include *maybe* to soften the advice if you wish.

Example: I'm sleepy.

SPEAKER A: I'm sleepy.

SPEAKER B: (Maybe) You should/ought to drink a cup of tea.

1. I'm hungry.

2. I'm cold.

3. I have a toothache.

4. I have the hiccups. What should I do?

5. I left my sunglasses at a restaurant yesterday. What should I do?

Switch roles.

6. I'm hot.

7. I have a headache.

8. Someone stole my bicycle. What should I do?

9. I bought a pair of pants that don't fit. They're too long.

10. I always make a lot of spelling mistakes when I write. I don't know what to do about it. What do you suggest?

7-8 EXPRESSING ADVICE: *HAD BETTER*

(a) My clothes are dirty. I $\left\{\begin{array}{l}\textbf{\textit{should}}\\ \textbf{\textit{ought to}}\\ \textbf{\textit{had better}}\end{array}\right\}$ *wash* them.	***Had better*** has the same basic meaning as *should* and *ought to:* "This is a good idea. This is good advice."
(b) You're driving too fast! You'***d better*** *slow* down.	***Had better*** usually implies a warning about possible bad consequences. In (b): If you don't slow down, there could be a bad result. You could get a speeding ticket or have an accident.
(c) You'***d better not*** *eat* that meat. It looks spoiled.	NEGATIVE: ***had better not***
(d) I'***d*** *better send* my boss an e-mail right away.	In speaking, ***had*** is usually contracted: *'d.*

☐ **EXERCISE 18. Expressing advice: HAD BETTER. (Chart 7-8)**

Directions: In the following, the speaker chooses to use ***had better***. What are some possible bad consequences the speaker might be thinking of?

1. The movie starts in ten minutes. We'*d better hurry.*
   → *Possible bad consequences: We'll be late if we don't hurry.*

2. You can't wear shorts and a T-shirt to a job interview! You'*d better change* clothes before you go.

3. I can't find my credit card. I have no idea where it is. I guess I'*d better call* the credit card company.

4. A: My ankle really hurts. I think I sprained it.
   B: You'*d better put* some ice on it right away.

5. You shouldn't leave your car unlocked in the middle of the city. You'*d better lock* it before we go into the restaurant.

☐ **EXERCISE 19. Expressing advice: HAD BETTER. (Chart 7-8)**

Directions: Give advice using ***had better***. Explain the possible bad consequence if your advice is not followed. Only the cuer's book is open.

Example: It's raining. I need to go out.
   ↪ *You'd better take your umbrella. If you don't, you'll get wet.*

1. I haven't paid my electric bill.
2. I need to be at the airport for a nine o'clock flight tonight.
3. (. . .) and I want to go out to dinner at *(name of a popular restaurant)* Saturday night, but we don't have reservations yet.
4. (. . .) wants to go to a movie tonight, but she/he has a test tomorrow.
5. I don't feel good today. I think I'm coming down with something.*
6. (. . .) has a job at *(name of a local place)*. She/He has been late to work three times in the last week. Her/His boss is very unhappy about that.

---

*The idiom "come down with something" means "get a sickness" like a cold or the flu.

☐ EXERCISE 20. Expressing advice: SHOULD, OUGHT TO, and HAD BETTER.
    (Charts 7-7 and 7-8)

Directions: Correct the errors.

1. You ~~will~~ ^{had} better not be late.

2. Anna shouldn't wears shorts into the restaurant.

3. I should to go to the post office today.

4. I ought paying my bills today.

5. You'd had better to call the doctor today.

6. You don't should stay up too late tonight.

7. You'd to better not leaving your key in the door.

8. Mr. Nguyen has a large family and a small apartment. He ought found a new
   apartment.

☐ EXERCISE 21. Giving advice. (Charts 7-7 and 7-8)

Directions: Work in pairs. Complete all of the dialogues. Make the dialogues longer if you
wish by adding more advice, and present one of your dialogues to the class.
    One of you is Speaker A, and the other is Speaker B.

Example:

SPEAKER A: I don't feel like studying tonight.
SPEAKER B: **Maybe** you **should** . . . . *go to a movie instead / take the night off / etc.*
SPEAKER A: I can't do that. I have a big test tomorrow.
SPEAKER B: Well, then you**'d better** . . . . *study tonight whether you feel like it or not / go to
    your room and get to work.*

1. A: I don't feel good. I think I'm getting a cold.
   B: That's too bad. You**'d better** . . . .
   A: That's probably a good idea.
   B: You **should** also . . . .
   A: Okay. I will. That's a good idea. And I suppose I**'d better not** . . . .
   B: No, you'd better not do that if you're getting a cold.

2. A: My English isn't progressing as fast as I'd like. What should I do?
   B: You **should** . . . . That's really important when you're learning a second language.
   A: Do you have any other suggestions?
   B: Yes, you **ought to** . . . .
   A: That's a good idea.
   B: And you **shouldn't** . . . .
   A: You're right. Good suggestion.

Switch roles.

3. A: My roommate snores really loudly. I'm losing sleep. I don't know what to do.
   B: **Maybe** you **should** . . . .
   A: I've thought of that, but . . . .
   B: Well then, **maybe** you**'d better** . . . .
   A: Maybe. I guess I really **ought to** . . . .
   B: That's a good idea.

4. A: The refrigerator in my apartment doesn't work. The air conditioner makes so much noise that I can't sleep. And there are cockroaches in the kitchen.
   B: Why do you stay there? You **should** . . . .
   A: I can't. I signed a lease.
   B: Oh. That's too bad. Well, if you have to stay there, you**'d better** . . . .
   A: I suppose I should do that.
   B: And you also **ought to** . . . .
   A: Good idea.

☐ EXERCISE 22. Giving advice. (Charts 7-7 and 7-8)
   Directions: Give advice using ***should, ought to,*** and ***had better***. Work in groups of four. Only Speaker A's book is open. Rotate the open book, using a new Speaker A for each item.

   Example:
   SPEAKER A *(book open):* I study, but I don't understand my physics class. It's the middle of the term, and I'm failing the course. I need a science course in order to graduate. What should I do?★
   SPEAKER B *(book closed):* You**'d better** get a tutor right away.
   SPEAKER C *(book closed):* You **should** make an appointment with your teacher and see if you can get some extra help.
   SPEAKER D *(book closed):* Maybe you **ought to** drop your physics course and enroll in a different science course next term.

   1. I forgot my dad's birthday yesterday. I feel terrible about it. What should I do?

   2. I just discovered that I made dinner plans for tonight with two different people. I'm supposed to meet my fiancée/fiancé at one restaurant at 7:00, and I'm supposed to meet my boss at a different restaurant across town at 8:00. What should I do?

   3. The boss wants me to finish my report before I go on vacation, but I don't have time. I might lose my job if I don't give him that report on time. What should I do?

   4. I borrowed Karen's favorite book of poems. It was special to her. A note on the inside cover said "To Karen." The poet's signature was at the bottom of the note. Now I can't find the book. I think I lost it. What am I going to do?

   ───────────

   ★*Should* (not *ought to* or *had better*) is usually used in a question that asks for advice. The answer, however, can contain *should, ought to,* or *had better*. For example:
   A: My houseplants always die. What ***should*** I do?
   B: You**'d better** get a book on plants. You ***should*** try to find out why they die. Maybe you **ought to** look on the Internet and see if you can find some information.

Directions: Discuss problems and give advice. Work in groups.

Speaker A: Think of a problem in your life or a friend's life. Tell your classmates about
the problem and then ask them for advice.

Group: Give Speaker A some advice. Use *should/ought to/had better.*

Example:

SPEAKER A: I can't study at night because the dorm is too noisy. What should I do?

SPEAKER B: You ought to study at the library.

SPEAKER C: You shouldn't stay in your dorm room in the evening.

SPEAKER D: You'd better get some ear plugs.

SPEAKER E: Etc.

7-9 EXPRESSING NECESSITY: *HAVE TO, HAVE GOT TO, MUST*

(a) I have a very important test tomorrow. I $\begin{cases} \textbf{\textit{have to}} \\ \textbf{\textit{have got to}} \\ \textbf{\textit{must}} \end{cases}$ *study* tonight.	***Have to, have got to***, and ***must*** have basically the same meaning. They express the idea that something is *necessary*.
(b) I'd like to go with you to the movie this evening, but I can't. I ***have to go*** to a meeting. (c) Bye now! I***'ve got to go***. My wife's waiting for me. I'll call you later. (d) All passengers ***must present*** their passports at customs upon arrival.	***Have to*** is used much more frequently in everyday speech and writing than ***must***. ***Have got to*** is typically used in informal conversation, as in (c). ***Must*** is typically found in written instructions, as in (d). It is usually a strong, serious, "no nonsense" word.
(e) ***Do*** we ***have to bring*** pencils to the test? (f) Why ***did*** he ***have to leave*** so early?	QUESTIONS: ***Have to*** is usually used in questions, not ***must*** or ***have got to***. Forms of ***do*** are used with ***have to*** in questions.
(g) I ***had to*** *study* last night.	The PAST form of ***have to, have got to***, and ***must*** (meaning necessity) is ***had to***.
(h) I ***have to*** ("hafta") *go* downtown today. (i) Rita ***has to*** ("hasta") *go* to the bank. (j) I've ***got to*** ("gotta") *study* tonight.	Usual PRONUNCIATION: ***have to*** = /hæftə/ OR /hæftu/ ***has to*** = /hæstə/ OR /hæstu/ *(have)* ***got to*** = /gadə/ OR /gɔtə/

☐ EXERCISE 24. HAVE TO, HAVE GOT TO, MUST, and SHOULD. (Charts 7-7 and 7-9)

Directions: Discuss the questions and the meanings of the auxiliaries.

1. What are some things you *have to do* today? tomorrow? every day?
2. What is something you *had to do* yesterday?
3. What is something you*'ve got to do* soon?
4. What is something you*'ve got to do* after class today or later tonight?
5. What is something a driver *must do*, according to the law?
6. What is something a driver *should* always *do* to be a safe driver?
7. What are some things a person *should do* to stay healthy?
8. What are some things a person *must do* to stay alive?

☐ EXERCISE 25. Summary: expressing advice and necessity. (Charts 7-7 → 7-9)
Directions: Read the passage, and then give advice either in a discussion group or in writing.

Mr. and Mrs. Hill don't know what to do about their fourteen-year-old son, Mark. He's very intelligent but has no interest in school or in learning. His grades are getting worse, but he won't do any homework. Sometimes he skips school without permission, and then he writes an excuse for the school and signs his mother's name.

His older sister, Kathy, is a good student and never causes any problems at home. Mark's parents keep asking him why he can't be more like Kathy. Kathy makes fun of Mark's school grades and tells him he's stupid.

All Mark does when he's home is stay in his room and listen to very loud music. Sometimes he doesn't even come downstairs to eat meals with his family. He argues with his parents whenever they ask him to do chores around the house, like taking out the trash.

Mr. and Mrs. Hill can't stay calm when they talk to him. Mrs. Hill is always yelling at her son. She nags him constantly to do his chores, clean up his room, finish his homework, stand up straight, get a haircut, wash his face, and tie his shoes. Mr. Hill is always making new rules. Some of the rules are unreasonable. For instance, one rule Mr. Hill made was that his son could not listen to music after five o'clock. Mark often becomes angry and goes up to his room and slams the door shut.

This family needs a lot of advice. Tell them what changes they should make. What should Mr. and Mrs. Hill do? What shouldn't they do? What about Kathy? What should she do? And what's Mark got to do to change his life for the better?

Use each of the following words at least once in the advice you give:
a. should
b. shouldn't
c. have got to/has got to
d. had better
e. ought to
f. have to/has to
g. must

7-10 EXPRESSING LACK OF NECESSITY: *DO NOT HAVE TO* EXPRESSING PROHIBITION: *MUST NOT*

(a) I finished all of my homework this afternoon. I *don't have to study* tonight. (b) Tomorrow is a holiday. Mary *doesn't have to go* to class.	*Don't/doesn't have to* expresses the idea that something is *not necessary*.
(c) Children, you *must not play* with matches! (d) We *must not use* that door. The sign says PRIVATE: DO NOT ENTER.	*Must not* expresses *prohibition* (DO NOT DO THIS!).
(e) You *mustn't play* with matches.	*Must* + *not* = *mustn't*. (Note: The first "t" is not pronounced.)

☐ **EXERCISE 26. Lack of necessity (DO NOT HAVE TO) and prohibition (MUST NOT).**
(Chart 7-10)

Directions: Complete the sentences with ***don't/doesn't have to*** or ***must not***.

1. You _____ must not _____ drive when you are tired. It's dangerous.

2. I live only a few blocks from my office. I _____ don't have to _____ drive to work.

3. Liz finally got a car, so now she usually drives to work. She _____
   take the bus.

4. Tommy, you _____ say that word. It's not a nice word.

5. Mr. Moneybags is very rich. He _____ work for a living.

6. A: You _____ tell Jim about the surprise birthday party. Do
   you promise?

   B: I promise.

7. According to the rules of the game, one player _____ hit or
   trip another player.

8. If you use a toll-free number, you _____ pay for the phone call.

9. A: Did Professor Adams make an assignment?

   B: Yes, she assigned Chapters 4 and 6, but we _____ read
   Chapter 5.

10. A: Listen carefully, Annie. If a stranger offers you a ride, you _____
    get in the car. Never get in a car with a stranger. Do you understand?

    B: Yes, Mom.

11. A: Do you have a stamp?

    B: Uh-huh. Here.

    A: Thanks. Now I _____ go to the post office to buy
    stamps.

12. A: Children, your mother and I are going out this evening. I want you to be good.
    You must do everything the baby-sitter tells you to do. You _____
    go outside after dark. It's Saturday night, so you _____
    go to bed at eight. You can stay up until eight-thirty. And remember: you
    _____ pull the cat's tail. Okay?

    B: Okay, Dad.

☐ EXERCISE 27. **Summary: expressing advice, possibility, and necessity.**
(Charts 7-4 and 7-7 → 7-10)

Directions: Read about each situation and discuss it, orally or in writing. In your discussion, include as many of the following expressions as possible.

should, shouldn't	have to, not have to
ought to	have got to, not have to
had better, had better not	must, must not
could	

Example: Carol is just recovering from the flu. She's at work today. She works for a big company. It's her first day back to work since she got ill. She tires easily and feels a little dizzy.

SPEAKER A: Carol **ought to** talk to her supervisor about leaving work early today.

SPEAKER B: I think Carol **should** go directly home from work, no matter what her boss says. She**'s got to** take care of her health.

SPEAKER C: I agree. She **doesn't have to** stay at work if she doesn't feel well, and she **shouldn't**.

SPEAKER D: She **could** explain to her boss that she doesn't feel well yet and see what her boss says.

SPEAKER E: I think she **should stay** at work until quitting time. If she was well enough to come to work, she's well enough to work a full day. Etc.

1. Steve is a biology major. Chemistry is a required course for biology majors. Steve doesn't want to take chemistry. He would rather take a course in art history or creative writing. His parents want him to become a doctor. He's not interested in medicine or science. He hasn't told his parents because he doesn't want to disappoint them.

2. Matt and Amy are eighteen years old. They are full-time students. Their parents are supporting their education. Matt and Amy met five weeks ago. They fell in love. Matt wants to get married next month. Amy wants to wait four years until they finish their education. Matt says he can't wait that long. Amy loves him desperately. She thinks maybe she should change her mind and marry Matt next month because love conquers all.

3. Georgia has just left the supermarket. She paid for her groceries in cash. When she got her change, the clerk made a mistake and gave her too much money. Georgia put the extra money in her purse. With her ten-year-old son beside her, she walked out of the store. Georgia needs the money and tells herself that the store won't miss it. Nobody needs to know.

4. This is a story about a rabbit named Rabbit and a frog named Frog. Rabbit and Frog are good friends, but Rabbit's family doesn't like Frog, and Frog's family doesn't like Rabbit.

Rabbit's family says, "You shouldn't be friends with Frog. He's too different from us. He's green and has big eyes. He looks strange. You should stay with your own kind."

And Frog's family says, "How can you be friends with Rabbit? He's big and clumsy. He's covered with hair and has funny ears. Don't bring Rabbit to our house. What will the neighbors think?"

7-11 MAKING LOGICAL CONCLUSIONS: *MUST*

(a) A: Nancy is yawning. B: She *must be* sleepy.	In (a): Speaker B is making a logical guess. He bases his guess on the information that Nancy is yawning. His logical conclusion, his "best guess," is that Nancy is sleepy. He uses *must* to express his logical conclusion.
(b) LOGICAL CONCLUSION: Amy plays tennis every day. She *must like* to play tennis. (c) NECESSITY: If you want to get into the movie theater, you *must buy* a ticket.	COMPARE: *Must* can express • a logical conclusion, as in (b). • necessity, as in (c).
(d) NEGATIVE LOGICAL CONCLUSION: Eric ate everything on his plate except the pickle. He *must not like* pickles. (e) PROHIBITION: There are sharks in the ocean near our hotel. We *must not go* swimming there.	COMPARE: *Must not* can express • a negative logical conclusion, as in (d). • prohibition, as in (e).

□ EXERCISE 28. Making logical conclusions: MUST and MUST NOT. (Chart 7-11)
Directions: Make a logical conclusion about each of the following situations. Use *must*.

Example: Emily is crying.
→ *She must be unhappy.*

1. Mrs. Chu has a big smile on her face.
2. Nadia is coughing and sneezing.
3. Rick is wearing a gold ring on the fourth finger of his left hand.
4. Sam is shivering.
5. Mr. Alvarez just bought three mouse traps.
6. James is sweating.
7. Rita rents ten movies every week.
8. Olga always gets the highest score on every test she takes.
9. Toshi can lift one end of a compact car by himself.

□ EXERCISE 29. Making logical conclusions: MUST and MUST NOT. (Chart 7-11)
Directions: Complete the dialogues with *must* or *must not*.

1. A: Did you offer our guests something to drink?
   B: Yes, but they didn't want anything. They ___must not___ be thirsty.

2. A: You've been out here working in the hot sun for hours. You ___must___ be thirsty.
   B: I am.

3. A: Adam has already eaten one sandwich. Now he's making another.
   B: He _____ be hungry.

4. A: I offered Holly something to eat, but she doesn't want anything.
   B: She _____ be hungry.

5. A: Brian has a red nose and has been coughing and sneezing.
   B: Poor fellow. He _____ have a cold.

6. A: Fido? What's wrong, old boy?
   B: What's the matter with the dog?
   A: He won't eat.
   B: He _____ feel well.

7. A: Erica's really bright. She always gets above ninety-five percent on her math tests.
   B: I'm sure she's bright, but she _____ also study a lot.

8. A: I've called the bank three times, but no one answers the phone. The bank
   _____ be open today. That's strange.
   B: Today's a holiday, remember?
   A: Oh, of course!

9. A: Listen. Someone is jumping on the floor in the apartment above us. Look. Your chandelier is shaking.

B: Mr. Silverberg _____ be doing his morning exercises. The same thing happens every morning.

☐ **EXERCISE 30. Making logical conclusions: MUST and MUST NOT. (Chart 7-11)**
Directions: Make logical conclusions. Use ***must*** or ***must not***. Use the suggested completions and/or your own words.

1. I am at **Eric**'s apartment door. I've knocked on the door and have rung the doorbell several times. Nobody has answered the door. *be at home? be out somewhere?*
   → *Eric must not be at home. He must be out somewhere.*

2. **Jennifer** reads all the time. She sits in a corner and reads even when people come to visit her. *love books? like books better than people? like to talk to people?*

3. **Kate** has a full academic schedule, plays on the volleyball team, has the lead in the school play, is a cheerleader, takes piano lessons, and has a part-time job at the ice cream store. *be busy all the time? have a lot of spare time?*

4. **David** gets on the Internet every day as soon as he gets home from work. He stays at his computer until he goes to bed. *be a computer addict? have a happy home life?*

5. **Betsy** just talked to Jake on the phone. He asked her to go to a movie. She told him that she had to study. She has just hung up, and now she's going to get ready for bed and go to sleep. *want to go a movie? be tired?*

6. **Debbie** just got home from school. She slammed the front door, threw her books on the floor, and ran to her room. Now her parents can hear music through Debbie's closed door. *be upset? want to talk to her parents right now? want to be alone?*

COMMAND
(a) *General:* **Open** the door!
  Soldier: Yes, sir!
 	
REQUEST
(b) *Teacher:* **Open** the door, please.
  Student: Okay, I'd be happy to.
 	
DIRECTIONS
(c) *Barbara:* Could you tell me how to get to the post office?
  Stranger: Certainly. **Walk** two blocks down this street. **Turn** left and **walk** three more blocks. It's on the right-hand side of the street.
		Imperative sentences are used to give commands, make polite requests, and give directions. The difference between a command and a request lies in the speaker's tone of voice and the use of **please**.
		Please can come at the beginning or end of a request:
		  Open the door, please.
		  Please open the door.

(d) **Close** the window. (e) Please **sit** down. (f) **Be** quiet! (g) **Don't walk** on the grass. (h) Please **don't wait** for me. (i) **Don't be** late.		The simple form of a verb is used in imperative sentences. The understood subject of the sentence is **you** (meaning the person the speaker is talking to): *(You) close the window.* NEGATIVE FORM: **Don't** + *the simple form of a verb*

□ EXERCISE 31. Imperative sentences. (Chart 7-12)

Directions: Complete the dialogues with imperative sentences. Try to figure out something the first speaker might say in the given situation.

1. THE TEACHER: <u>Read this sentence, please. /Look at page 33. /Etc.</u>
    THE STUDENT: Okay.

2. THE DOCTOR: _____
    THE PATIENT: All right.

3. THE MOTHER: _____
    THE SON: I will. Don't worry.

4. MRS. JONES: _____
    THE CHILDREN: Yes, ma'am.

5. THE GENERAL: _____
    THE SOLDIER: Yes, sir! Right away, sir!

6. THE FATHER: _____
    THE DAUGHTER: Okay, Dad.

7. A FRIEND: _____
    A FRIEND: Why not?

8. THE WIFE: _____
    THE HUSBAND: Okay.

9.   THE HUSBAND: _____

         THE WIFE: Why?

10.   THE BOSS: _____

  THE EMPLOYEE: I'll do it immediately.

11.   THE FATHER: _____

      THE SON: Okay. I won't.

☐ **EXERCISE 32. Imperative sentences. (Chart 7-12)**

Directions: Pair up with a classmate.
Student A: Your book is open. Read the directions to Student B.
Student B: Your book is closed. Follow the directions.

STUDENT A TO B: Follow these steps to find the answer to a number puzzle.
- Write down the number of the month you were born. (For example, write "2" if you were born in February. Write "3" if you were born in March.)
- Double it.
- Add 5.
- Multiply by 50.
- Add your age.
- Subtract 250.
- In the final number, the last two digits on the right will be your age, and the one or two digits on the left will be the month you were born.

Switch roles.
STUDENT B TO A: Repeat the directions to the number puzzle to Student A.

☐ **EXERCISE 33. Writing activity. (Chart 7-12)**

Directions: Write about one or more of the following.

Give general advice to people who want to
1. improve their health.
2. get good grades.
3. improve their English.
4. make a good first impression.
5. find a job.
6. live life fully every day.
7. get married.
8. help preserve the earth's environment.

Example: handle stress
    Do you want to handle stress in your life? Here are some suggestions for you to consider.
- Be sure to get daily exercise. You should devote at least half an hour to physical activity every day.
- Don't overload your daily schedule. Learn to manage your time efficiently.
- You have to take time for yourself. Don't keep yourself busy doing things for everyone else from morning until night. Do things that are just for you. Read, reflect, listen to music, or just do nothing for a period every day.
- Don't waste time worrying about things you can't change. Recognize the things you can't change and accept them. Change only the things you can change.

□ EXERCISE 34. Writing activity. (Charts 7-1 → 7-12)
Directions: One of your friends wants to come to this city, either to go to school or get a job. Write your friend a letter. Give your friend advice about coming to this city to study or work.

7-13 MAKING SUGGESTIONS: *LET'S* AND *WHY DON'T*

(a) A: It's hot today. ***Let's go*** to the beach. B: Okay. Good idea. (b) A: It's hot today. ***Why don't we go*** to the beach? B: Okay. Good idea.	***Let's*** *(do something)* and ***why don't we*** *(do something)* have the same meaning. They are used to make suggestions about activities for you and me. ***Let's*** = *let us.*
(c) A: I'm tired. B: ***Why don't you take*** a nap? A: That's a good idea. I think I will.	***Why don't you*** *(do something)* is used to make a friendly suggestion, to give friendly advice.

□ EXERCISE 35. Making suggestions with LET'S and WHY DON'T WE. (Chart 7-13)
Directions: Make suggestions using ***let's*** and/or ***why don't we***. Work in pairs or as a class.

Example:
SPEAKER A: What would you like to do today?
SPEAKER B: Why don't we go for a walk in the park? / Let's go for a walk in the park.

1. Would you like to do this exercise in pairs or as a class?
2. What would you like to do this afternoon?
3. What do you want to do this weekend?
4. Where should we go for dinner tonight?
5. Who should we ask to join us for dinner tonight?
6. What time should we meet at the restaurant?

□ EXERCISE 36. Making suggestions with WHY DON'T YOU. (Chart 7-13)
Directions: Make suggestions using ***why don't you***. Work in pairs or as a class.

Example:
SPEAKER A: I'm hungry,
SPEAKER B: Why don't you have a candy bar?

1. I'm thirsty.
2. I'm sleepy.
3. I have a toothache.
4. It's too hot in this room.
5. I have to take a science course next semester. What should I take?
6. Tomorrow is my sister's birthday. What should I give her?

Directions: Two students, books open, will read a dialogue aloud. Listen to the dialogue, books closed, and then repeat or write down the suggestion(s) you hear in the dialogue.

Example:

SPEAKER A (Yoko): Are you done with your work?

SPEAKER B (Talal): Yes.

SPEAKER A (Yoko): Good. Let's go to the market. I'm hungry for some fresh fruit.

SPEAKER B (Talal): Okay.

→ (repeated or written): Yoko said, "Let's go to the market."

1. A: I'm getting sleepy.
   B: Why don't you have a strong cup of tea?
   A: I suppose I could.

2. A: Are you busy tonight?
   B: No. Why?
   A: Let's rent a video.
   B: Okay.

3. A: Brrr. I'm cold.
   B: Why don't you put on a sweater?
   A: I don't have a sweater.

4. A: Where do you want to go for lunch?
   B: Why don't we go to *(name of a local place)*?
   A: That's too crowded at lunch time. Let's go to *(name of a local place)* instead.
   B: Okay.

5. A: I have a headache.
   B: Why don't you take some aspirin?
   A: I don't like to take aspirin.
   B: Why not?
   A: It upsets my stomach.
   B: Then why don't you lie down and rest? Sometimes that's all it takes to get rid of a headache.

6. A: Why don't we go dancing tonight?
   B: I don't know how to dance.
   A: Oh. Then why don't we go to a movie?
   B: I don't like movies.
   A: You don't like movies?!
   B: No.
   A: Well then, let's go to a restaurant for dinner.
   B: That's a waste of money.
   A: Well, you do what you want to tonight, but I'm going to go to a restaurant for dinner. And after that I'm going to go to a movie. And then I'm going to go dancing!

□ EXERCISE 38. Making suggestions with LET'S and WHY DON'T WE. (Chart 7-13)
Directions: Complete the dialogues. Use *let's* or *why don't we*.

1. A: The weather's beautiful today. <u>Let's/Why don't we go on a picnic?</u>
   B: Good idea.

2. A: I'm bored.
   B: Me too. _____
   A: Great idea!

3. A: Are you hungry?
   B: Yes. Are you?
   A: Yes. _____
   B: Okay.

4. A: What are you going to do over the holiday?
   B: I don't know. What are you going to do?
   A: I haven't made any plans.
   B: _____
   A: That sounds like a terrific idea, but I can't afford it.
   B: Actually, I can't either.

5. A: I need to go shopping.
   B: So do I.
   A: _____
   B: I can't go then. _____
   A: Okay. That's fine with me.

6. A: Do you have any plans for this weekend?
   B: Not really.
   A: I don't either. _____
   B: Okay. Good idea.

7. A: What time should we leave for the airport?
   B: _____
   A: Okay.

8. A: What should we do tonight?
   B: _____
   A: Sounds okay to me.

9. A: _____
   B: Let's not. _____ instead.
   A: Okay.

□ **EXERCISE 39. Making suggestions with WHY DON'T YOU.** (Chart 7-13)

Directions: Work in groups. Make suggestions using *why don't you*. Speaker A states the problem, and then others offer suggestions. Only Speaker A's book is open. Rotate the open book, using a new Speaker A for each item.

Example: I'm at a restaurant with some business clients. I left my wallet at home. I don't have enough money to pay the bill. What am I going to do?

SPEAKER A: Okay, here's the situation. I'm at a restaurant with some business customers. I sell computer parts. I need to impress my clients. I have to pay for dinner, but I left my wallet at home. I'm really embarrassed. What am I going to do?

SPEAKER B: Why don't you call your office and ask someone to bring you some money?

SPEAKER C: Why don't you borrow the money from one of your customers?

SPEAKER D: Why don't you excuse yourself and go home to get your wallet?

SPEAKER E: Why don't you have a private discussion with the manager and arrange to pay the bill later?

1. I feel like doing something interesting and fun tonight. Any suggestions?

2. I need regular physical exercise. What would you suggest?

3. An important assignment is due in Professor Black's history class today. I haven't done it. Class starts in an hour. What am I going to do?

4. I've lost the key to my apartment, so I can't get in. My roommate is at the library. What am I going to do?

5. My friend and I had an argument. We stopped talking to each other. Now I'm sorry about the argument. I want to be friends again. What should I do?

6. I work hard all day, every day. I never take time to relax and enjoy myself. I need some recreation in my life. What do think I should do?

7. I'm trying to learn English, but I'm making slow progress. What can I do to learn English faster?

7-14 STATING PREFERENCES: *PREFER, LIKE . . . BETTER, WOULD RATHER*

(a) I *prefer* apples *to* oranges. (b) I *prefer* watching TV *to studying*.	*prefer* + *noun* + *to* + *noun* *prefer* + *-ing* verb + *to* + *-ing* verb
(c) I *like* apples *better than* oranges. (d) I *like* watching TV *better than* studying.	*like* + *noun* + *better than* + *noun* *like* + *-ing* verb + *better than* + *-ing* verb
(e) Ann *would rather have* an apple than an orange. (f) INCORRECT: *Ann would rather has an apple.* (g) I'd rather visit a big city *than live* there. (h) INCORRECT: *I'd rather visit a big city than to live there.* INCORRECT: *I'd rather visit a big city than living there.*	*Would rather* is followed immediately by the simple form of a verb (e.g., *have, visit, live*). Verbs following *than* are also in the simple form.
(i) *I'd/You'd/She'd/He'd/We'd/They'd* rather have an apple.	Contraction of *would* = *'d*.
(j) *Would you rather* have an apple *or* an orange?	In (j): In a polite question, *would rather* can be followed by *or* to offer someone a choice.

□ **EXERCISE 40. Expressing preferences. (Chart 7-14)**
Directions: Complete the sentences with *than* or *to*.

1. When I'm hot and thirsty, I **prefer** cold drinks _____to_____ hot drinks.

2. When I'm hot and thirsty, I **like** cold drinks **better** _____than_____ hot drinks.

3. When I'm hot and thirsty, I**'d rather have** a cold drink _____than_____ a hot drink.

4. I **prefer** tea _____ coffee.

5. I **like** tea **better** _____ coffee.

6. I**'d rather** drink tea _____ coffee.

7. When I choose a book, I **prefer** nonfiction _____ fiction.

8. I **like** rock-and-roll **better** _____ classical music.

9. My parents **would rather work** _____ retire. They enjoy their jobs.

10. Do you **like** fresh vegetables **better** _____ frozen or canned vegetables?

11. I **prefer visiting** my friends in the evening _____ watching TV by myself.

12. I **would rather read** a book in the evening _____ visit with friends.

□ **EXERCISE 41. Expressing preferences: WOULD RATHER. (Chart 7-14)**
Directions: Answer the questions **in complete sentences**. Work in pairs or as a class.

Example: Which do you prefer, apples or oranges?*
→ *I prefer (oranges) to (apples).*

Example: Which do you like better, bananas or strawberries?
→ *I like (bananas) better than (strawberries).*

Example: Which would you rather have right now, an apple or a banana?
→ *I'd rather have (a banana).*

1. Which do you like better, rice or potatoes?

2. Which do you prefer, peas or corn?

3. Which would you rather have for dinner tonight, beans or potatoes?

4. Name two sports. Which do you like better?

5. Name two movies. Which one would you rather see?

(Switch roles if working in pairs.)

6. What kind of music would you rather listen to, rock or classical?

7. Name two vegetables. Which do you prefer?

8. Which do you like better, Chinese food or Mexican food?

9. Name two sports that you play. Which sport would you rather play this afternoon?

10. Name two TV programs. Which do you like better?

---

*Use a rising intonation on the first choice and a falling intonation on the second choice.
Which do you prefer, apples or oranges?*

☐ EXERCISE 42. Expressing preferences: WOULD RATHER. (Chart 7-14)
Directions: Use **would rather . . . than . . . .** in your answers. Work in pairs, in small groups, or as a class.

Would you rather . . .
1. live in an apartment or (live) in a house?* Why?
2. be a doctor or (be) a dentist? Why?
3. be married or (be) single? Why?
4. be ugly and intelligent or (be) handsome/beautiful and stupid? Why?
5. have a car or (have) an airplane? Why?
6. be rich and unlucky in love or (be) poor and lucky in love? Why?

(Switch roles if working in pairs.)
7. get on the Internet or read a good book? Why?
8. go to Moscow or (go) to London for your vacation? Why?
9. go to a football game or (go) to a soccer game? Why?
10. go to *(name of a place in this city)* or go to *(name of a place in this city)?* Why?
11. have six children or (have) two children? Why?
12. be a bird or (be) a fish? Why?

☐ EXERCISE 43. Cumulative review. (Chapter 7)
Directions: Each of the following has a short dialogue. Try to imagine a situation in which the dialogue could take place, and then choose the best completion.

Example: "My horse is sick."
"Oh? What's the matter? You ___B___ call the vet."
A. will   B. had better   C. may

1. "Does this pen belong to you?"
"No. It _____ be Susan's. She was sitting at that desk."
A. had better   B. will   C. must

2. "Let's go to a movie this evening."
"That sounds like fun, but I can't. I _____ finish a report before I go to bed tonight."
A. have got to   B. would rather   C. ought to

3. "Hey, Ted. What's up with Ken? Is he upset about something?"
"He's angry because you recommended Ann instead of him for the promotion. You _____ sit down with him and explain your reasons. At least that's what I think."
A. should   B. will   C. can

---
*It is possible but not necessary to repeat a preposition after *than*.
CORRECT: *I'd rather live in an apartment **than in a house**.*
CORRECT: *I'd rather live in an apartment **than a house**.*

4. "Does Tom want to go with us to the film festival tonight?"
   "No. He _____ go to a wrestling match than the film festival."
       A. could   B. would rather   C. prefers

5. "I did it! I did it! I got my driver's license!"
   "Congratulations, Michelle. I'm really proud of you."
   "Thanks, Dad. Now _____ I have the car tonight? Please, please!"
   "No. You're not ready for that quite yet."
       A. will   B. should   C. may

6. "I just tripped on your carpet and almost fell! There's a hole in it. You _____ fix that before someone gets hurt."
   "Yes, Uncle Ben. I should. I will. I'm sorry. Are you all right?"
       A. can   B. ought to   C. may

7. "Are you going to the conference in Atlanta next month?"
   "I _____ . It's sort of iffy right now. I've applied for travel money, but who knows what my supervisor will do."
       A. will   B. have to   C. might

8. "What shall we do after the meeting this evening?"
   "_____ pick Jan up and all go out to dinner together."
       A. Why don't   B. Let's   C. Should

9. "Have you seen my denim jacket? I _____ find it."
   "Look in the hall closet."
       A. may not   B. won't   C. can't

10. "Bye, Mom! I'm going to go play soccer with my friends."
    "Wait a minute, young man! You _____ do your chores first."
        A. had better not   B. have to   C. would rather

11. "Do you think that Scott will quit his job?"
    "I don't know. He _____ . He's very angry. We'll just have to wait and see."
        A. must   B. may   C. will

12. "The hotel supplies towels, you know. You _____ pack a towel in your suitcase."
    "This is my bathrobe, not a towel."
        A. don't have to   B. must not   C. couldn't

13. "I heard that Bill was seriously ill."
    "Really? Well, he _____ be sick anymore. I just saw him riding his bike to work."
        A. won't   B. doesn't have to   C. must not

14. "Do you understand how this computer program works?"
    "Sort of, but not really. _____ you explain it to me one more time? Thanks."
        A. Could   B. Should   C. Must

15. "Did you climb to the top of the Statue of Liberty when you were in New York?"

"No, I didn't. My knee was very sore, and I _____ climb all those stairs."

    A. might not   B. couldn't   C. must not

16. "Rick, _____ work for me this evening? I'll take your shift tomorrow."

"Sure. I was going to ask you to work for me tomorrow anyway."

    A. should you   B. would you   C. do you have to

17. "How are we going to take care of your little brother and go to the concert at the same time?"

"I have an idea. _____ we take him with us?"

    A. Why don't   B. Let's   C. Will

18. "Meet me at Tony's at five. Please! I _____ talk to you. It's important."

"Is something wrong?"

    A. could   B. will   C. must

19. "What are you children doing? Stop! You _____ play with sharp knives."

"What?"

    A. mustn't   B. couldn't   C. don't have to

20. "Don't wait for me. I _____ late."

"Okay."

    A. maybe   B. may to be   C. may be

21. "Mr. Wells can't figure out how to assemble his daughter's tricycle."

"He _____ read the instructions very carefully."

    A. had better   B. can't   C. would rather

Directions: Complete the sentences with any appropriate auxiliary verb in the list. There may be more than one possible completion. Also include any words in parentheses.

am	*do*	*has to*	*might*	*was*
are	*does*	*have to*	*must*	*were*
can	*did*	*is*	*ought to*	*will*
could	*had better*	*may*	*should*	*would*

1. A: Hello?

   B: Hello. This is Gisella Milazzo. _____May (Could/Can)_____ I speak with

   Ms. Morgan, please?

2. A: Where's the newspaper?

   B: I *(not)* _____don't_____ have it. Ask Kevin.

3. A: _____ you rather go downtown today or tomorrow?

   B: Tomorrow.

4. A: Stop! You *(not)* _____ pick those flowers! It's against the law

   to pick flowers in a national park.

   B: Really? I didn't know that.

5. A: _____ you talk to Amanda yesterday?

   B: Yes. Why?

6. A: _____ I help you, sir?

   B: Yes. _____ you show me the third watch from the left on the

   top shelf?

   A: Of course.

7. A: I'm sorry. _____ you repeat that? I can't hear you because

   my dog _____ barking.

   B: I said, "Why is your dog making all that noise?"

8. A: I don't know whether to turn left or right at the next intersection.

   B: I think you _____ pull over and look at the map.

9. A: Hurry up. Kate and Greg _____ waiting for us.

   B: I _____ hurrying!

10. A: Andy can't teach his class tonight.

    B: He _____ teach tonight! He'll be fired if he doesn't show up.

11. A: Stop! *(not)* _____ touch that pan! It's hot! You'll burn

    yourself.

    B: Relax. I had no intention of touching it.

12. A: What _____ you carrying? _____ you

    want some help?

    B: It's a box of books. _____ you open the door for me, please?

13. A: Hello?

    B: Hello. _____ I please speak to Sandra Wilson?

    A: I'm sorry. There's no one here by that name. You _____ have

    the wrong number.

14. A: _____ Nick going to be at the meeting tomorrow?

    B: I hope so.

15. A: Everyone _____ work toward

    cleaning up the environment.

    B: I agree. Life on earth *(not)* _____

    survive if we continue to poison the land, water,

    and air.

Index

After, *(Look on pages 48, 65, and 161.)*	The numbers following the words listed in the index refer to page numbers in the text.
Consonants, 13*fn.* *(Look at the footnote on page 13.)*	The letters *fn.* mean "footnote." Footnotes are at the bottom of a page or the bottom of a chart.

1

NOTES

NOTES